HTML and CSS

9th Edition

JOE CASABONA

 Peachpit Press

Visual QuickStart Guide
HTML and CSS, 9th Edition
Joe Casabona

Peachpit Press
www.peachpit.com

San Francisco, CA

Peachpit Press is an imprint of Pearson Education, Inc.

To report errors, please send a note to errata@peachpit.com

Executive Editor: Laura Norman
Development Editor: Victor Gavenda
Senior Production Editor: Tracey Croom
Copy Editor: Scout Festa
Proofreader: Becky Winter
Compositor: Danielle Foster
Indexer: Valerie Haynes-Perry
Cover Design: RHDG / Riezebos Holzbaur Design Group, Peachpit Press
Interior Design: Peachpit Press with Danielle Foster
Logo Design: MINE™ www.minesf.com

ISBN-13:   978-0-13-670256-6
ISBN-10:   0-13-670256-2

7 2022

Dedication

To my wife, Erin. Your love and support has allowed me not only to write this book, but to have the life I've always wanted.

To my daughter, Teresa. You make me smile and laugh every day. And to my son, Louis. Welcome to the world, buddy.

I love you all.

Acknowledgments

Writing a book, especially a good one, takes time and a group of solid people. And this one wouldn't have happened without the great team I got to be a part of. I want to extend a special thank you to:

- Laura Norman, who helped me get back in the book writing game with this title, for her support and guidance along the way.

- Victor Gavenda, for his development editing and deep knowledge of the VQS format, and for making it seem like I have good control over the English language.

- Faraz Kelhini, the tech editor. His feedback and suggestions made for a much better read.

- Scout Festa, for excellent copyediting.

- Tracey Croom and the entire Pearson design team, for making this book look fantastic.

- Shawn Hesketh, a friend and mentor who taught me all the good things I know about screencasts.

- Brian Richards, for helping me work though some of the more advanced topics in this book.

- My friends and family, for the support and encouragement throughout the writing process.

- Everyone who has contributed by letting me use a screenshot, image, or resource that they created.

- To TT at my local Starbucks. He always saw me coming and had my order ready.

- To you, the readers. Thank you for allowing me to contribute to your learning journey.

- Finally, to Elizabeth Castro for creating this title, and to Bruce Hyslop for passing me the torch.

Contents at a Glance

Table of Contents

Introduction

When I started making websites, back in 2000, it was a much simpler time. I was able to build a full website with just HTML and CSS and a few images. There were also fewer browsers and devices. But as the web evolved and computers got smarter and more powerful, the needs of both web users and web developers changed. This made some things easier. It also made learning more complicated.

Today, a website that doesn't use any JavaScript is a rare sight (and site!). There are so many build tools, libraries, and development philosophies that learning how to make a website can seem overwhelming.

But there's good news: at the heart of it all are still just plain and simple HTML and CSS.

In This Introduction

What You Will Learn

The building blocks of the web are plain HTML and CSS—and you can make a website knowing just those two technologies. That's what you learn in this book. Specifically, you'll get the ins and outs of what it takes to write good, meaningful, and well-structured HTML. You'll learn how to write proper, maintainable CSS to make your HTML look nice. And you'll learn how to get it all online.

Websites are meant to be universal files that can be accessed and displayed everywhere by everyone. *Accessibility*—in multiple senses of the word—is the name of the game, and learning to design and build websites that can be reached by all users, regardless of their personal abilities, using any device they choose.

To make a webpage, you need only what you already have on your computer: a text editor, a place to save files, and a browser. This book teaches you how to put all those pieces together.

Current technologies

On top of learning how to write HTML and CSS (and get it online), you'll get a crash course in what it's like to build a professional website today. You'll learn about important aspects of web design, such as performance (making sure your website loads quickly and doesn't burden the user). You'll learn about how to make your website accessible so that anyone can use it, including those who are color blind or rely on a screen reader.

This book also explores modern tools like CSS preprocessors, JavaScript libraries, and version control. It's good to know these things as you move forward because they will probably be the next step on your learning journey. This brings us to the next question: who is this book for?

Who Is This Book For?

In short, this book is written for anyone who wants to learn HTML and CSS. It assumes no prior knowledge.

That means that if you want to make a website for your hobby, this book is for you. If you're taking a beginner course (or teaching a beginner course), it's for you too. Or if you want to become a professional web developer, hey, it's for you too. After all, books like this are how I got my start. You'll get all the tools you need to get a website online. And then I'll give you some options for what you can learn next.

However, if you're looking for advanced techniques, like using HTML Canvas, writing JavaScript from scratch, or using advanced build tools like node.js, this book is not for you. Though I will say that after reading through the official HTML and CSS documentation thoroughly, you'll probably pick up some new things. I know I did.

How This Book Is Structured

This book is structured so that each chapter builds on the last. That means you'll first learn exactly what HTML and CSS are and what the purpose of each is. Then you'll learn about how to organize your website's files and directories. Then, on to the crux of the matter!

Both the HTML and CSS sections of the book start with the most basic markup or code and move to more complex techniques. If you're starting with no knowledge, it's best to take the chapters in order.

This book, like others in the Visual Quick-Start Guide series, uses a combination of explanatory text and step-by-step tasks to teach you HTML and CSS. Each chapter begins with text that introduces a topic, and a series of short sections present specific features within that topic.

These sections typically begin with an explanation of the feature, which is followed by one or more tasks that walk you through implementing the feature. Code samples and images accompany each task to show you what to do.

If you're brushing up or using this book as a reference, each chapter also stands alone—so if you need a refresher on forms or on the box model, you can just check out those chapters. While the book is not comprehensive, it covers all the important parts and it points you in the right direction for the rest.

The book ends with some bigger concepts to consider once you're comfortable putting an entire website together.

Although you'll get all the building blocks to make a full site, we won't build a single site from scratch. There will, however, be full-page examples for you to follow, as well as starter files to work from.

Code

There are three ways code is presented in the book.

Code within regular narrative text (which you'll usually see in numbered steps) is set in a distinctive font. Here are a couple of examples: `</head>` and `.nav-main {`.

Blocks of code appear as standalone paragraphs within the flow of text, or as separate numbered Code samples (**CODE00.1**).

Both of the previous types can include small portions that are highlighted in red to draw your attention to them:

```
<a href="#contact">Jump to Contact
  Form</a>
```

You'll encounter most of the code in the step-by-step tasks. They'll show you exactly what to type and then show you the results. So please follow along— there's nothing like learning by doing!

In the actual code files, I include inline comments to help you understand what's going on. These comments use special markup to prevent them from appearing on the page when it's rendered in a web browser.

CODE 00.1 A sample code block

```
p.introduction {
    color: red;
    font-family: Monaco, monospace;
    font-size: 16px;
}
```

HTML comments look like this:

```
<!-- This is an HTML comment -->
```

CSS comments look like this:

```
/* This is a CSS comment */
```

Much of the code is available for download at peachpit.com (see "Online Content," below). You can also find it, along with links and other useful resources, at casabona.org/vqs/.

Supplemental information

Throughout the book there are two other elements to look out for: tips and sidebars.

> **TIP** Tips are formatted like this and include helpful notes, links, and other information that's good to know.

This Is a Sidebar

Sidebars, as the name implies, include more information than a tip but don't really fit in the main body of the text, which is designed to give you hands-on experience.

Sidebars support the step-by-step tasks and are designed to enhance and strengthen the skills you're learning.

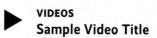

VIDEOS
Sample Video Title

This book is heavily supplemented with videos, which you can access via the online Web Edition (see "Online Content"). The videos reinforce bigger points, expand on skills taught in step-by-step tasks, and highlight topics that are more easily demonstrated in video than in static images.

Online Content

Your purchase of this Visual QuickStart Guide includes online materials provided by way of your Account page on peachpit.com.

Code samples

Some of the code examples shown in the book are provided for your personal use and study. They're organized in folders by chapter.

Web Edition

The Web Edition is an online interactive version of the book, providing an enhanced learning experience. Your Web Edition can be accessed from any device with a connection to the internet, and it contains the following:

- The complete text of the book
- Hours of instructional video keyed to the text

Accessing the code samples and Web Edition

Note: If you encounter problems registering your product or accessing the code samples or Web Edition, go to www.peachpit.com/support for assistance.

You must **register** your purchase on peachpit.com in order to access the online content:

1. Go to www.peachpit.com/htmlvqs.
2. Sign in or create a new account.
3. Click Submit.
4. Answer the question as proof of purchase.
5. The **code samples** can be accessed from the Registered Products tab on your Account page. Click the Access Bonus Content link below the title of your product to proceed to the download page. Click the lesson file links to download them to your computer. As a courtesy, the code samples are also available—along with other useful learning resources—from casabona.org/vqs/.

   The **Web Edition** can be accessed from the Digital Purchases tab on your Account page. Click the **Launch** link to access the product.

Note that if you purchased a digital product directly from peachpit.com, your product will already be registered. However, you still need to follow the registration steps and answer the proof of purchase question before the Access Bonus Content link will appear under the product on your Registered Products tab.

Errata

Finally, try as I might to get rid of them all, there still may be some errors in the final, printed text. You can find a list of those on the book's page at www.peachpit.com/title/9780136702566. Click the Updates tab to report an error or to see any corrections that are available.

I hope you enjoy the book and get a lot out of it, whether you're learning or using it as a reference.

What Are HTML and CSS?

The web has come a long way since it launched, in 1991. We've seen some big evolutions: from plain, static pages to slightly nicer-looking websites, to fully interactive web-based applications that we can access from anywhere in the world—including the device in our pocket.

And while the web has evolved considerably over that time, at its very core are still two important technologies: HTML and CSS. But what are they, and why should you know them?

What Is HTML?

HTML stands for *HyperText Markup Language* and it does two important things: it describes how webpages should look, and it defines the semantics of those pages.

But what is a *markup* language? Well, websites are made up of a bunch of different components. A variety of kinds of data—text, images, audio, video, and downloadable media—are part of a website. Those files—every component of the website—are stored on a server for you and other people to access.

Think of it this way: imagine that accessing a website from a server is like ordering takeout. You order from your favorite restaurant (sending a request across the internet), the kitchen staff (the server) selects the items you need, and then the delivery person (the internet again) brings the food (the files for the website) to your door (your computer).

All of this data is presented to you in your browser (Chrome, Firefox, Safari, Microsoft Edge, etc.) in a human-readable way.

Because humans and computers don't read data the same way, there needs to be something that tells computers how to display all of this data in a structured way—to *render* it—so humans can read it.

The raw data files that the server sends you come with one or more files written in HTML. To continue our takeout analogy, you can think of an HTML file like a bento box (or, if you're not into Japanese cuisine, like a cafeteria tray). It acts as a container that keeps the different types of data organized and presents them in a useful arrangement.

That's where *markup* comes in. An HTML file is simply a text file *marked up* with special codes that tell the web browser how to display the data it's receiving from the server on the computer's screen. HTML markup draws from a large collection of text *tags* that are embedded in the text and tell the computer—specifically the browser—how a website should look.

Semantics in this context is important because it gives meaning to those tags (also known as *elements*). For example, there's an **<h1>** HTML element (for Heading 1) (**FIGURE 1.1**), which tells the browser and search engines that the enclosed text is a heading—and not just any heading, but the most important heading. The browser then knows to display it in big bold letters ... that is, unless you use *CSS*, or *Cascading Style Sheets* (which you'll learn about later), to tell the browser to display it differently.

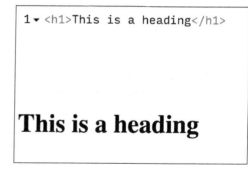

```
1 ▾ <h1>This is a heading</h1>
```

This is a heading

FIGURE 1.1 A heading tag in HTML

While you could just put a bunch of plain text into a file and open it in a browser, that text will have no structure or meaning. It will all run together, and there will be no visual hierarchy. It will just be a blob of text.

Let's start by looking at the simple Word document in **FIGURE 1.2**. You can see there are multiple headings at different sizes, paragraphs with spacing, and text that's formatted as bold or italic type.

This visual hierarchy gives the reader an idea of how they should approach the text: when a new section starts, where emphasis in the text lies, and more. In Word you do this using the Styles pane. On a webpage, you do that by adding HTML tags to the HTML file.

To create a simple hierarchy with HTML:

1. Open Notepad on Windows, or TextEdit on Mac.
2. Type `<h1>Bigger headings are more important</h1>`.
3. Type `<h2>This is smaller</h2>`.
4. Type `<h3>This is smaller still</h3>`.
5. `<p>This is body copy, and is most common.</p>`.
6. Save the file as **hierarchy.html**.
7. Double-click the file to open it in your browser.

   Your browser should display four paragraphs of text, decreasing in size from top to bottom (**FIGURE 1.3**).

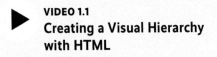

VIDEO 1.1
Creating a Visual Hierarchy with HTML

See how you can create an outline, or visual hierarchy, using only HTML markup.

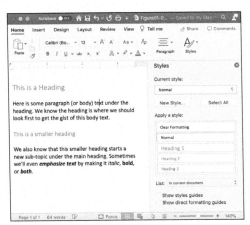

FIGURE 1.2 A Microsoft Word document

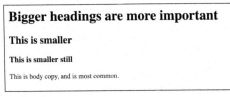

FIGURE 1.3 A simple hierarchy in HTML

Current version: HTML5

At the time of this writing, the current version of HTML is HTML5. This version introduced lots of new elements and simplified a lot of the markup.

Because it's likely that you're just entering the wonderful world of HTML, using HTML5 mostly means you have a ton of great features at your disposal, and that those features are well supported. But it is good to know that HTML5 is backwards compatible, and much of it works with old and new browsers.

Luckily, browsers are pretty forgiving of HTML versions and even of errors in your markup, so you won't have to worry about completely breaking anything with your code!

What Is CSS?

If HTML provides the structure for a webpage, then CSS supplies the style—and it's right in the name! CSS stands for Cascading Style Sheets, and it describes how a webpage should look: it prescribes colors, fonts, spacing, and much more. In short, you can make your website look however you want.

While HTML uses tags, CSS uses *rulesets*. They look like this:

```
h1 {
    color: black;
    font-size: 30px;
}
```

A great example of how CSS works is the website CSS Zen Garden. You can visit the site at csszengarden.com and, by changing the CSS, completely change the look and feel of the pages without changing the underlying HTML markup. Much like when you apply different themes or layouts to documents in Microsoft Word,

▶ **VIDEO 1.2**

Changing Styles on CSS Zen Garden

Let's take a look at CSS Zen Garden in action! You'll see how to change a bunch of styles to see how the appearance of the site changes. And then you'll take a quick peek at the markup to see that it's *not* changing.

▶ **VIDEO 1.3**

Applying Simple Styles to Markup

Start with your HTML markup from earlier and add some styles to it.

changing the CSS styles on a webpage makes the page look different, but the hierarchy of the content stays the same (**FIGURE 1.4**).

While browsers come with their own default styles, you can easily override them with your own styles, in the form of CSS files called *style sheets*.

Current version: CSS3

CSS is currently on version 3 (CSS3) and is constantly evolving as browsers and computers get more powerful.

With CSS3 you get animations, more visual effects, and much, much better support for layout features like columns and grids, among other features.

For feature support, CSS3 is more dependent on the user's browser than is HTML. With HTML, browsers treat unknown tags as plain text, so they still render properly. But older browsers likely will not support newer features in CSS3—and that will affect how your pages look and function. You'll learn more about that later in the book.

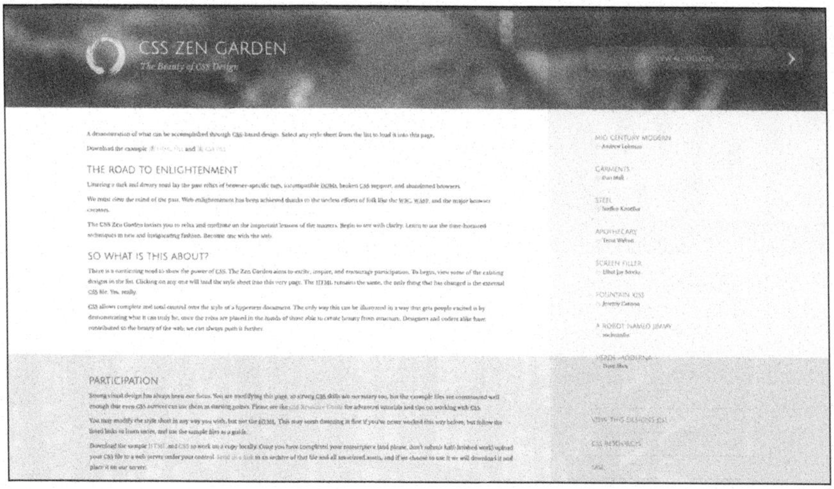

FIGURE 1.4 CSS Zen Garden

How HTML and CSS Work Together

Even though HTML and CSS perform different functions for a website, they are almost always coupled in learning materials such as this book.

That's because they are the two core languages necessary for making modern websites. Although technically only HTML is required to make a webpage, without CSS you'll get a bland website that doesn't look like much more than a Word document (**FIGURE 1.5**).

VIDEO 1.4
Styles vs. No Styles

First, I'll show you a plain website with no CSS, and then I'll apply a style sheet to show you how dramatically it can change.

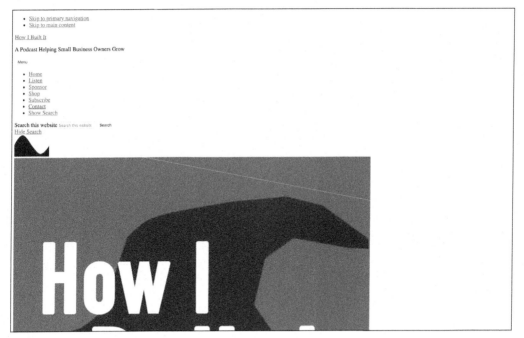

FIGURE 1.5 HTML, no CSS

These days, with the power of HTML5 and CSS3, we can create with our websites unique experiences that would have required a true programming language like JavaScript just a few years ago (**FIGURE 1.6**).

Exciting times

Because of the synergy between HTML5 and CSS3, we live in a pretty exciting time for website creation. Things we once had to hack together are now natively supported (like columns of text), and HTML is getting more semantic and accessible.

That means more people with different abilities can use websites, search engines are getting more useful information, and websites should load faster, because you don't need to add workarounds or extra processing to make certain aspects of your website work.

Much of that has to do with advancements in web browser development.

FIGURE 1.6 The HTML page from Figure 1.5, this time with CSS

Wrapping Up

Another reason HTML and CSS are so often discussed together is that they're both processed by the user's browser. Other web technologies, programs, and apps work differently. Some might be processed by a server, or some on a developer's computer and exported. HTML and CSS are uniquely positioned because the source code is accessible to the user in the browser.

When something new gets added to HTML or CSS, it's up to each individual browser to implement the changes. That means that Google Chrome, Firefox, Safari, and Microsoft Edge may implement the new features at different times.

As a result, the websites you create might look different in each browser.

We'll talk more about testing your websites in a later chapter, but knowing this will help you understand the true power of HTML and CSS: any device that has a browser can view your website.

It also means that you don't need any additional tools, equipment, or expenses to start making websites. You can do it right from your computer.

Let's do that now.

▶ **VIDEO 1.5**
Browser Comparison

See how one website can look different when viewed in Chrome, Safari, and Microsoft Edge.

Creating a Website on Your Computer

The beauty of HTML and CSS being interpreted by the browser is that you can basically create HTML and CSS on *anything* that has a browser. Although this book focuses on working on a Mac or a Windows computer, you can definitely get it done on a Chromebook, an iPad, or, in a pinch, even your phone.

It also means that (assuming you have a device with a browser on it) you can do it at no initial cost. In Chapter 21 you'll learn about the two components you need to get your website online: a *server* (also known as a *hosting service*) and an *address* for that server (known as a *domain*). You don't need either of them to start working with HTML and CSS, nor do you need to pay for any other software. Everything used in this chapter is free!

There are three components to creating a website on your computer:

- A text editor
- A folder structure
- A web browser

Using a Text Editor

A text editor is a program that lets you write plain text (that is, text without any formatting) on your computer. In Windows, Notepad serves that purpose, and macOS ships with TextEdit (**FIGURE 2.1**). Be careful: TextEdit lets you add simple formatting to plain text, so you'll need to make sure to save the file in plain text format and add the .html extension to the file name. Don't save the file in the default rich text format (.rtf).

To create a new webpage:

1. Open Notepad on Windows, or TextEdit on macOS.

   In the following steps, enter each tag on a separate line of code.

2. Type **<html>**.

3. Type **<head>**.

4. Type **</head>**.

5. Type **<body>**.

6. Type **</body>**.

7. Type **</html>**.

8. Save the file as **index.html**.

VIDEO 2.1
Creating a New Webpage

Use a simple text editor to create a basic HTML webpage and save the file.

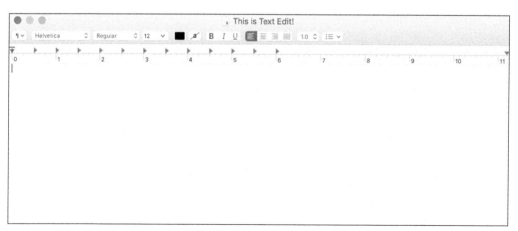

FIGURE 2.1 TextEdit for macOS

▶ **VIDEO 2.2**

Installing VS Code

Download, install, and customize Visual Studio Code.

FIGURE 2.2 HTML markup in VS Code showing syntax highlighting in action

Using Advanced Tools

There are also a multitude of advanced tools specifically for writing code and markup. They include features like:

- **Syntax highlighting** to make your code easier to read
- **Autocompletion** to allow you to write code faster
- **Real-time compiling**
- **Error checking**
- **Version control**

Some are souped-up text editors, like Notepad++ (for Windows) and Atom and Visual Studio Code (VS Code), which are both cross-platform.

Some are integrated development environments (IDEs) that have whole suites of tools built in. Coda for Mac is a popular one, but there's also the cross-platform PHPStorm. These are generally used for programming in languages like PHP or Python.

I recommend VS Code (**FIGURE 2.2**). It's free, well made, and stable, and the user interface is completely customizable. The ability to customize the interface of VS Code will make reading HTML and CSS easier, and it allows you to highlight the markup for an HTML tag or CSS statement, which we'll cover in later chapters.

Website Directory Structures and File Extensions

With a code editor in place, it's time to talk about the actual files you'll need for your website, and the folder, or *directory*, structure you'll use to store them.

Since you're developing right on your computer, you could technically just throw all the files onto the desktop and work from there. But I *strongly recommend against that*. Instead, you should create a proper directory structure.

Your initial examples and projects will use only one or two files. But as your websites get more complex, you'll need more files (and more types of files). Having a good file structure will keep your site organized. It will help you, and anyone else who might maintain your code, find things easily.

Naming conventions

Before you set up the directory on your computer, let's talk about naming conventions. When it comes to naming files, you'll use one file extension for HTML files (`.html`) and one for CSS files (`.css`).

All file names should be lowercase and should use hyphens (-) in place of spaces. So "My Cool File" would have the file name `my-cool-file.html`.

The same convention goes for directories: their names should be all lowercase, and if you're going to use multiple words, use hyphens to separate them.

TIP A file extension tells the computer how to handle the file. Usually this means telling the computer which program should open the file, or what kind of information the file contains.

 VIDEO 2.3
Setting Up a Directory Structure

Your website will end up using a lot of files on your computer, and the way you organize those files into directories is important.

To set up a directory structure:

1. If you're on Windows, go to and open the My Documents folder. On macOS, open the Documents folder in your home, or user, folder.

2. Right-click in the folder window and choose New Folder. This is the top-most folder in your directory structure, which is also called the *root folder* of the website.

3. Name that folder **website**.

   You can name the folder anything you'd like.

4. Double-click the new folder to open it.

5. Create a new folder called **images**.

6. Find the index.html file you created in the previous task. Move it into the website folder.

TIP This book uses Google Chrome throughout to test web pages that we create, but you can use Safari, Edge, Firefox, or the latest version of any modern browser you'd like!

Accessing your files

When you want to open an HTML file, you can double-click its icon on your computer to open it in the browser. Taking files online so that other people can open them is a bit of a different story, and I'll talk more about that in Chapter 21. But there is one important piece of information you should know.

To access a file online, you need to know its *path*—that is, its location in the file system hierarchy. File paths use the format `/directory/file-name`. Many times, when we use a browser to visit a website, we don't specify the name of the file we wish to access. The browser could be visiting a *domain* (peachpit.com) or a specific subfolder in that domain (peachpit.com/store/). A domain serves as the "address" for a website. You can think of it the same way you'd think of a mailing address for house.

Continuing the home address analogy, to get to a specific file on the web you have to know the route to follow to reach it. This is provided by the file's Uniform Resource Locator (URL). The URL of a file incorporates the name of its domain and the file's path (**FIGURE 2.3**).

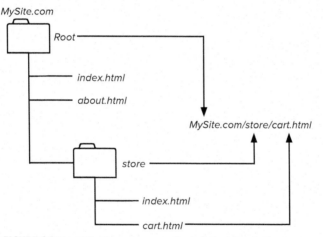

FIGURE 2.3 The URL of a webpage reflects its location in the website's directory structure.

What if you don't know the exact URL of the page you want to visit, but you know the domain name of its website? In these cases, most web servers will choose a default file to show you. This default file is most often named `index.html` and sits at the root of the directory we're accessing. So the main page for your website (its *home page*) will have the file name `index.html`.

Mimicking a web server

Another reason to forge good organizational habits early in this process is that web servers—where your files will eventually live—are organized in a specific way, with your site's files living in some publicly available folder, usually named `public_html`, `public`, `html`, or even `root`.

If you'd like to get a good idea of how web servers work (although it isn't necessary to understand this now), you could download a program that creates a small server on your computer. For Windows, that will be the software bundle WAMP (Windows, Apache, MySQL, PHP). For macOS, that will be MAMP (Mac, Apache, MySQL, PHP). Don't worry. In both cases, all four components come in a single installer.

This is definitely overkill for what we need right now, but let's file it under "good to know."

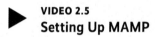

VIDEO 2.4
How Default Files Work

To see how default files work, you'll first visit a website where you specify the file name, and then you'll visit two different URLs where the file name is not specified.

VIDEO 2.5
Setting Up MAMP

Install MAMP on a Mac, and then look at how the file structure lines up with the URL structure.

Using CodePen for Quick Tests

There's one more option for quickly testing code without the need for a web server, but you will need an internet connection.

The popular website CodePen provides an interface that lets you write and test code in a single window. You can see how this works in **FIGURE 2.4**.

You enter your HTML and CSS into one of the panels at the top of the page, while the bottom of the page displays the results in real time. So if you want to rapidly see the effects of what you're writing without opening and refreshing your browser, CodePen is a great option. It's especially good for rapid prototyping.

FIGURE 2.4 The CodePen code editing interface

Wrapping Up

Now that you have your text editor, your local website directory, and a fast way to test code, you're ready to start writing HTML.

In the next chapter we're going to dive into how HTML works. Let's do it!

HTML Syntax

As mentioned in Chapter 1, HTML is the language that defines every webpage. But what exactly does that mean, and what are the terms we should use when talking about HTML?

HTML is a set of text *tags*. These tags are inserted into the content of the HTML files that create your webpages, and they define the type of content being displayed in the browser.

In this chapter you will learn all about HTML, from the terms you need to know, to how to write tags, to the general makeup of an HTML document.

How HTML Tags Work

Take a look at one of the most common HTML tags (**FIGURE 3.1**). The **<p>** is a standard HTML tag. It starts with a less-than sign (<), followed by the letter *p* (the name of the tag), and ends with a greater-than sign (>). Taken together, these constitute an HTML tag.

Note that HTML tags usually work in pairs that frame the content to which they apply. The only difference between the first and second **p** tags is the addition of the forward slash (/) after the left angle bracket that encloses the second **p** tag. This denotes the closing tag, and treated as a unit, the whole statement creates an HTML *element*: opening tag, content, and closing tag.

The **p** in between the angle brackets is the character—this tells the browser what the content is. In this case, **"p"** stands for "paragraph" and causes the browser to display the content between the tags as a block of text.

One might read this aloud as, "An opening paragraph tag, followed by text, then a closing paragraph tag." Depending on the tag, the browser will display the text differently.

TIP You'll often see the less-than and greater-than symbols that enclose a tag referred to as *left* and *right angle brackets*, respectively, even though they're not technically equivalent. Another convenient way to refer to the symbols collectively is to call them *inequality symbols*.

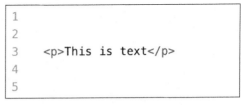

```
42
43
44
45
46    <p>This is a paragraph</p>
47
48
49
50
51
```

FIGURE 3.1 An HTML element

```
1
2
3    <p>This is text</p>
4
5
```

FIGURE 3.2 Using HTML tags to define text as a paragraph

This is text

FIGURE 3.3 How the tagged text looks in a browser

```
1
2
3    <h1>This is text</h1>
4
5
```

FIGURE 3.4 The same bit of text but with **<h1>** tags replacing the **<p>** tags

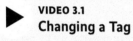

FIGURE 3.5 Our familiar text, now rendered as a top-level heading

 VIDEO 3.1
Changing a Tag

I'll demonstrate how changing a tag changes the way the browser displays text.

 VIDEO 3.2
Excluding Necessary Attributes

See what happens if you exclude a necessary attribute from an HTML tag, such as <**img**> or <**a**>.

To change an HTML tag and see the result in the browser:

1. In your text editor, type <p>This is text</p> (**FIGURE 3.2**).

2. Save the file as **tag.html**.

3. Double-click the file to open it in your browser (**FIGURE 3.3**).

4. Back in the editor, replace **<p>** with **<h1>**.

5. Replace **</p>** with **</h1>** (**FIGURE 3.4**).

6. Save the file.

7. In the browser, refresh the page to see how the text changes size and style (**FIGURE 3.5**).

Attributes

There's one more key piece of text you might find in HTML tags: *attributes*. Attributes provide additional information about the element they're being applied to. Let's look at our paragraph tag again, this time with an attribute:

<p lang="en">This is a paragraph.</p>

The attribute should go after the character in the opening tag. There are two parts to an attribute: the name (**lang**) and the value (**en**). This attribute tells the browser, "This paragraph is in English."

Two other notes about attributes:

- Elements can have any number of attributes.

- Some elements, like images (**<img>**) or hyperlinks (**<a>**), require specific attributes to work properly.

Adding Comments

Finally, it's considered a best practice to annotate your HTML code with information about the code itself by adding *comments*. You can do this to label sections of the code or to explain the purpose of individual pieces of code. These comments are helpful when you revisit the code later to update it, or especially when someone else works on the code.

Comments don't appear on the page when it's rendered in a browser. This is useful during development, because you can "comment out" a piece of code to try out the effect of turning it off temporarily without actually deleting it from the file.

To add comments to HTML:

1. In your HTML file, find the spot where you want the comment to start and type `<!--`.

2. Do one of the following:

    If you're adding a comment, type the text of the comment followed by `-->`.

    If you're commenting out existing code, place the insertion point at the end of the code and type `-->`.

See **CODE 3.1** for an example of commented code. **FIGURE 3.6** shows the rendered page.

> **TIP** Even though commented code doesn't appear when a browser renders the page, the comments are not completely hidden! Any user can view the page's source code (you'll learn how to do that in Chapter 22) and see the full text of any comments, so be careful not to store anything embarrassing or offensive in comment text.

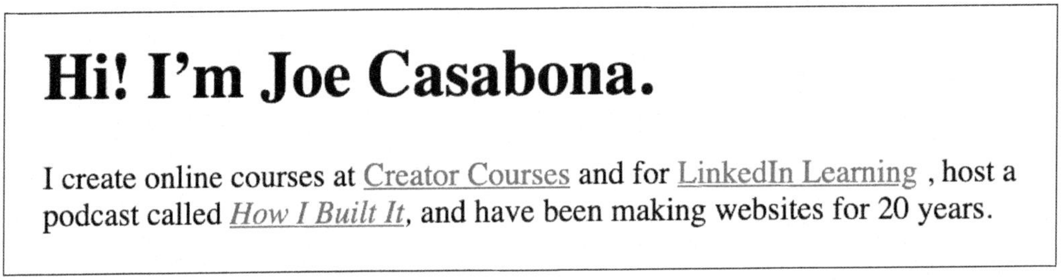

Hi! I'm Joe Casabona.

I create online courses at <u>Creator Courses</u> and for <u>LinkedIn Learning</u> , host a podcast called *<u>How I Built It</u>*, and have been making websites for 20 years.

FIGURE 3.6 When Code 3.1 is rendered in a user's browser, the commented code is invisible to the user.

CODE 3.1 This code contains two comments that mark the beginning and end of a section of the page, and one paragraph element that's been commented out.

```
<!doctype html>
<html class="no-js" lang="">
    <head>
        <link href="style.css" rel="stylesheet" type="text/css" />
        <title>Joe Casabona - Done for You Podcasts and Courses</title>
    </head>
    <body>
        <main>
            <h1>Hi! I'm Joe Casabona.</h1>
<!-- Start of Site Description -->
<div>
    <p>I create online courses at
        <a href="https://creatorcourses.com/">Creator Courses</a>
 and for
        <a href="https://www.linkedin.com/learning/instructors/joe-casabona">LinkedIn
        ➝ Learning</a>
, host a podcast called
<em><a href="https://howibuilt.it/">How I Built It</a>, </em>
and have been making websites for 20 years.</p>
</div>
<!--
<p>This content won't display because it's been commented out.</p>
-->
<!-- End of Site Description -->
        </main>
    </body>
```

Structuring an HTML Page

Now that you have a basic understanding of how HTML tags work, you need an understanding of the structure of an entire page. The essential components of a standard HTML page can be distilled into a boilerplate file. You can use this boilerplate file as a template for new HTML documents (**FIGURE 3.7**).

These components should exist on every HTML page:

- A **DOCTYPE** declaration (to tell the browser what version of HTML we're using) as the very first line.

- An opening **<html>** tag. All other tags on the page will be placed between the opening and closing **html** tags.

- Opening and closing **<head>** tags.

- Opening and closing **<body>** tags.

- A closing **</html>** tag ends the document. Nothing should come after that.

TIP Older versions of HTML required that "DOCTYPE" be set in all uppercase letters, but in HTML5 the term is case-insensitive.

```
<> boilerplate.html  ✕
1    <!doctype html>
2    <html class="no-js" lang="">
3
4        <head>
5
6        </head>
7
8        <body>
9
10       </body>
11   </html>
```

FIGURE 3.7 HTML boilerplate file markup

<html>, <head>, and <body> tags

Aside from the DOCTYPE, three different tags define the overall structure of a webpage:

- The **<html>** tags mark the opening and closing of the entire document. Every other tag (aside from DOCTYPE) will go between these tags.

- The **<head>** element is where information *about* the page goes. In most cases, none of this information will be displayed in the browser window.

- The **<body>** element is where all the page content goes. If there's text between the **<body>** and **</body>** tags, it will likely be displayed to the user.

There are some exceptions to these rules about the **<head>** and **<body>** and what gets displayed. A good example for the **<head>** is the **<title>** element. The **<title></title>** tags go in the **<head>** and define the text that gets displayed in the tab of your browser (**FIGURE 3.8**).

FIGURE 3.8 The **<title>** element as displayed in the browser

The \<meta> Tag

The \<meta> tag, much like the \<title> tag, belongs in the \<head> of the document. However, unlike \<title>, this displays no information to the user.

Instead, the \<meta> tag is used to send information about the web page to search engines. Its most common attributes are **name** and **content**, which are used for name-value pairs. One example of this is to provide the description of a document:

```
<meta name="description" content="A
 basic HTML boilerplate file.">
```

A list of common values for the **name** attribute are:

- **author**: Defines the name of the author of the document

- **description**: Provides the description of the document that should show up in search engine results

- **color-scheme**: Determines whether a page supports dark mode on devices that allow it.

- **viewport**: Gives information about the initial size of the document. This is used on mobile devices only.

- **robots**: Determines whether the document should be included in search engine results.

TIP The \<meta> tag does not use a closing tag or slash.

TIP The **name/content** combination for the \<meta> tag is the most common. But there are other attributes for more advanced definitions and functionality. You can find them here: developer.mozilla.org/en-US/docs/Web/HTML/Element/meta

To create an HTML boilerplate file:

1. Create a new file in your text editor.

2. Type \<!DOCTYPE html>.

   This is the DOCTYPE declaration. In HTML5, just "html" is used. In older versions, the definition is a bit more verbose.

3. Type \<html> to start the document.

4. Type \<head>.

5. Type \<title>HTML Boilerplate\</title>.

6. Type \<meta name="author" content="*your name*">.

   Be sure to replace *your name* with your own name.

7. Type \</head>.

8. Type \<body>.

9. Type \</body>.

10. Type \</html> to close the document.

11. Save the file as **boilerplate.html** in your website folder.

▶ **VIDEO 3.3**
Creating an HTML Boilerplate File

I'll walk you through creating an HTML boilerplate file.

What Is Semantic Markup?

As you've learned, the tags tell the browser the kind of content being presented. But why is that important?

By using the appropriate tags, we're describing our content—to the user, to the browser, and to search engines and other computer-based processors. This allows each to interpret the information the way they see fit. This could mean displaying it in a certain color, or highlighting it in specific search results.

For example, Google displays site navigation directly in search results, as long as the appropriate semantic tags are used (**FIGURE 3.9**).

In short, semantic markup means our webpage is more accessible to everyone. It can be more easily translated for international visitors, and assistive technology (like screen readers) can understand its content better.

Wrapping Up

HTML tags are the building blocks of the web. They create structure and assign meaning to our text. This helps everything and everyone who visits your webpage understand it better.

Now that you have a basic understanding of how HTML works and why we should use it, let's use it for our most common task: formatting content.

▶ **VIDEO 3.4**
Screen Reader in Action

Let's see how assistive technology takes advantage of semantic markup.

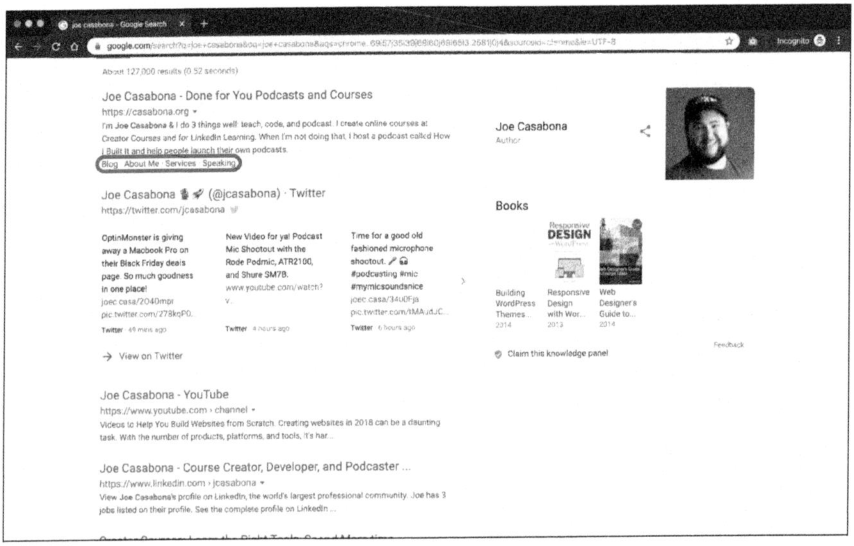

FIGURE 3.9 Site navigation links can be displayed in search results.

Basic HTML Elements

There's a wide range of HTML elements, and technically all formatting of those elements happens in CSS. But certain HTML elements come with semantic meaning for how text should be presented on the screen.

In this chapter, we look at the most basic elements, and how they can come together to create a well-formatted, readable, and meaningful page.

HTML Text Formatting

If you've created text in Word or Google Docs, you'll know that formatting can be done with the press of a few buttons. Select the text and choose a style from the menu, and formatting is applied. White space is added between paragraphs and headings, bullets are added to unordered lists, you can change the color of text, and more.

It's not quite like that in HTML. If you just write text in an HTML document, there will be no formatting. All the text will run together, new lines will be ignored, and certain characters will not display properly.

While browsers do use a default style sheet to format all HTML elements, we still need to use HTML to describe every piece of content on the page. Without the HTML, the browser won't know what kind of text is on the page.

So let's start with the most common elements: headings and paragraphs.

Paragraphs and Headings

You were introduced to paragraphs in the last chapter. They are blocks of text that generally contain one idea, in one or more sentences.

To create paragraphs:

1. Open the boilerplate.html file and save it as **chapter4.html**.
2. On a new line after the opening **<body>** tag, type **<p>**.
3. Type `This is a paragraph!`.
4. Type `</p>`.
5. On a new line, type **<p>This is another paragraph.</p>**.
6. On a new line, type **<p>This is a third paragraph.</p>**.
7. Save the file, then open it in your browser.

   You'll end up with what you see in **FIGURE 4.1**.

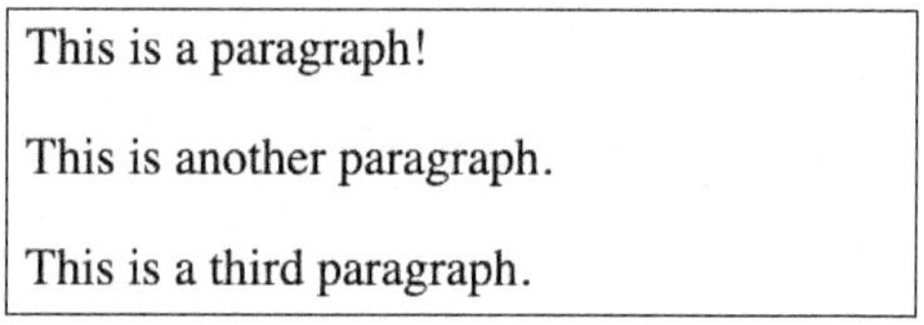

This is a paragraph!

This is another paragraph.

This is a third paragraph.

FIGURE 4.1 Three blocks of text, formatted as paragraphs in HTML

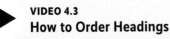

VIDEO 4.1
HTML with No Elements

To see how much of an impact elements have on a webpage, let's look at an HTML page that has no markup.

VIDEO 4.2
Creating Paragraphs

As an exercise, create a few paragraphs on a page and then see what they look like in the browser.

VIDEO 4.3
How to Order Headings

Because of the strong semantic meaning associated with headings, they need to be ordered properly.

Headings are slightly different. HTML allows for six levels of headings, with Heading 1 (<h1>) being the most important and Heading 6 (<h6>) the least important (**FIGURE 4.2**).

The principal role of headings is to create a visual hierarchy on a page. Paragraphs should be organized into sections, with headings at the top of those sections.

Headings also add meaning to the text—meaning that's important to search engines.

Semantically, there should only be one Heading 1 on a page. As we move down the page, we should make sure to keep our headings in the right hierarchical order.

The smaller the heading number, the bigger the idea it should represent. So <h2> tags should represent only the big ideas on a page.

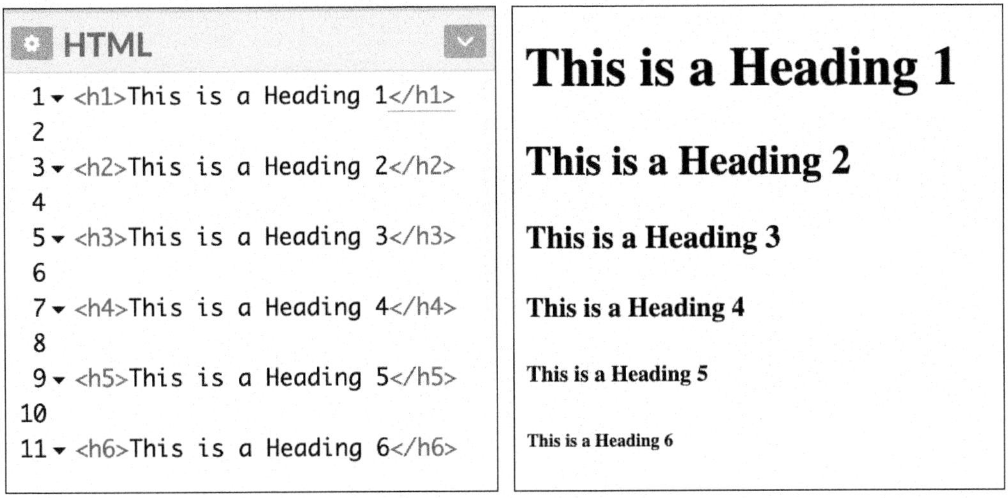

```
HTML
1 ▾ <h1>This is a Heading 1</h1>
2
3 ▾ <h2>This is a Heading 2</h2>
4
5 ▾ <h3>This is a Heading 3</h3>
6
7 ▾ <h4>This is a Heading 4</h4>
8
9 ▾ <h5>This is a Heading 5</h5>
10
11 ▾ <h6>This is a Heading 6</h6>
```

This is a Heading 1

This is a Heading 2

This is a Heading 3

This is a Heading 4

This is a Heading 5

This is a Heading 6

FIGURE 4.2 All the headings available in HTML, from <h1> to <h6>

Lists

After paragraphs and headings, the next most common element you'll find in text is a list. If you look back at a Word or Google Doc you've done recently, you'll likely find bulleted lists show up at least a few times.

There are two different types of lists you can create in HTML: *ordered* and *unordered*.

Ordered lists (by default) are prefixed by numbers. Unordered lists have bullets (●) prefixed.

Depending on the type of list you want to create, use an <ol> tag (for an ordered list) or a <ul> tag (for an unordered list). Between the opening and closing tags, each item on the list will be enclosed in <li> tags (for list item).

To create an unordered list:

1. In your HTML file, type <ul> to begin the list.
2. Type <li>Apples</li> to create the first of three items on the list.
3. Type <li>Bananas</li>.
4. Type <li>Cherries</li>.
5. Type </ul> to end the list.

   And in **FIGURE 4.3**, you see how it looks.

TIP You'll learn how to change the default symbol for bullets when we talk about **CSS**, but you can use anything to represent the bullets, even your own images. Visually, though, ordered lists should always be represented with numbers.

TIP Notice that list items are indented. When embedding HTML elements within other elements, it's common to indent them to make the markup more readable.

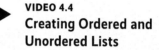

VIDEO 4.4
Creating Ordered and Unordered Lists

Learn how to create both types of lists, and nest one list within another.

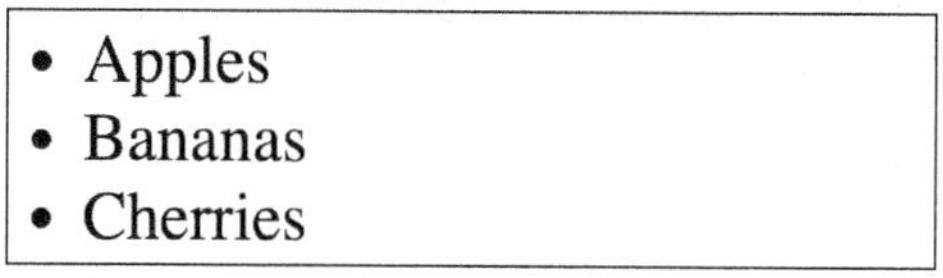

- Apples
- Bananas
- Cherries

FIGURE 4.3 The unordered list you created, as rendered in the browser

CODE 4.1 An example of a `<blockquote>` with the `cite` attribute together with an example of the `<cite>` element

```
<p><cite>The Importance of Being Earnest
→ </cite> is only one of many sources of
→ witty sayings by Oscar Wilde. To take
→ one example:</p>

<blockquote cite="https://en.wikiquote.org
→ /wiki/Oscar_Wilde">
<p>I never travel without my diary. One
→ should always have something sensational
→ to read in the train.</p>
</blockquote>
```

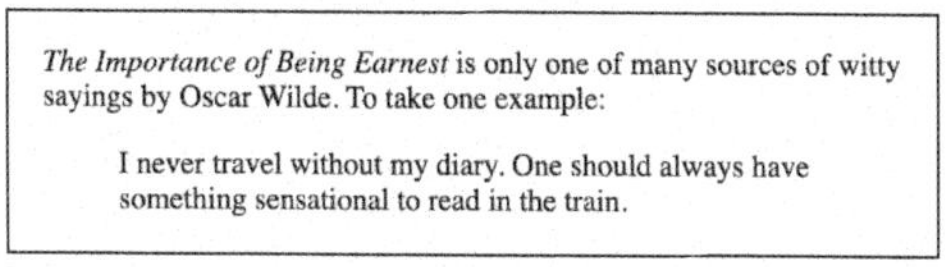
The Importance of Being Earnest is only one of many sources of witty sayings by Oscar Wilde. To take one example:

I never travel without my diary. One should always have something sensational to read in the train.

FIGURE 4.4 Code 4.1 as rendered in a browser

Quoting a Block of Text

Traditionally, in printed material, quotations of substantial amounts of text are set apart from the surrounding content by indentations or changing the type style. HTML includes the block-level element `<blockquote>` (which conveniently contains "block" in its name) to accomplish the same thing in the browser. By default, `<blockquote>` elements are indented compared to other block elements, but you can use CSS to change the indentation.

To provide a source for the quotation, include the `cite` attribute with the URL of the source as its value. You can also use the `<cite>` element to give the title of the source in text (**CODE 4.1**, **FIGURE 4.4**). It's normally styled in italics by the browser, but you can change that with CSS. If you wish to provide a link to the source as well, combine the `<cite>` element with an `<a>` element.

To quote a paragraph with citation:

1. Type `<blockquote>`.
2. Type `<p>`.
3. Type the quote.
4. Type `</p>`.
5. Type `<cite>`.
6. Type the source of the quote.
7. Type `</cite>`.
8. Type `</blockquote>`.

Formatting Text Inline

The last of the basic elements we'll cover are inline elements—that is, elements that are used inside other elements.

Paragraphs, headings, and lists are "block-level" elements. They are self-contained sections that start on a new line and take up the entire width of the container. But inline elements do not start on a new line and are only as wide as the content. An example is the `<strong>` tag.

In the following task you'll create a short paragraph (a block element) and change the formatting of some of the text in the middle of it (an inline element).

To bold text with the `<strong>` tag:

1. Type `<p>We use the strong tag to`.
2. Type `<strong>draw attention</strong>`.
3. Type `to text by bolding it.</p>`.

    You can see the result in **FIGURE 4.5**.

Notice that the `<strong>` tag is inside the `<p>` tag but still inline with the text. And by default, the browser bolds `<strong>` text. However, there's another benefit to using the `<strong>` tag. It tells browsers and search engines that this text is slightly more important than the normally formatted text.

TIP To draw attention to text without making it semantically more important, you can use the `<b>` tag instead. In HTML5 this is the Bring Attention To element; previously it was known as the Boldface element. It should be noted that you shouldn't rely on either one (`<strong>` or `<b>`) to bold text. That should be done with CSS.

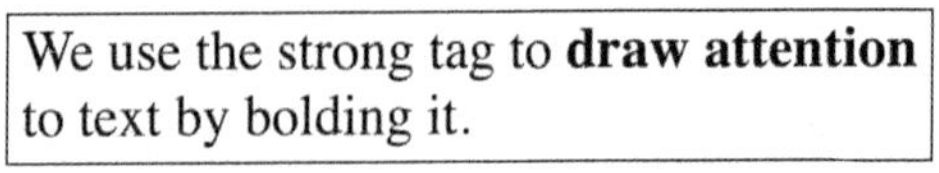

> We use the strong tag to **draw attention** to text by bolding it.

FIGURE 4.5 The paragraph produced by the code in this example

The catalog of tags for formatting inline text is extensive; here are the most common ones (**FIGURE 4.6**):

- `<em>` is used for emphasis. It shows as italicized text. Use the `<i>` tag if you want to set the text apart without semantically noting "emphasis."

- `<u>` is used to underline text. It shows as text with a line drawn under it.

- `<s>` is used to cross something out because it is no longer correct. It shows as text with a line through it. You may also come across `<strike>` in older code, but it's now been replaced by `<s>`.

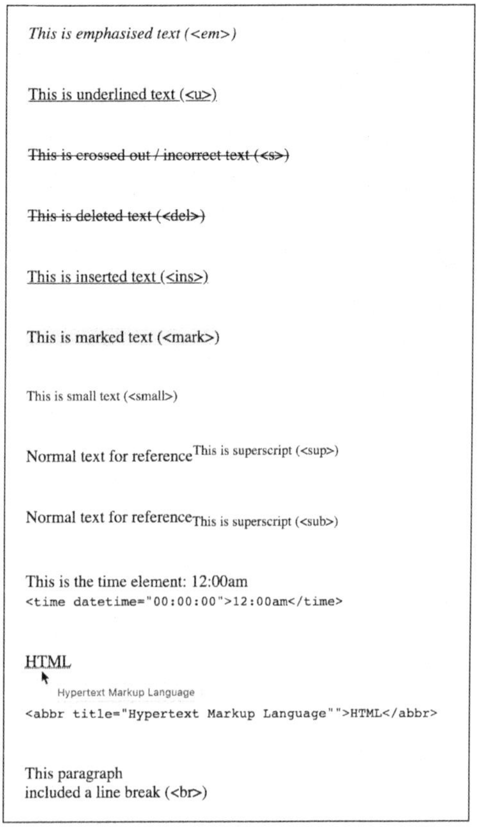

This is emphasised text (<em>)

This is underlined text (<u>)

~~This is crossed out / incorrect text (<s>)~~

~~This is deleted text (<del>)~~

This is inserted text (<ins>)

This is marked text (<mark>)

This is small text (<small>)

Normal text for reference^This is superscript (<sup>)

Normal text for reference_This is superscript (<sub>)

This is the time element: 12:00am
`<time datetime="00:00:00">12:00am</time>`

HTML
  Hypertext Markup Language
`<abbr title="Hypertext Markup Language"">HTML</abbr>`

This paragraph
included a line break (<br>)

FIGURE 4.6 All of the listed formatting markup and their default styles in Chrome.

- `<del>` looks similar to `<s>`, but lends a slightly different meaning to text. `<del>` marks something that has been deleted from the original document.

- `<ins>`, which is usually underlined by default, notes something that has been inserted into the document.

- `<mark>` is used to highlight text. It adds a yellow background to text, as if a highlighter pen has been drawn across it.

- `<small>`, which renders text smaller than the default size, is used for notes, side comments, and fine print.

- `<sup>` is superscript, and makes text appear smaller and raised slightly above the baseline. This is often used for exponents, or bibliographic citations.

- `<sub>` is used to display subscript text. Like `<sup>` reduces text size but is lowered below the baseline than normal text.

- `<time>` represents a specific time and is often combined with the `datetime` attribute to convert human readable time into a machine-readable format.

   You'll find a list of valid `datetime` values here: developer.mozilla.org/en-US/docs/Web/HTML/Element/time.

- `<abbr>` represents an abbreviation and is usually rendered with a dotted underline. You can include the fully expanded version of the abbreviation in the `title` attribute, which is usually displayed in a tooltip on mouseover.

- `<br>` creates a line break. It's useful for situations when you want to make lines a specific length, as in poetry or in a mailing address.

TIP This is only a sampling of the tags available in HTML for formatting inline text. You can find a more comprehensive list of tags at developer.mozilla.org/en-US/docs/Web/HTML/Element#Inline_text_semantics

▶ VIDEO 4.5
Converting a Fully Formatted Word Doc to HTML

You've learned enough formatting in HTML to start with a Word document and convert it to HTML.

Marking Up Code

There are also two HTML tags specifically used for marking up code:

- **<code>** is displayed in a monospace font and is used to represent a short snippet of computer code.

- **<pre>** is also displayed in a monospace font and represents preformatted text. That means any text, including white spaces, appears exactly as it was typed.

TIP When using < and > in the **<code>** element, you should use the HTML entities: **<** and **>**, respectively. To learn about HTML entities visit **developer.mozilla.org/en-US/docs/Glossary/Entity.**

If you need to display multiple lines of code, place the **<code>** element inside a **<pre>** element. The only time you should use **<code>** by itself is for an inline element (**CODE 4.2**, **FIGURE 4.7**).

CODE 4.2 Examples of a **<code>** element inline in a paragraph, and another where it contains several lines of code inside a **<pre>** element.

```
<p>If you need to display multiple lines of code, place the <code> &lt;code&gt; </code>element
 inside a <code> &lt;pre&gt;</code> element. </p>

<p>In completely unrelated news, here's a bit of the code for a table that you'll encounter
 again in Chapter 8:</p>

<pre><code>
&lt;table border="1"&gt;
    &lt;thead&gt;
        &lt;th colspan="4"&gt;Aaron Judge&lt;/th&gt;
        &lt;th&gt;RF&lt;/th&gt;
    &lt;/thead&gt;
    &lt;tbody&gt;
        &lt;tr role="header"&gt;
            &lt;td&gt;Year&lt;/td&gt;
</code></pre>
```

If you need to display multiple lines of code, place the <code> element inside a <pre> element.

In completely unrelated news, here's a bit of the code for a table that you'll encounter again in Chapter 8:

```
<table border="1">
    <thead>
        <th colspan="4">Aaron Judge</th>
        <th>RF</th>
    </thead>
    <tbody>
        <tr role="header">
         <td>Year</td>
```

FIGURE 4.7 Code 4.2 as rendered in Chrome.

Working with Other Languages

If you're working with languages that use a right-to-left (RTL) script like Arabic or Hebrew, then there are two elements that will be helpful to you: **<bdi>** and **<bdo>**.

<bdi> is the Bidirectional Isolate element. Place text within it to isolate it from the rest of the text around it to prevent rendering issues. This is helpful if your main text uses a left-to-right (LTR) script but you want to include a quotation or a name written in a right-to-left script.

If you want to override the current directionality of the text (which is generally defined by the browser), you can use the Bidirectional Text Override element (**<bdo>**) element with the `dir` attribute. It accepts the values `rtl` or `ltr`.

Finally, if the entire direction of the page is RTL, you can apply the `dir="rtl"` attribute to the **<html>** element.

There's a thorough explanation at w3.org: www.w3.org/International/questions/qa-html-dir.

Wrapping Up

With that, you have the basics down. You know how to format text and create a nice visual hierarchy in the browser. This will make your website much easier to read. Now let's talk about what makes the web ... well, the web: hyperlinks!

5

Links

The element that has made the web at least somewhat interactive since the very beginning is the *hyperlink*.

Hyperlinks, or simply *links*, allow us to connect pages to each other to form a website, and let us send visitors to pages that are external to our website. They play an important role in the organization and SEO (search engine optimization) of websites. But how exactly do they work? What can we link to?

In This Chapter

Link Markup

A link (or hyperlink) is a way to connect one webpage to another. Links also allow users to jump to a different section of a webpage, download documents, and more. To distinguish them visually from other webpage content, textual links are usually given a distinctive appearance, using color (typically blue for a link that has not yet been visited), special text formatting, or both.

Links are represented in HTML by the <a> (or *anchor*) tag. The <a> tag is one of those HTML tags that can include a number of attributes.

In this case, the link takes users to a page on a different website, so we need to include the attribute **href**, for *hypertext reference*. The value of the **href** attribute is the URL (Uniform Resource Locator) of the *destination*—the page you're linking to. The enclosed content of the <a> element is typically some *label* text—usually the name of the page the link will take the user to. This label is the only part of the link that the user sees.

TIP The <a> tag does not absolutely require the **href** attribute, but it must be present for the tag to work correctly as a hyperlink.

Let's see how to set up the markup for a link to Google.

To create a hyperlink:

1. In your HTML file, type <a to start the anchor element.

2. Type href="https://google.com"> to define the destination of the link.

3. Type **Visit Google** to provide a label for the user to click.

4. Type </a> to finish the link (**FIGURE 5.1**).

5. Save the file and view it in your browser (**FIGURE 5.2**).

TIP Link labels don't have to be text. As you'll learn in Chapter 7, you can use an image as a clickable link too.

While the markup for a link may look straightforward, there are several nuances to creating links. Key to creating links is understanding how URLs are structured.

▶ VIDEO 5.1
The Components of Hyperlink Markup

Create a simple link to a different (external) website.

```
<a href="https://google.com">Visit Google</a>
```

FIGURE 5.1 The markup for the link to google.com

Visit Google

FIGURE 5.2 This hyperlink to google.com stands out by its color and underline.

VIDEO 5.2
Walking Through a URL

Take a closer look at Figure 5.3, and learn more about each section in detail.

VIDEO 5.3
HTTP vs. HTTPS

Learn how the HTTP and HTTPS protocols are different.

URL Structure

At this point, it's worth taking a closer look at URLs. In **FIGURE 5.3**, you'll see the components of a common URL.

TIP **URLs are the most common type of a broader set of Uniform Resource Identifiers (URIs). URIs tell the browser how to handle the resources that are being linked to.**

URLs are made up of these sections:

- The *protocol* (either http or https).
- The *subdomain* (optional).
- The *name* of the website.
- The *top-level domain* (or TLD). This is also known as the *extension*.

To link to a specific file within a site, you need to provide these items as well:

- The path (folder hierarchy) containing the file.
- The file name.

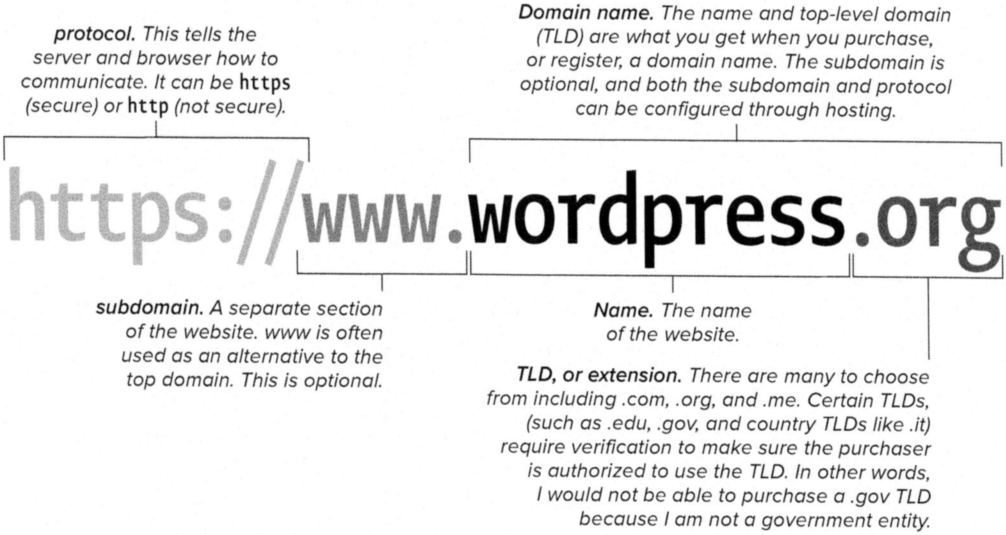

protocol. This tells the server and browser how to communicate. It can be https *(secure) or* http *(not secure).*

Domain name. The name and top-level domain (TLD) are what you get when you purchase, or register, a domain name. The subdomain is optional, and both the subdomain and protocol can be configured through hosting.

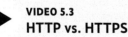

https://www.wordpress.org

subdomain. A separate section of the website. www is often used as an alternative to the top domain. This is optional.

Name. The name of the website.

TLD, or extension. There are many to choose from including .com, .org, and .me. Certain TLDs, (such as .edu, .gov, and country TLDs like .it) require verification to make sure the purchaser is authorized to use the TLD. In other words, I would not be able to purchase a .gov TLD because I am not a government entity.

FIGURE 5.3 The components of the URL https://www.wordpress.org

In order to reach a website at all, you need to provide at least these three parts of the URL: the protocol, the name, and the TLD. Paths, subdomains, and file names need to be included only when you want to reach those specific areas of the website.

Ultimately, where a link sends your users is based on what kind of URL—or how much of the URL—you include.

First, let's look at how linking to pages within your website compares with linking to pages outside your website.

Internal vs. External Linking

This concept is pretty clear. *Internal* links are links to pages within your own website (or on the same domain). *External* links are links to someone else's webpage.

TIP **Even though subdomains appear to be part of your website, they are still considered external. For example, sub.casabona.org is not the same site as casabona.org.**

As far as markup goes, internal and external links use exactly the same structure, except (as you'll learn later in this chapter) external links are always *absolute*. That is, they need to include the entire URL, including the protocol. If one of those items is missing or incomplete, the link will not work.

If you're linking internally, there's something else to consider: you don't always need to include the entire URL, because it's implied. This is the result of the difference between absolute and relative links.

VIDEO 5.4
Errors in External Links

How important is it to include the protocol? This video shows what happens when an external link isn't structured properly.

Relative vs. Absolute Linking

Back in Chapter 2, you learned about file structures and how websites are organized (**FIGURE 5.4**). You also saw how URLs incorporate part of a file's directory structure. When we talk about *relative* versus *absolute* linking, we're talking about how much of the URL and directory structure we want to include.

With an *absolute* link, you include the entire URL in the anchor element markup. Always use an absolute link when linking to an external site, but you'll usually use relative links for files on your own site.

TIP There are times when an absolute link is appropriate even for files within your own site. This is generally the case with dynamically generated content—that is, content generated automatically by a script.

Say you want to link to a specific file called cart.html on the website mysite.com. You'll need to know the location of the file in the site's directory structure to link to it. If cart.html is in a top-level folder (i.e., a folder in the root directory) called /store/, then the absolute link for this file is https://mysite.com/store/cart.html.

Relative links, on the other hand, don't include the complete URL of the location you're linking to. The structure of the link markup is based only on where the linked file is relative to the current file. So relative links are commonly used to link within pages on a single website, whose files share one common directory.

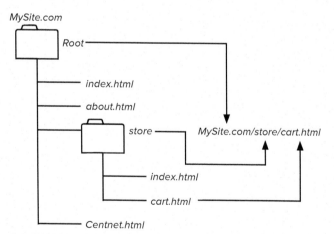

FIGURE 5.4 The directory structure we created in Chapter 2

There are several different types of relative links we can create, as shown in **TABLE 5.1**.

- **Same folder:** The linked file is in the same folder as the linking file. The relative link would just be the file name (e.g., file.html).

- **Child folder:** The linked file is one folder down from the linking file (in other words, in a folder contained in the linking file's folder). The relative link starts with a forward slash (/), then includes the folder name, another forward slash, and the file name (/folder-name/file.html).

- **Parent folder:** The linked file is one folder up from the linking file. The relative link would be two periods and a forward slash (../) and then the file name (../file.html).

These patterns can be repeated for any number of folders. So if a file is three folders up from the current file, the relative link would be ../../../file.html. And there can be great-, great-great-, great-great-great-grandchildren, and so on.

Looking at our example website again, to make a link from the home page (mysite.com/index.html in the root directory) to cart.html, you could use a relative link. Since cart.html is in the child folder /store/, we could link to it using a relative path: /store/cart.html.

TABLE 5.1 **Types of relative links**

Relative link type	Relative path	Example from our sample directory
Same Folder: Both files are in same folder	file.html	From the home page: about.html
Child: Linked file is in next folder down	/folder-name/file.html	From home: /store/cart.html
Grandchild: Linked file is two folders down	/child-folder/folder-name/file.html	From home: /store/orders/001.html
Parent: Linked file is next folder up	../file.html	From /store/ to home: ../index.html
Grandparent: Linked file is two folders up	../../file.html	From /store/orders/ to home: ../../index.html

To create a relative link:

1. In your website folder on your computer, create a new folder called **images**.

2. Go to unsplash.com and download any image you'd like. Save it into the images folder you just created and name the image file **unsplash.jpg**.

3. In the website folder, make a duplicate of the file boilerplate.html and rename the new file **5.html**.

4. Open the file **5.html**.

5. Right after the opening **<body>** tag, type **<a href="**.

6. Type **/images/unsplash.jpg">**.

7. Type **Check out this image!**.

8. Type **</a>**.

9. Save the file and open it in your browser.

10. Click the link to display the image in the webpage.

> ▶ **VIDEO 5.5**
> **Creating Relative Links**

Let's take a closer look at the markup for creating relative links, and learn how those links behave in the browser.

Other Types of Links

Aside from internal and external links, here are two other types of links you can add to a webpage. You can link to a specific section of a page, and you can link to other applications, like email.

Linking to a specific section of the page

This is a great way to highlight specific content or drive a user to a pertinent area. There are two parts to this link:

- Assign a unique name to the section you want to link to by including the **id** attribute. For example, say you want to add a link to your page that takes people to a contact form. If the contact form is under the heading "Contact Me!" you would assign an **id** attribute (**"contact"**, perhaps) to the heading:

  <h3 id="contact">Contact Me!</h3>

- Link to that **id** in the anchor tag:

  <a href="#contact">Jump to Contact ⇢ Form</a>

The **id** attribute is often assigned to a heading tag (as in the "Contact Me!" example) because heading tags denote the beginnings of sections. But **id** is a standard attribute that can be applied to any HTML element.

In our link, we identify the section using the hash tag, or number sign (#), followed by the value of the **id** attribute (e.g., #contact). The hash tag tells the browser "this is a specific location on the page."

▶ **VIDEO 5.6**
Link to a Specific Location on a Page

You'll see the markup for linking to a page section, as well as how the browser behaves when you link to a page section.

To create a link to a specific location on a page:

1. In your HTML file, type or copy and paste several text paragraphs (be sure to enclose them in **<p>** tags) between the opening and closing **<body>** tags. If you wish, make the last paragraph a brief biographical sketch of yourself.

2. Place the insertion point in front of the last <p> tag to create a heading before the last paragraph. Type **<h3>About Me</h3>** to define the heading.

   Now, add an **id** attribute to this heading so you can link directly to it.

3. Place the insertion point in the opening tag of the heading element and type **id="aboutme"**.

   The entire line of code should look like this:

   <h3 id="aboutme"

4. Go back to the top of the document, and right after the opening **<body>** tag, type **<a href="**.

5. Type **#aboutme">** to tell the link to jump to the anchor you just created.

6. Type **Skip to "About Me"** to create the label for the link that will be displayed to the user.

7. Type **</a>** to close the anchor element.

8. Save the file and open it in a browser to test the link.

In many real-world implementations, you'll see the browser smoothly scroll to the linked section. In order to achieve that effect, you'll need to add some CSS to your website.

Linking to more than just webpages

Finally, links can do more than just take you from one webpage to another. There is a growing set of Uniform Resource Identifiers (URIs) that tell the browser which specific applications a link should open in. While email links are the most common, you can also specify telephone numbers (`tel:`), file servers (`ftp:`), and more.

Email links are links that will open an email app on your device, with the email address (and potentially other information) filled in. To create one, you structure the link like this:

```
<a href="mailto:joe@casabona.org">
→ Email Joe</a>
```

Notice that there's no URL here, just the prefix `mailto:` and the email address.

TIP Using `mailto:` is a great way to get a lot of spam email. A much more secure and user-friendly way to add an email form to your webpage is to use a form. You'll learn about forms in Chapter 9.

 VIDEO 5.7
Advanced Mailto Links

You can include more than just the main recipient's email address in email links. You can also add CC and BCC addresses, attach a subject line to the message, and even include message text.

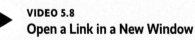 **VIDEO 5.8**
Open a Link in a New Window

Construct a link that opens a page in a new window.

Link Targets

Before we wrap up the chapter, there's one more attribute you should know about, and that's `target`.

You've likely browsed websites on which the links opened in new tabs or windows. A common reason is that the webpage author hopes the user will close the new tab when they're done and return to their site.

That's achieved by using the `target` attribute and the value `blank`. For example, to open casabona.org in a new tab, use this link:

```
<a href="https://casabona.org"
→ target="_blank">Link that opens in a
→ new tab</a>.
```

Other Link Targets

While not as common as `_blank`, several other link targets can be used in HTML:

- `_self` opens the link in the same window (the default).

- `_parent`: If the current page was opened in a new window, you can use this to open subsequent links in the original window.

- `_top` opens the page in the full body of the window (useful if using the `<iframe>` element).

- An `<iframe>` is a way to embed the content of one page into another, and is now used much less often than in the past. Today, you're most likely to encounter them when you embed a YouTube video on a page, which you'll learn about in Chapter 7.

- `framename` opens the page in a specific `<iframe>`.

To create a link that opens in a new window:

1. In your HTML file, type `<a href= "https://google.com"`.

2. Type `target="_blank">`.

3. Type `Visit Google</a>`.

4. Save the file.

5. Open the file in your browser and click the link to see it open the home page of google.com in a new window.

While it's considered best practice to open links in the same window, there might be legitimate reasons to send the user to a new window. If you do decide to open links in new windows, you should at least let the user know what to expect. You can do so by adding simple text (like "new window") to the link label or by adding an icon, as shown in **FIGURE 5.5**.

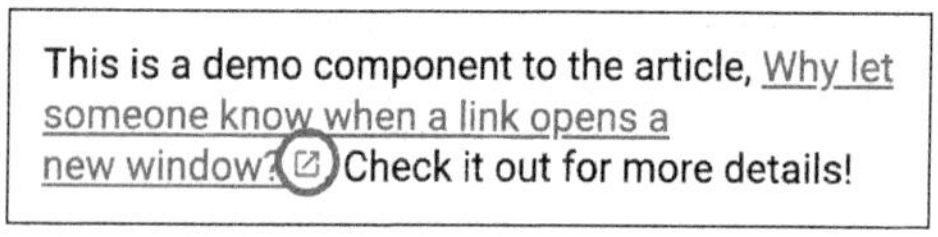

This is a demo component to the article, Why let someone know when a link opens a new window? Check it out for more details!

FIGURE 5.5 An example of a new window indicator icon from CodePen (codepen.io/svinkle/pen/BreKRJ)

Wrapping Up

With your knowledge of formatting, organization, and now linking, you're ready to move into the structure and layout side of HTML.

In the next chapter, you'll learn about the building blocks that are used to lay out a webpage.

Structure and Layout with HTML

Aside from formatting text, HTML gives us a set of tools for defining areas of a webpage. While they don't affect the way a page looks (that's what CSS is for), it's yet another way to apply semantic meaning to webpages for users and anything else that's reading the page.

In this chapter, you'll learn the kinds of areas you can create on a page, find out more about block versus inline elements, and get a preview of the CSS box model. Let's dive in!

Webpage Layout

If you've been to any website, you'll know that the items on a page are grouped into areas with specific functions, such as a header, a footer, a main area (which can contain several elements), and a sidebar. As an example, take a look at the home page of the *New York Times* with a box drawn around each item (**FIGURE 6.1**).

Each of these boxes is an area defined in HTML and styled with CSS. But the browser knows how to arrange the areas thanks to the HTML elements used to define them.

If you'd like to see how a page is structured in the Chrome browser, you can do so using the Web Developer extension. This extension adds a number of developer-friendly tools to Chrome, including options for drawing an outline around individual webpage elements.

You'll start by downloading the extension from the Chrome Store and installing it.

VIDEO 6.1
Preview of the Box Model

The term *box model* is used for CSS. It defines the box around each element—its padding (spacing from content to borders), margins (spacing around the outside of the box), borders, and content. It's integral to understanding how to best style a page.

But its building blocks (pun a little intended) are here in the HTML. Each element can be considered its own box. How it looks, and how it's positioned, is defined by the CSS.

FIGURE 6.1 The layout for the *New York Times* home page

FIGURE 6.2 The Chrome Store offers a wide range of extensions that add functionality to the browser.

FIGURE 6.3 Searching for "Web Developer" returns a long list of results.

FIGURE 6.4 The Web Developer page in the Chrome Store

To outline webpage elements in Chrome:

1. Open the Google Chrome web browser and go to the Extensions section of the Chrome Store: chrome.google.com/webstore/category/extensions (**FIGURE 6.2**).

2. Enter **Web Developer** into the Search field and press Return/Enter. The page displays the results of the search (**FIGURE 6.3**).

3. Find Web Developer by chrispederick. com in the results (it should be near the top) and click it to load its page into the browser (**FIGURE 6.4**).

4. Click the Add To Chrome button and follow the installation instructions.

   When the installation is complete, you'll notice a new cog icon in the toolbar ⚙.

5. Click the cog icon. A tabbed set of controls appears.

6. Click the Outline tab. A menu lists sets of elements that can be outlined (**FIGURE 6.5**).

7. Click to select the elements you want to outline. Outline Block Level Elements is a good starting point, so select that item in the menu.

An outline is drawn around each block-level element on the page (**FIGURE 6.6**).

▶ **VIDEO 6.2**
Outlining Elements with the Web Developer Extension

In this video, you'll see how to use the Web Developer extension for Chrome to outline elements of a webpage.

FIGURE 6.5 Select Outline Block Level Elements on the Outline tab to draw a box around each block-level element.

FIGURE 6.6 The home page of nytimes.com with elements outlined using the Web Developer extension in Chrome

Block vs. Inline Elements

Chapter 4 touched on this a bit, but there are essentially two kinds of HTML elements: block elements and inline elements. The best way to think about them is by how much page width they take up.

Block elements take up the full available width, thus creating their own block on a page. Style-wise, each element fits into the box model and has its own spacing. A paragraph is a block element (**FIGURE 6.7**).

Inline elements, on the other hand, take up only the width they need. Again, looking at this stylistically, by default there is no spacing applied directly to inline elements. `<strong>`, `<em>`, and `<a>` are all inline elements (**FIGURE 6.8**).

All the elements that we consider "layout elements" in the next section are block elements.

TIP One caveat, which will come up in the CSS chapters: you can change the default type of any element. So if you want to turn links into block elements, adding a little CSS will make it happen.

VIDEO 6.3

Outlining Block and Inline Elements Together

The Web Developer extension doesn't outline inline elements, so here I apply CSS to block and inline elements so that you can see more clearly how they work with each other.

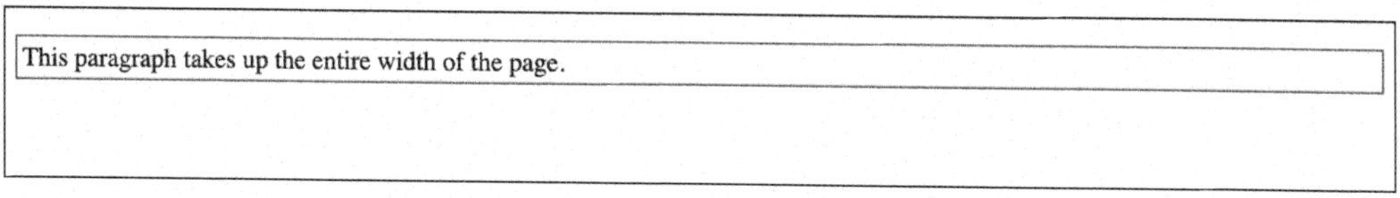
This paragraph takes up the entire width of the page.

FIGURE 6.7 A paragraph takes up the full available width.

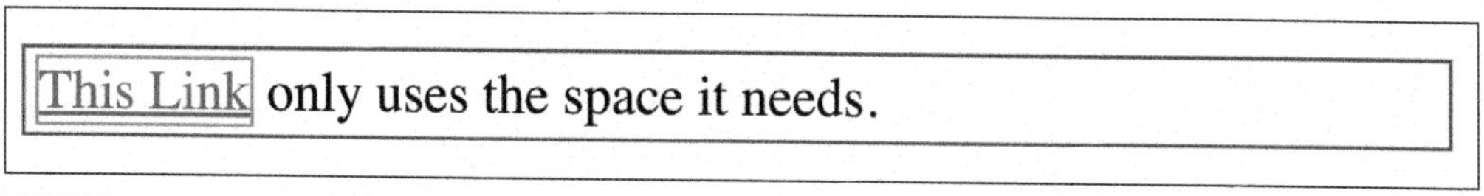
This Link only uses the space it needs.

FIGURE 6.8 A link takes up only the width that it needs to take up.

Page Sections

Before diving into the actual elements, it's important to define (at least loosely) the areas that will be included in the page design. A good way to get an idea of a page's design and layout is to sketch out a *wireframe*. A wireframe is a blueprint or a general framework of a webpage. Its focus is on content priority and lacks the niceties of visual design, like text styling or colors. In short, it should tell us where content and elements go. A typical webpage layout includes a few basic areas (**FIGURE 6.9**).

Now that you have a better understanding of how a page is laid out, here are the seven HTML elements that define these areas.

▶ **VIDEO 6.4**
Walking Through the Wireframe

This wireframe has several areas that are worth pointing out, along with some caveats and nice-to-knows. Let's take a closer look at it.

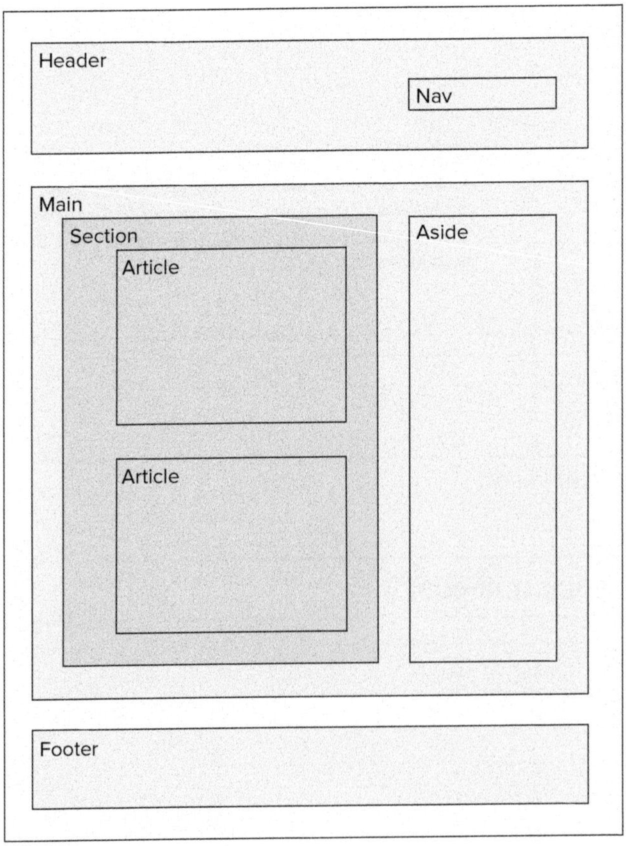

FIGURE 6.9 A wireframe of a webpage that uses common page sections

Header, footer, nav

The first areas to examine are the header, footer, and navigation. They are grouped because you can have each on a macro (site-wide) level and a micro (area-specific) level.

The *header* is the area that contains information at the top of a webpage or section of a webpage. A site's header generally includes the site title and maybe a tagline or logo. Other elements, like articles, can also have a **header** tag, which might include the title, date, and author's name. The navigation is also usually found in the header. The tag for this element is **<header>**.

FIGURE 6.10 The HTML markup for a simple navigation element

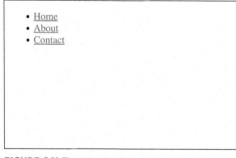

FIGURE 6.11 The simple navigation element as rendered in a web browser

The *navigation* includes links to other important pages on the site. On a micro level, groups of pages or articles can have their own navigation (if an article is spread across several pages, for example). Its tag is **<nav>**.

The *footer* is at the bottom of the page or section of a page and is generally used to provide extra information. For a section of a page, it could display the date it was published or tags or keywords. For the entire site, the footer can include additional links, copyrights, or other legal disclosures. You can get really creative with this section! Its tag is **<footer>**.

Both the header and footer can be pretty flexible as far as content and layout, but navigation tends to follow a more specific structure. That's because unordered lists (which use the **<ul>** element) are recommended for navigation, since they are an unordered list of links!

Lists for Navigation

Over the years, the use of unordered lists for navigation has been hotly debated. There are several arguments for and against.

The recommendation here comes from the HTML5 specification explicitly using lists in their nav examples (html.spec.whatwg.org/multipage/sections.html#the-nav-element) and from accessibility experts stating their importance in relation to screen readers.

Several years ago, CSS-Tricks published an article about it that garnered a lot of strong opinions. Their postmortem on the article is a great summary of the pros and cons of lists in nav: css-tricks.com/wrapup-of-navigation-in-lists/.

A simple site navigation element might have links to the home, about, and contact pages (**FIGURES 6.10** and **6.11**).

To create simple site navigation:

For this task, assume there are three pages: a home page (index.html), an about page (about.html), and a contact page (contact.html).

1. Type **<nav** to create the opening of the navigation element.

2. Type the attribute **role="main"** because this will be the page's primary navigation element.

3. Type **>** to close the opening tag.

4. Type **<ul>** to begin the unordered list of links to other pages in the site.

5. Create a navigation item for the home page by typing

   <li><a href="index.html">Home
   ↪ </a></li>.

6. Do the same for the about page; type

   <li><a href="about.html">About
   ↪ </a></li>.

7. Add the last link, for the contact page. Type

   <li><a href="contact.html">
   ↪ Contact</a></li>.

8. Type **</ul>**.

9. Type **</nav>**.

> **TIP** If you're creating links but you don't have a target URL or file name yet, you can use the hash symbol (#). This tells the browser "this is a link, but it doesn't go anywhere."

Section, article, aside, main

With the more general areas of a website covered, let's move to the content that changes with each page.

A *section* (tag: **<section>**) is any discrete area of a website with related content. For example, on a home page there might be an "about me" section, an "articles" section, and a "photo gallery" section. You have a lot of flexibility here.

An *article* (tag: **<article>**) is an area that is often self-contained and can stand on its own (and is often related to syndication). Blog posts or a page's main copy are usually described as articles.

An *aside* (tag: **<aside>**) is auxiliary information that's related to, but not integral to, the main content. Asides are often described as "sidebars," but they don't need to be physically to the side of the content. The tips in this book can be considered asides.

VIDEO 6.5
Making a Header with Navigation

Take your site navigation one step further and put it in a full header, with a site title.

ID and class

id and class are two attributes that can be applied to any element. They're used to apply some definition to the element they're assigned to.

Generally, each ID is unique (as in, only one element has a specific ID), and a class can be assigned to multiple elements.

In practice, IDs are usually used by JavaScript, and classes are used by CSS.

With all of our building blocks in place, you can create a simple blog layout. You can use a sample content generator (like loremipsum.io) or come up with your own.

To match the aside tag, there's also a <main> tag, which would denote the *main* content of the page. This will likely be a wrapper for your articles or sections.

If you're looking at other websites' markup, you might have noticed a very common tag: <div>. This tag, short for "division," predates the ones we've talked about and is often used for areas of a website that don't have an otherwise clearly defined purpose. Really, it's an all-purpose tag, if you're not sure what to use.

TIP I'd recommend giving divs an ID or class to make it clearer to those reading your code what kind of content they're looking at.

Building a Blog Article Layout

Now that you have all the building blocks (pun totally intended), you can put together a simple blog article page (**CODE 6.1**). Anything not relevant to this chapter is omitted and replaced with three dots (. . .).

To create a page header:

1. Type <header to open the **header** tag.

2. Type role="banner".

3. Type > to close the opening header tag.

4. On a new line, type <h1 id="site-title">Welcome to my Site!</h1>.

   We've added the ID site-title to tell browsers and search engines "this is the name of the site."

5. Add the navigation created earlier in this chapter.

6. Type </header> to close the page header tag.

> **TIP** As you become familiar with more samples of code from pages around the web, you might notice that sometimes they use "**id**," and sometimes they use "**role**" instead. That's because there are specific roles defined for accessibility. We'll talk about that more in Chapter 24, but for now, you can get a full list of roles at developer. mozilla.org/en-US/docs/Web/Accessibility/ ARIA/ARIA_Techniques.

> **TIP** Some HTML elements will not have a role assigned to them, because they already communicate a role. For example, we don't need to assign the role "main" to the <**main**> element.

To create the main article section:

1. Open the wrapper for the content by typing <div class="wrapper">.

   You're opening the wrapper **div** element here, but you'll close it when we create the <aside> element.

2. Open the main section by typing <**main**>.

3. Type <article>.

4. Type <header> to open the article's header.

5. Add a headline using the <**h2**> tag: type <h2>10 Reasons HTML is so great!</h2>.

   Use an **h2** tag here because the site title should be the only **h1** on the page.

6. Type </header>.

7. Type all of the content for the article. This should include text like paragraphs, lists, images, and hyperlinks.

8. Type <footer> to open the article's footer.

9. The publish date will go here. Type <p>Published March 6 at 11:06pm</p>.

10. Type </footer>.

11. Type </article> and then </main> to close out the rest of the elements.

CODE 6.1 The markup for a simple blog article

```html
<html>
    ...
    <body>
        <header role="banner">
            <h1 class="site-title">Welcome to my site!</h1>
            <nav>
                <ul role="main">
                    <li><a href="index.html">Home</a></li>
                    <li><a href="about.html">About</a></li>
                    <li><a href="contact.html">Contact</a></li>
                </ul>
            </nav>
        </header>

        <div class="wrapper">
            <main role="main">
                <article role="article">
                    <header>
                        <h2>10 Reasons HTML is so great!</h2>
                    </header>
                        ...
                    <footer>
                        <p>Published March 6th at 11:06pm</p>
                    </footer>
                </article>
                ...
            </main>

            <aside>
                <h3>Related Articles</h3>
                <ul>
                    <li><a href="/articles/css.html">Wait until you see CSS</li>
                        ...
                </ul>
            </aside>
        </div>

        <footer>
            <p>Copyright Joe Casabona</p>
        </footer>
    </body>
</html>
```

To create a sidebar:

1. Type `<aside>`.

2. Type the heading `<h3>Related Articles </h3>`.

3. Created an unordered list of articles. Type `<ul>`.

4. Add the first item: type `<li><a href= "/articles/css.html">Wait until you see CSS</a></li>`.

5. Add as many related articles as you'd like.

6. Type `</ul>`.

7. Type `</aside>` to close the **aside** element.

8. Type `</div>` to close the wrapper **div**.

To create a site footer:

1. Type `<footer>`.

2. Add one paragraph for the copyright line. Type `<p>Copyright [YOUR NAME]</p>`.

3. Type `</footer>`.

For the complete markup, see Code 6.1. To see the page rendered in a browser, see **FIGURE 6.12**.

> **TIP** Reminder: all the source code for this book can be found at GitHub.com/jcasabona/html-css-VQS.

Wrapping Up

You now have the basic HTML elements that are necessary to semantically lay out a page. You can find a complete list of semantic elements available in HTML5 at www.w3schools.com/html/html5_semantic_elements.asp.

Up until now we've focused a lot on text and how it's laid out. Now let's turn our attention to something more visually appealing: media.

VIDEO 6.6
Building a Blog Article Layout

In this video, you'll go through all the markup that's required to create a single blog article. You'll also see how the article looks in the browser.

Welcome to my site!

- Home
- About
- Contact

10 Reasons HTML is so great!

Lorem ipsum dolor sit amet, consectetur adipiscing elit, sed do eiusmod tempor incididunt ut labore et dolore magna aliqua. Ultricies tristique nulla aliquet enim. Nisi lacus sed viverra tellus in hac. Metus aliquam eleifend mi in nulla posuere. Sit amet cursus sit amet dictum sit amet justo donec. Nulla posuere sollicitudin aliquam ultrices. Sed risus ultricies tristique nulla aliquet enim tortor at. Egestas egestas fringilla phasellus faucibus. Pharetra massa massa ultricies mi quis hendrerit dolor magna. Faucibus vitae aliquet nec ullamcorper sit amet risus. Semper quis lectus nulla at volutpat diam ut. Ut consequat semper viverra nam libero justo laoreet sit amet.

Eleifend quam adipiscing vitae proin sagittis nisl. At ultrices mi tempus imperdiet. Mi eget mauris pharetra et ultrices neque. Risus pretium quam vulputate dignissim suspendisse in est. Venenatis urna cursus eget nunc scelerisque viverra. Integer quis auctor elit sed vulputate mi sit. In ornare quam viverra orci sagittis eu volutpat odio. Nibh tellus molestie nunc non blandit. Fermentum dui faucibus in ornare quam viverra. Faucibus in ornare quam viverra orci sagittis eu volutpat odio.

Published March 6th at 11:06pm

Related Articles

- Wait until you see CSS

Copyright Joe Casabona

FIGURE 6.12 A sample blog article page containing a header, site navigation, a main article section, a sidebar, and a footer

---

Media

You've learned how to add text and create semantic layouts, and that's great! But media—images, video, and audio—is what makes websites really stand out.

Media in this case refers to any non-plain-text file. And in this chapter, you'll learn how to embed images, videos, and audio. You'll also learn the ins and outs of finding good resources and where to host multimedia.

How Does Media Work on the Web?

The nice thing about using media on a webpage is that all you have to do is store the media files on your web server and insert links to them into your HTML files. The browser will know how to open most common forms of media (**FIGURE 7.1**).

But if you use HTML tags to tell the browser the type of media you're linking to, you can display that media directly on the page—without having to open separate windows or applications (**FIGURE 7.2**).

This is known as *embedding* the media file. The media can be viewed, watched, or listened to without the user leaving the page.

space.jpg (1920×1920)
File | /Users/joecasabona/Dropbox/books/HTML%20and%20CSS%20Visual%20Quick%20Start/Chapters/Chapter%207/space.jpg
Guest

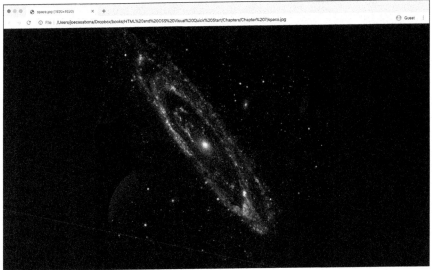

FIGURE 7.1 An image open in a browser window

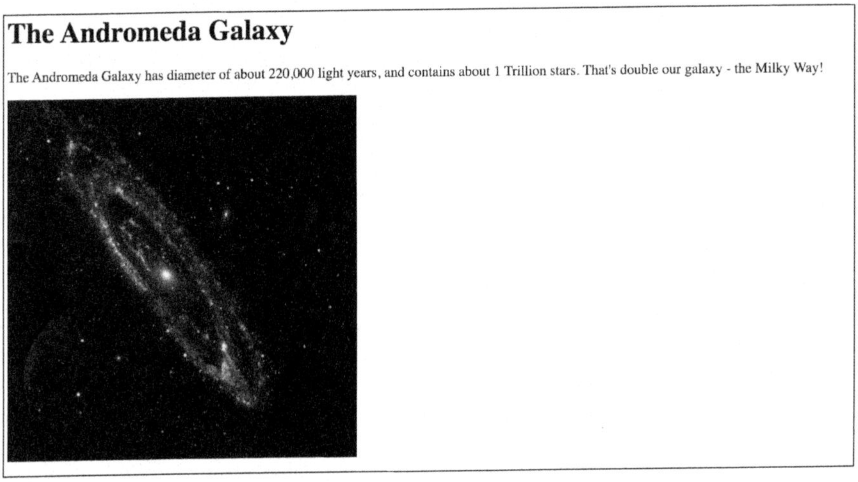
The Andromeda Galaxy
The Andromeda Galaxy has diameter of about 220,000 light years, and contains about 1 Trillion stars. That's double our galaxy - the Milky Way!

FIGURE 7.2 An image embedded on a page

Thanks to features of HTML5, you can tell the browser how to handle images, video, and audio. You can embed them directly into the page, and even give some instruction on how to display or control them—play, pause, mute, rewind, and more.

Other forms of media, like Microsoft Word documents, PDFs, and presentation software slide shows, can be linked in the browser but not embedded. The browser will rely on another program on the device to handle opening the file.

Web Image Format Acronyms

The image formats most commonly used on websites are usually referred to by cryptic acronyms. Here they are, along with what they stand for:

- **JPG/JPEG:** Joint Photographic Experts Group, in honor of the organization that invented the format
- **GIF:** Graphics Interchange Format
- **PNG:** Portable Network Graphic
- **SVG:** Scalable Vector Graphic

Images

Chances are that of all the types of media, you'll work with images the most, so that's a fantastic starting point.

Types of images

There are lots of different types of image that can be stored in a variety of file formats; these formats serve different purposes. For example, the most common type of image used on webpages is photos. They are typically in JPEG format, which compresses them so that their file sizes are not gigantic. Simple animated images will be in GIF format. Lightweight graphics will often be in PNG format; they can use transparent backgrounds. And more complex graphics that need to be displayed at several different sizes are usually in scalable vector format (or SVG). You can resize SVGs without worrying that you will lose image quality.

The types of images supported in HTML are determined by the browser, and as a result, certain file types will work only in certain browsers.

Pixel vs. Vector Graphics

As far as the web is concerned, there are two basic categories of graphics: pixel (JPEG, PNG, GIF) and vector (SVG).

Pixel graphics are made up of a grid of colored dots (*pixels*, short for "picture elements"), so an 800×600 pixel graphic is 800 dots wide by 600 dots tall. If you try to display a pixel graphic at a bigger size ("Scale it up"), you'll run into *pixelation*. In other words, the browser will actually increase the size of each pixel, so you will start to see big colored squares.

Vector graphics aren't stored as those dots. They are a set of instructions to the browser for *how to draw* the image. That means that there's no inherent size associated with it. You tell the browser the image dimensions you want, and it will adjust the instructions accordingly.

While pixel graphics are great for images with continuous tones of color like photos, vector graphics are much better for sharp-edged graphics like logos, icons, and images representing data.

To understand why SVGs are an important part of web design, you'll see the effects of scaling a JPEG versus scaling an SVG.

The most common image types will work in all browsers: JPEG, GIF, PNG, and SVG. These images use the file name extensions .jpg, .gif, .png, and .svg, respectively (**FIGURE 7.3**).

TIP For a full table of image types, file name extensions, and supported browsers, see developer.mozilla.org/en-US/docs/Web/HTML/Element/img.

Adding Images to a Page

Once you've got the images you want to use in the right format, it's time to add code to your HTML to insert the images into the page's flow. Next, you'll learn about two elements you can use to place an image on a page: `<img>` and `<figure>`.

The `<img>` tag

For all supported image types except SVG (that's coming later), you will use the image embed tag `<img>`. This tag is unique because in addition to requiring an attribute (`src`), it has no end tag. Here's some sample markup:

```
<img src="space.jpg" alt="A view
 of the Andromeda Galaxy"
 title="A view of the Andromeda
 Galaxy" />.
```

FIGURE 7.3 This image of space is called *space.jpg*.

All images should also include an **alt** attribute, whose value is text that describes the image. While this isn't required for the tag to work, it is required to make your website accessible (for more on website accessibility, see Chapter 24).

The **title** attribute can also include this text. The main difference (besides semantic meaning) is that the title will appear in a tool tip when you hover over an image (**FIGURE 7.4**).

▶ **VIDEO 7.2**
Adding an Image to a Webpage

You will see how to add an image to a page, as well as how to design the folder structure of the website to make sure the image appears properly.

To add an image to a webpage:

1. Type **<img** to open the image embed tag.

2. Type **src=** followed by the path to the image. In this example, type **"space.jpg"**.

3. Add the **alt** and **title** attributes. Type **alt="A view of the Andromeda Galaxy" title="A view of the Andromeda Galaxy"**.

4. Close the **img** tag by typing **/>**.

5. Save the file and open it in your browser to see the result (Figure 7.2).

FIGURE 7.4 The image's title showing on hover

The `<figure>` tag

If you want to make meaningful additions to the flow of your page, or group an image with a caption, you'll use a figure with an optional caption element. Its tag is `<figure>`, and to associate a caption with it you insert the element `<figcaption>` inside it. The structure looks like this:

```
<figure>
    <img src="space.jpg" alt="A view
    of the Andromeda Galaxy" />
    <figcaption>A view of the
    Andromeda Galaxy</figcaption>
</figure>
```

Note these points about the use of the `figure` tag:

- You can put more than one image in a `<figure>` tag if they make sense together in context.

- Everything inside the opening and closing `<figure>` tags creates a single, self-contained unit.

- Since figures are self-contained, you should be able to move a figure up or down on a page without changing the meaning of the page.

That last point also means that not all images are figures.

Figures: Not Just for Images

As it turns out, the `<figure>` tag can be a pretty flexible element. Since it's a self-contained piece of content that should add value to the document, a figure doesn't just need to be an image or set of images.

You can put code, audio, video, or even ads (which can have their own specific requirements) in figures.

To add a figure to the page:

1. Type `<figure>` to open the `figure` element.

2. Add the image from earlier, without the `title` attribute. Type `<img src="space.jpg" alt="A view of the Andromeda Galaxy." />`.

3. Type `<figcaption>A view of the Andromeda Galaxy.</figcaption>` to add a caption to the image.

4. Type `</figure>` to close the `figure` element.

5. Save the file and open it in your browser (**FIGURE 7.5**).

VIDEO 7.3
Using Figures for Code Samples

Figures aren't just for images. In this video, you learn how to use the `<code>` tag to add a figure that contains code to a webpage.

A view of the Andromeda Galaxy.

FIGURE 7.5 Our photo of the Andromeda galaxy, now with a caption

Responsive Images: Considering Different Devices and Connections

One of the biggest issues with adding images to webpages is that, depending on the file size of the images, they can unnecessarily bloat the site and make it very slow to download. Here's an example: the full size of the space image is 6200×6200, coming in at 4.2MB (4200KB).

If we resize it to 1920×1920, 30 percent of the original size, the file size is 415KB. That's 9 percent of the original file size!

That size difference will have a considerable effect on the time it takes to download the page, and it will have little to no effect on how most visitors see the image; 1920 pixels is still overkill if you consider that most mobile screen sizes are considerably smaller.

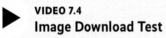

VIDEO 7.4
Image Download Test

Seeing is believing! Here's a download test comparing the performance of different image sizes and connection speeds.

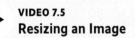

VIDEO 7.5
Resizing an Image

Using the srcset attribute requires that multiple versions of the same image be available to the browser. In this video, you'll learn how to use a couple of popular applications to resize an image.

However, you might wonder what happens if someone is viewing the page on a big monitor or even a TV, where they would rather take advantage of the full size of the screen. That's where the srcset attribute comes in.

This attribute tells the browser that it has a range of image files to choose from when rendering the <img> element.

Here's an example:

```
<img srcset="
    space-original.jpg 4x,
    space-large.jpg 3x,
    space-medium.jpg 2x,
    space-small.jpg 1x"
src="space-medium.jpg" />
```

Note that src is included to provide a fallback for browsers that don't support srcset yet.

Within the srcset attribute, include a comma-separated list of different images (or the same image at different sizes). For each image, provide its path as well as a relative size value (that is, 4 times, 3 times, etc.) notated as 4x, 3x, etc. (Note that 1x is implied and not required).

These numbers represent the *pixel density* of the user's browser (the number of pixels available in a chosen area of the display), and they tell the browser how to choose which image to download and serve to the user depending on the device's pixel density. If the device has a very high pixel density, it can choose to display the 4x image. If its display has a lower resolution, it might download and display only the 2x or 1x image. This will save on load time and bandwidth.

Alternatively, you can specify the image widths in pixels instead of expecting the browser to use pixel density to decide which file to use. So you would replace 4x with 6200w (6200 pixels is the original image's width), 3x could be replaced with 4650w, and so on. This gives the browser more information about the image, so it can replace the images while taking into account both the characteristics of the device and the image width.

To add an image using `srcset`:

1. Create three sizes for your image: 1024, 800, and 600 pixels wide.

   See Video 7.5 to learn how, if you need to.

2. Save them in the same folder as your HTML file.

   For the purposes of this task, name the images following the pattern **space-[size].jpg**, which gives us **space-original.jpg**, **space-1024.jpg**, and so on.

3. In your HTML document, type `<img srcset="`.

4. On the next line, type `space-original.jpg 6200w,`.

5. Press Return or Enter, then type `space-1024.jpg 1024w,`.

6. Press Return or Enter, then type `space-800.jpg 800w,`.

7. Press Return or Enter, then type `space-600.jpg 600w"`.

8. We also need a fallback for older browsers that don't support `srcset`. Type `src="space-1024.jpg"`.

9. Type `/>` to close the image tag.

> **TIP** If you want to learn a lot more about optimizing images, especially for mobile, Smashing Magazine has a fantastic write-up: **www.smashingmagazine.com/2019/10/ imagekit-guide-optimizing-images-mobile/.**

The `<picture>` Element

If you want more fine-grained control of when images show up, you could use the `<picture>` element. It's very similar to using `srcset`, but the markup is a bit different.

One thing it makes use of is *media queries*, which you'll learn more about in Chapter 17. The quick explanation is that you can use CSS to get information about the browser, like screen width, and then adjust the display of your website based on that information.

To use the `<picture>` element to show different images:

1. Create three sizes for your image: 1024, 800, and 600 pixels wide.

   See Video 7.5 to learn how to create these versions of your image if you need to.

2. Save them in the same folder as your HTML file.

   For the purposes of this task, the images will be named following the pattern **space-[size].jpg**, which gives us **space-original.jpg**, **space-1024.jpg**, and so on.

3. In your HTML document, type `<picture>`.

4. On a new line, type `<source`.

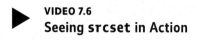

VIDEO 7.6
Seeing `srcset` in Action

This video shows you how to add a responsive image using `srcset`, and then you'll see what happens as the browser is resized.

5. Type `media="(min-width: 1025px)"`.

   This is the media query. It says, "If the browser has a minimum width of 1025px, use this image."

6. Type `srcset="space-original.jpg">`.

7. On a new line, type `<source media="(min-width: 801px)" srcset="space-1024.jpg">`.

8. On a new line, type `<source media="(min-width: 601px)" srcset="space-800.jpg">`.

9. On a new line, type `<img src="space-600.jpg" />`.

   This serves as a fallback in two cases: for browsers that don't support the **picture** and **source** elements, and for when every media query returns **false**. In this case, it's for when the browser window has a width of 600px or smaller.

10. Type `</picture>`.

Ultimately, there's no major difference between **srcset** and **picture**, except that **srcset** does a bit more of the work for you; **srcset** is the method more commonly used today.

Using SVG

If you can use Scalable Vector Graphics (SVG), that would go a long way in saving you on file size. But SVGs may not be as straightforward to use, mostly because they have to be designed in a program like Adobe Illustrator.

SVGs are best used for illustrations or logos and can't be used for photographs (**FIGURE 7.6**). These are computer-generated graphics that are more abstract than photographs, which accurately depict real life. Illustrations and logos can be described as rules more efficiently.

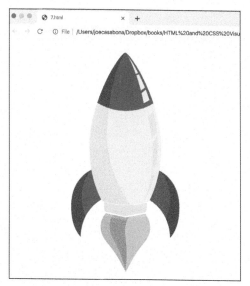

FIGURE 7.6 This image is a good example of an SVG.

The reason for that is the same reason they scale so well: the image data is stored not as pixels, but by mathematical instructions for drawing the image. That means that if you resize the image, the display pixels are recalculated for the resolution of the screen. So the image is sharp and crisp at any size, without pixelation. See **FIGURE 7.7** for an example of the source code for Figure 7.6.

Another nice thing about SVGs is that they can be treated like any other image, using the img tag. Here's the HTML for including Figure 7.6 on a webpage:

```
<img src="rocket.svg" alt="my rocket
 ship" />
```

But when you add a size to it, the graphic scales appropriately (**FIGURE 7.8**):

```
<img src="rocket.svg" width="9001px"
 alt="my rocket ship" />
```

You can also add an SVG directly to a webpage using the **<svg>** tag. Here's what that could look like:

```
<svg>
  <circle cx="100" cy="100" r="50"
  fill="red" />
</svg>
```

The result is shown in **FIGURE 7.9**.

```
<svg version="1.1" id="Layer_1" xmlns:x="&ns_extend;" xmlns:i="&ns_ai;" xmlns:graph="&ns_graphs;"
    xmlns="http://www.w3.org/2000/svg" xmlns:xlink="http://www.w3.org/1999/xlink" x="0px" y="0px" viewBox="0 0 595.28 595.28"
    enable-background="new 0 0 595.28 595.28" xml:space="preserve">
<switch>
    <foreignObject requiredExtensions="&ns_ai;" x="0" y="0" width="1" height="1">
        <i:pgfRef xlink:href="#adobe_illustrator_pgf">
        </i:pgfRef>
    </foreignObject>
    <g i:extraneous="self">
        <g>
            <rect x="0.003" y="0.002" fill="#FFFFFF" width="595.274" height="595.275"/>
            <g>
                <path fill="#E1E5DF" d="M297.747,403.664c29.556,0,54.446-5.031,61.986-10.525c17.453-33.18,31.096-78.607,31.096-132.696
                    c0-118.29-78.843-235.861-93.03-236.425v-0.015c-0.015,0-0.037,0.007-0.052,0.007c-0.022,0-0.037-0.007-0.059-0.007v0.015
                    c-14.188,0.564-93.031,118.135-93.031,236.425c0,54.088,13.643,99.516,31.096,132.696
                    C243.301,398.633,268.184,403.664,297.747,403.664z"/>
                <path fill="#D7D8D6" d="M308.257,401.289c-23.061-29.555-44.547-71.848-54.136-125.073
                    c-20.807-115.441,34.804-243.917,49.25-249.054c-2.344-2.012-4.246-3.088-5.572-3.144v-0.015c-0.015,0-0.037,0.007-0.052,0.007
                    c-0.022,0-0.037-0.007-0.059-0.007v0.015c-14.188,0.564-93.031,118.135-93.031,236.425c0,54.088,13.643,99.516,31.096,132.696
                    c7.548,5.494,32.431,10.525,61.994,10.525c5.749,0,11.313-0.195,16.613-0.547C311.84,402.631,309.767,402.02,308.257,401.289z"
                    />
```

FIGURE 7.7 A sample of source code for an SVG

FIGURE 7.8 What happens when you scale an SVG to over 9000px. Notice there is no pixelation.

FIGURE 7.9 Embedding an SVG circle directly on a webpage

FIGURE 7.10 Your code created this blue SVG square.

To use SVG to draw a square:

Here, you'll make a blue square.

1. Type `<svg id="square">`.

   The `id` can be anything. I used `square` to clearly describe what is being drawn.

2. On the next line, type `<rect`.

3. Type `x="0" y="0"`.

   This tells the browser the starting coordinates of the shape. In this case, you want the shape to be in the upper-left corner of the page, so you can start at 0, 0 (as in 0 pixels to the left, and 0 pixels down). I encourage you to experiment with these numbers to see what they do.

4. Type `width="100" height="100"`.

   This sets the dimensions of the square.

5. Type `fill="blue"`.

   This defines the color of the fill.

6. Close the `rect` element by typing `/>`.

7. Close the SVG by typing `</svg>`.

See the resulting image in **FIGURE 7.10**.

> **TIP** SVG is a great format to use for icons on your website because their code is lightweight. The other way is to use icon fonts, which you'll learn about in Chapter 13.

HTML Shapes

To help draw SVGs, HTML has a set of elements for basic shapes. They are `circle`, `rect` (for rectangles), `line`, `polyline`, `polygon`, and `path`. You can learn more about each of these at https://developer.mozilla.org/en-US/docs/Web/SVG/Tutorial/Basic_Shapes.

This book does not go into depth about these elements, because in general you can use tools like Illustrator to create SVGs.

Other Media

Aside from images, you can embed videos and audio directly into a webpage. In this section, you'll learn not only how to do that, but also the kinds of video and audio files that can be displayed by common modern web browsers. You'll also learn about factors to consider when storing large media on your server.

Video and audio file "formats"

When web developers talk about embedding video and audio files in webpages, they generally refer to a file's *format* to distinguish one kind of file from another. Yet web developers use "format" in a general sense to describe a combination of characteristics of a file, whereas video and audio professionals use the word in a stricter sense. These divergent uses of the word can lead to confusion and misunderstanding, so it's worth taking a moment to try to sort out the issue.

What distinguishes one kind of media file from another is a complex mix of technical parameters, which can be broken down into *file type*, *codec*, and *format*:

File type: Also called a *file container*, this is the way that the video or audio data is packaged into a file that a computer can read. Anything with a file extension is a file type, like .MOV, .MP4, etc. Each of these file types can contain video or audio data stored in one of several different ways (or even other kinds of data, like image data, subtitles, etc.). These file types are often called "formats," even though the video in one .MP4 file, for example, might be of a very different type from the video in another .MP4 file.

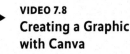

VIDEO 7.8
Creating a Graphic with Canva

In this video, you'll learn how to use Canva to make a simple image, which you can then use on your website.

Finding and Making Images

Finding the right images has gotten considerably easier over the last few years, but it can still be a slog.

First and foremost, don't just do a Google search. The images you'll find that way can be subject to copyright, and it's not always the safest way to get what you're looking for: royalty-free images. These are images you can get for free, or pay for, and use on your own websites.

A great source for free royalty-free images is Unsplash (https://unsplash.com). There's lots of fantastic stuff here. If you don't find what you're looking for there, both https://depositphotos.com/ and https://istock.com are good sources, but you will have to pay.

If you want to make your own images, apps like Photoshop and Affinity Photo are popular choices. But I love https://canva.com. You can easily create graphics of any size, use their templates, and find great stock photos there too. You can use it for free, and you can pay for upgrades that give you more features.

Codec: Recording video or audio data directly from a camera or a microphone produces truly vast amounts of digital data. To make this data more manageable, it's almost always compressed for storage, then decompressed when it's needed for editing or playback. The media industry uses numerous standards for this process; these are known as *codecs* short for "compressor/decompressor." You can think of the codec as the "language" in which the video or audio data is stored. H.264 is a very common video codec, and MP3 is an audio codec. Confusingly, H.264 video is usually stored in a .MP4 or .MOV file, but MP3 audio is often stored in a .MP3 file. (Note that not all video in a .MP4 or .MOV file uses the H.264 codec).

Format: This refers to the internal structure of the media data. For video, this includes frame size, frame rate, and pixel aspect ratio. Features of audio formats include the number of channels and configuration of those channels (whether stereo, multiple-mono, 5.1 surround-sound, etc.).

Like most of the web world, in this book I'll use "format" in a more general sense. When I talk about files in the MP4 format, I mean "video encoded using the H.264 codec and using MP4 as the file type."

When you embed video or audio in your webpage, take care to choose files in formats that the most common browsers support. The best solution for video is usually to choose MP4, because all browsers support it, with some exceptions (**TABLE 7.1**).

If you use MP4, be sure your video is encoded with H.264. Quite a bit of video created on Apple iPhones since 2017 uses the H.265 codec (or HEVC) which is incompatible with some browsers. You might also consider either Ogg or WebM for performance or for reasons of personal preference.

As with embedding video, when you embed audio in your webpage you need to be mindful of the formats that are supported. WAV is supported by all browsers except Internet Explorer. The MP3 format is supported by all browsers (**TABLE 7.2**).

You'll notice that Ogg is both a video and audio format.

TIP It's possible WebM will overtake Ogg because it has big names (like Google) behind it. There are also some clear performance benefits to using it.

TABLE 7.1 Video Formats

Format	Supported Browsers
MP4*	All (Internet Explorer, Firefox, Chrome, Safari, Opera)
WebM	Chrome, Firefox, Opera
Ogg	Chrome, Firefox, Opera

*Except for H.265-encoded video

TABLE 7.2 Audio Formats

Format	Supported Browsers
MP3	All (Internet Explorer, Edge, Firefox, Chrome, Safari, Opera)
WAV	Chrome, Firefox, Safari, Opera, Edge
Ogg	Chrome, Firefox, Opera

Embedding Video

You can embed a video on your webpage with the `<video>` element. There are a few attributes to know as well: `width`, `height`, and `controls`. The `controls` attribute has no value, but adding it tells the browser to include the play, pause, and volume buttons (**FIGURE 7.11**).

> **TIP** Current browsers don't natively support responsive (i.e., resizeable) videos like they do with images, but there are a few third-party options you can try. The best option at the time of this writing is the JavaScript library fitvids.js: fitvidsjs.com/.

Between the opening and closing `<video>` tags, you need to include the video source.

Luckily, you can add multiple video sources (which can use different formats), and the browser will pick the best one.

You should always include an MP4, since that is supported by all browsers.

To embed a video on a webpage:

> **TIP** If you need a free stock video for this task, check out www.pexels.com/videos. Here, the file is named moon.mp4.

1. Type `<video`.
2. Type `width="800px"`.

   You can skip the `height` attribute since the browser will intelligently resize the video to the appropriate height based on the width.

3. Type `controls>`.
4. Type `<source src="moon.mp4"`.
5. Type `type="video/mp4">`.

   This is not completely necessary in modern browsers, but it's still good to include, especially if you use multiple sources.

6. Type `</video>`.

The final result is what you see in Figure 7.11.

▶ **VIDEO 7.9**
Embedding a Video

In this video, in addition to adding a video to your webpage, you'll see how different attributes affect the display.

FIGURE 7.11 This webpage has an embedded video with playback controls displayed.

Converting and Embedding Audio

In this video, you'll not only add an audio file to your webpage, you'll also see how to convert an audio clip to the MP3 format.

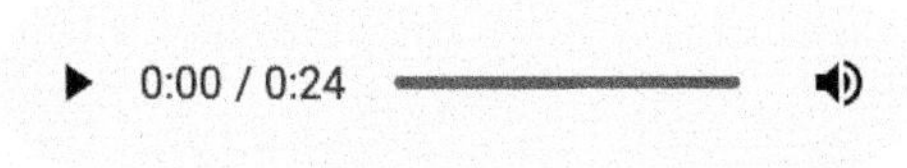

▶ 0:00 / 0:24 ──────── ◀))

FIGURE 7.12 This is the player for an embedded audio clip.

Embedding Audio

Adding audio to a webpage is very similar to adding video. The HTML is formatted exactly the same, except you'll use the `<audio>` tag instead of the `<video>` tag:

```
<audio controls>
    <source src="small-step.wav"
    → type="audio/wav">
    <source src="small-step.mp3"
    → type="audio/mp3">
</audio>
```

TIP Note that in this code sample I covered my bases by using both **WAV** and **MP3** sources. If you don't have an MP3 version of your audio, you can use a free online converter like **online-audio-converter.com/**. Free programs like Audacity (which is also cross-platform) can also do it for you. You can download it from **www.audacityteam.org**.

To embed audio on a webpage:

1. Type `<audio`.

2. Type `controls>`.

3. Type `<source src="small-step.wav" type="audio/wav">`.

   As a reminder, this relative path means the WAV file is in the same directory as the HTML file.

4. Type `<source src="small-step.mp3" type="audio/mp3">`.

5. Type `</audio>`.

The result will display a simple audio player in the page (**FIGURE 7.12**).

TIP If you need audio for this task, check out **www.free-stock-music.com/**. The sample file here is from **NASA** and is named *small-step.mp3*.

Storing Multimedia Files

Small files like images, SVGs, and PDFs can be stored directly on your server, in the same folder as your website. That's because these files don't require the user to interact with them and therefore are not resource intensive. In other words, they don't require a lot of computing power (as would playing a video game), so they won't cause stress on your website.

Multimedia—audio and video—will use considerable resources and bandwidth that your web server is likely not specialized for. This can lead to your website crashing or quickly running out of storage and bandwidth.

Instead, you should use specialized services to host your media, and then embed links to those services into your website using the embed code provided by the service. You can also get plain links (directly to an .mp3 or .mp4 file) and embed them using the `audio` or `video` element.

For video, many great services are available. Both YouTube (**FIGURE 7.13**) and Vimeo are free. If you need more in terms of features or control, Vimeo also offers paid plans (**FIGURE 7.14**).

For hosting audio, things are a little tough. SoundCloud is a popular free option, but it comes with limitations. Podbean is a podcasting service that has a free tier, but you're probably better off paying for a service.

Libsyn is a great audio hosting service that starts at $5 a month (**FIGURE 7.15**).

Any of these services will save you time and bandwidth (and probably a little strife too).

FIGURE 7.13 YouTube provides a great service for hosting free videos.

FIGURE 7.14 Vimeo offers hosting plans at a variety of price points.

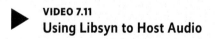

FIGURE 7.15 Libsyn offers a variety of audio hosting plans.

▶ **VIDEO 7.11**
Using Libsyn to Host Audio

In this video, you'll get a quick look at using Libsyn for audio hosting, and you'll learn how to embed a Libsyn file on a website.

FIGURE 7.16 The YouTube share dialog

FIGURE 7.17 The YouTube Embed screen with embed code

FIGURE 7.18 The YouTube embed code in an HTML file

FIGURE 7.19 A YouTube video embedded on a webpage

TIP A bonus of Libsyn (and most audio hosting services) is that you'll get a direct download link. This is a full URL that you can use with the <audio> tag to embed the audio in your webpage. You're not required to use Libsyn's embeddable player, like with some services.

To embed a YouTube video on your site:

1. Go to YouTube.com and find a video you'd like to embed.

2. Click the Share button (⤴ SHARE) to open the Share dialog (**FIGURE 7.16**).

3. Click Embed. The Embed Video dialog opens (**FIGURE 7.17**).

4. Copy the code in the top half of the dialog (it starts with <iframe and ends with </iframe>).

5. Open your HTML file.

6. Paste the embed code you just copied into the HTML file after the opening <body> tag, and save the file (**FIGURE 7.18**).

7. Open the HTML file in a web browser.

   You should see your YouTube video appear on a webpage as shown in **FIGURE 7.19**.

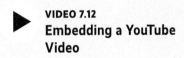

VIDEO 7.12
Embedding a YouTube Video

This video will show you how to grab any public YouTube video and embed it on your webpage.

Wrapping Up

Phew! That was a lot to take in—but now you know how to add all sorts of media to your website. This will make it more visually appealing and interactive, and it will add something beyond just text. After all, a picture's worth a thousand words, right?

Tables and Other Structured Data Elements

The main goal of HTML is to structure, define, and describe content. At this point you've seen most types of data: paragraphs and headings, images and other media, links, and layout elements. But there's a whole world of data out there that enhances websites by being described properly.

In this chapter, you'll learn about some of the more advanced types of structured data, like tables and definition lists. You'll also learn about schemas, a way for you to describe your own data.

Tables

Tables have been used on webpages as long as there have been webpages. They are used to display "tabular" data, which is data that is presented in rows and columns (**FIGURE 8.1**).

TIP Before the adoption of CSS and more modern web standards, tables were used for layout. This is considered very bad practice now. As you saw in Chapter 6, there are a whole host of tags dedicated to creating semantic layouts.

Table markup

Several elements go into making a table:

- **<table>**: This is the parent element. All the data in the table will be wrapped in the opening and closing **table** tags.

- **<caption>**: Specifies a title or caption for the table. If included, this should be the first child element of the table.

- **<thead>**: This stands for "table header" and will contain the column headings.

- **<tbody>**: Stands for "table body" and contains the primary content (or data) of the table.

- **<tr>**: Short for "table row." Each row of data goes in between opening and close **tr** tags.

- **<td>**: This is a cell of data (**td** stands for "table data").

- **<th>**: If contained inside **<thead>**, **th** (table heading) can replace **td** as the table cell. Data tagged with **<th>** will usually appear in bold by default.

- **<tfoot>**: The "table footer," this contains the table's footer (example in **FIGURE 8.2**).

Team	Location
Yankees	Bronx, NY
Red Sox	Boston, MA
Dodgers	Los Angeles, CA
Phillies	Philadelphia, PA

FIGURE 8.1 A basic table in HTML

Team	Home Runs
Yankees	306
Red Sox	245
Dodgers	279
Phillies	215
Total:	1,045

FIGURE 8.2 This table shows the sum of the values in each column at its bottom, so using **<tfoot>** for the totals is appropriate.

The <span> Element

As you learn about more specific types of elements, note that there's one that is used almost like a wildcard: the **<span>** element.

This is a generic inline element that has no inherent meaning, much like **<div>** at the block level. It's often used to apply classes or other helpful attributes to content, in the event that there is not a specific HTML element for it.

CODE 8.1 The HTML markup behind the baseball table shown in **FIGURE 8.3**

```
<table border="1">
    <caption>Baseball players with their
    → teams and numbers.</caption>
    <thead>
        <tr>
            <th>Player</th>
            <th>Team</th>
            <th>Number</th>
        </tr>
    </thead>
    <tbody>
        <tr>
            <td>Derek Jeter</td>
            <td>Yankees</td>
            <td>2</td>
        </tr>
        <tr>
            <td>David Ortiz</td>
            <td>Red Sox</td>
            <td>34</td>
        </tr>
        <tr>
            <td>Roy Halladay</td>
            <td>Phillies</td>
            <td>34</td>
        </tr>
        <tr>
            <td>Mike Piazza</td>
            <td>Mets</td>
            <td>31</td>
        </tr>
    </tbody>
</table>
```

Sample table markup

CODE 8.1 shows the markup for a simple table that lists baseball players, the teams they were on when they retired, and their uniform numbers.

A quick note on this code: the **border** attribute is actually deprecated in HTML5. You should use CSS to define borders. It's used here only so you can see the different cells in the table.

Let's take it one section at a time, beginning with the header. Adding this header will make three columns with bold text, denoting column headings (**FIGURE 8.4**).

A table header and a table row will look very similar in markup, but both should be included. We'll walk through both so you can see how a table is built. The main difference is that **th** cells will appear in bold.

TIP You can use CSS to move the caption to the bottom of the table.

Baseball players with their teams and numbers.		
Player	**Team**	**Number**
Derek Jeter	Yankees	2
David Ortiz	Red Sox	34
Roy Halladay	Phillies	34
Mike Piazza	Mets	31

FIGURE 8.3 A table of baseball players, their teams, and their numbers

Player	**Team**	**Number**

FIGURE 8.4 The header for the baseball players table as it will appear when rendered in a browser

To create the table header:

1. Type `<table border="1">`.

   The **border** attribute here would normally be excluded in favor of adding it via CSS, but it will make reading the table much easier for the purposes of this example. The **1** means "1 pixel" and it will create a border around the entire table and around each cell and header.

2. Type `<thead>` to begin the header.

3. Type `<tr>` to start the row within the header.

4. Type `<th>Player</th>` to enter the first of the three column heads.

5. Type `<th>Team</th>`.

6. Type `<th>Number</th>`.

7. Type `</tr>` to close off the row of column heads.

8. Type `</thead>` to mark the end of the header.

To create a table row:

1. Type `<tbody>`.

2. Type `<tr>`.

3. Type `<td>Derek Jeter</td>`.

4. Type `<td>Yankees</td>`.

5. Type `<td>2</td>`.

6. Type `</tbody>`.

7. Type `</table>`.

> **TIP** To avoid repetition, I've shown you how to code only the first row of the table. Repeat these steps (changing the data in the cells each time) to add as many rows as you'd like!

VIDEO 8.1
Building a Table

In this video, you will see in real time what happens as I build a table in CodePen.

```
<table border="1">
    <thead>
        <th colspan="4">Aaron Judge</th>
        <th>RF</th>
    </thead>
    <tbody>
        <tr role="header">
            <td>Year</td>
            <td>Team</td>
            <td>BA</td>
            <td>HR</td>
            <td>RBI</td>
        </tr>
        <tr>
            <td>2017</td>
            <td rowspan="3">NYY</td>
            <td>.284</td>
            <td>52</td>
            <td>114</td>
        </tr>
        <tr>
            <td>2018</td>
            <td>.278</td>
            <td>27</td>
            <td>67</td>
        </tr>
        <tr>
            <td>2019</td>
            <td>.272</td>
            <td>27</td>
            <td>55</td>
        </tr>
        <tfoot>
            <tr>
                <td colspan="2">Totals:</td>
                <td>.278</td>
                <td>106</td>
                <td>236</td>
            </tr>
        </tfoot>
    </tbody>
</table>
```

Extending rows and columns

You aren't limited to strictly structured rows and columns. Thanks to the attributes **colspan** and **rowspan**, which accept a numeric value for the number of cells the column or row should span (or take up), you can tell the table "this cell should take up two columns" or "this cell should take up three rows":

```
<th colspan="2">
<th rowspan="3">
```

These attributes come in handy when you want to build a more complicated table—one that mimics a baseball card, for example (**FIGURE 8.5** and **CODE 8.2**).

Doing this takes a little bit of math to get right, but it can make your tables look better and help you align data just the way you want to.

Aaron Judge				RF
Year	Team	BA	HR	RBI
2017		.284	52	114
2018	NYY	.278	27	67
2019		.272	27	55
Totals:		.278	106	236

FIGURE 8.5 A complex, baseball card–like table for Aaron Judge (batting average, home runs, and runs batted in). However, the table header has the player's name spanning four columns. The Totals cell in the footer spans two columns. And since he's played for the same team for his entire career, the first Team entry takes up three rows.

Miscalculating the **rowspan** can make a trainwreck of your table (**FIGURE 8.6**). Since the table is expecting another cell to fill the 2019 row, the cells no longer line up and there's a random blank space.

Similar problems arise when a column spans one too many cells (**FIGURE 8.7**). In this instance, the browser creates an entirely new column with a single cell to account for the overflow.

To add **colspan** to a table header:

1. Type `<thead>`.
2. Type `<tr>`.
3. Type `<th` but don't add the closing `>`.
4. Type `colspan="4">`.

   Since the head has two columns but it's a five-column table, this **colspan** should be **4**—one for the cell and three for the cells that are skipped.

5. Type `Aaron Judge`.
6. Type `<th>RF</th>`.
7. Type `</tr>`.
8. Type `</thead>`.

The result is the heading you see in Figure 8.5.

Aaron Judge				RF
Year	Team	BA	HR	RBI
2017	NYY	.284	52	114
2018		.278	27	67
2019	.272	27	55	
Totals:		.278	106	236

FIGURE 8.6 What happens when a **rowspan** is short by one row

Aaron Judge				RF
Year	Team	BA	HR	RBI
2017		.284	52	114
2018	NYY	.278	27	67
2019		.272	27	55
Totals:		.278	106	236	

FIGURE 8.7 What happens when a **colspan** spans one column too many

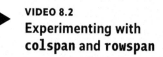

VIDEO 8.2
Experimenting with **colspan** and **rowspan**

In this video you will start with a basic table and incorporate **rowspan** and **colspan** into the code to see how the table changes in real time.

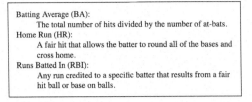

Batting Average (BA):
    The total number of hits divided by the number of at-bats.
Home Run (HR):
    A fair hit that allows the batter to round all of the bases and
    cross home.
Runs Batted In (RBI):
    Any run credited to a specific batter that results from a fair
    hit ball or base on balls.

FIGURE 8.8 A description list of baseball terms and their definitions

CODE 8.3 The markup that creates the description list in Figure 8.8

```
<dl>
    <dt>Batting Average (BA):</dt>
    <dd>The total number of hits divided
    → by the number of at-bats.</dd>

    <dt>Home Run (HR):</dt>
    <dd>A fair hit that allows the batter
    → to round all of the bases and cross
    → home.</dd>

    <dt>Runs Batted In (RBI):</dt>
    <dd>Any run credited to a specific
    → batter that results from a fair hit
    → ball or base on balls.</dd>
</dl>
```

Description Lists

A description list is a fantastic example of structured, defined data. It's an element that contains a list of terms and descriptions (or definitions) for those terms. A glossary is a perfect example (**FIGURE 8.8**).

TIP Prior to HTML5, description lists were called definition lists.

The markup for a description list includes three tags:

- **<dl>**: This is the container for the entire list. **dl** stands for "description list."

- **<dt>**: The **dt** (description term) is the term being described.

- **<dd>**: This is the "description details." It's the text that describes the term.

CODE 8.3 shows you the code for the description list in Figure 8.8.

Description lists aren't limited to definition/term lists. You can also use them for recipes, upcoming events, or dialogue (like in a script).

Semantically, a **<dd>** will be associated with the preceding **<dt>**. That means that you can have multiple **<dd>** elements following a single **<dt>**, and vice versa. If you have two **<dt>**s in a row, the very next **<dd>** will be associated with both of them.

To create an events list using a description list:

1. Type `<dl>` to start the list.

2. Type `<dt>Opening Day</dt>` to enter the first term to be described.

3. Type `<dd>April 1, 2021</dd>` to enter the description for the term you just added.

4. Type `<dt>All-Star Game</dt>` to add a new term to the list.

5. Type `<dd>July 13, 2021</dd>`.

6. Type `<dd>Game held at Truist Park, home of the Atlanta Braves</dd>` to add a second line of information about the term.

7. Type `<dt>Postseason</dt>`.

8. Type `<dd>October 2021</dd>`.

9. Type `<dd>Rounds: Wild Card, Division Series, League Championship, World Series</dd>`.

10. Type `<dd> The winners in each league will play in the World Series. </dd>`.

11. Type `</dl>` to close the description list.

The resulting list is shown in **FIGURE 8.9**.

This example shows that, by default, every `<dd>` is indented under the most recent `<dt>`, creating a nice visual hierarchy of terms and descriptions.

> **TIP** You can even use other HTML elements, like <p> or <ul>, inside description lists!

▶ **VIDEO 8.3**
Writing a Script with a Description List

Even though description lists are not often used, they have many applications that can be creative as well as practical. This video will show you how to use one to write dialogue in a TV script.

Opening Day
    April 1, 2021
All-Star Game
    July 13, 2021
    Game held at Truist Park, home of the Atlanta Braves
Postseason
    October 2021
    Rounds: Wild Card, Division Series, League Championship, World Series
    The winners in each league will play in the World Series

FIGURE 8.9 A description list of upcoming events in Major League Baseball

On Indenting Your Code

HTML does not require that code use any particular style of indentation. I add indents manually in my code. Some HTML editing software will add them for you.

Through the book, you'll notice the use of indentation for each child element, like so:

```
<parent>
    <child>
        <grandchild>
```

This makes the code easier to follow, and you can quickly locate opening and closing tags.

```
Yankee Stadium
1 E 161 St.
The Bronx, NY 10451
```

FIGURE 8.10 The <address>
tag in action

Why Is Structured Data Important?

You might be wondering why we need to use specific structures for different kinds of data. After all, we could easily use an unordered list for description lists.

But using the right tags to define data is important for browsers, users, and search engines. A great example of defining data in HTML is the **<address>** tag:

```
<address>
    Yankee Stadium<br/>
    1 E 161 St.<br/>
    The Bronx, NY 10451
</address>
```

... which renders as **FIGURE 8.10**.

Aside from it being italicized, there's not much visually different about an address. You could easily use a **<p>** or **<div>**. But the **<address>** tag tells the browser and search engines, "This is the contact information for this page." Even better, if the **<address>** tag is nested in an **<article>** tag, it indicates contact information specifically for that article.

What this ultimately leads to is better, more informative search results for users. Here's what happens if you search online for "Yankee Stadium address" (**FIGURE 8.11**).

FIGURE 8.11 The answer shows up directly on the search results page.

Without semantic meaning applied to the text (in this case, as an `<address>` tag), Google would have a much harder time knowing which data on the page contained the correct answer.

Using Schema.org vocabulary for custom structured data

This is a bit beyond the scope of "basic HTML and CSS," but it's important to know in the context of this conversation.

There are a number of different ways of annotating your structured content. By annotating your data, you help search engines better understand your page content and enable them to display your site with interesting search appearance elements. While there are several types of specifications, Schema.org is the commonly used type we'll use in this book. These sets of markup are called schemas. Driven primarily by Schema.org, these schemas provide a vocabulary that search engines can potentially use to better understand what you're presenting.

TIP Yoast, a company that specializes in search engine optimization (SEO), has a fantastic write-up on schema: yoast.com/structured-data-schema-ultimate-guide/.

Common examples of schemas drive search engine results that you regularly see: information on movies and TV shows, recipes, and so on (**FIGURES 8.12** and **8.13**).

If you wanted to, you could create a more meaningful event list. The main driver is an attribute called `itemscope`, which states that the element is about a specific item. Then we'd use the attribute `itemtype` to get the right schema from Schema.org to go with it. We can add more information to an element with `itemprop`, which allows you to set item properties based on the type of data represented (e.g., events will have a date; recipes will not).

TIP Two hugely helpful resources are schema.org/docs/gs.html, for getting started, and schema.org/docs/full.html, which lists all the types of data.

FIGURE 8.12 Google uses movie schema from several different sites (IMDB, Wikipedia, and YouTube, to name a few) to build a special display for movies to show up in searches.

FIGURE 8.13 Recipes show up in a card format on Google, allowing users to see what looks best to them and then click through to the recipe.

To create an event with Schema.org vocabulary:

This task uses the following markup for an event that, alas, never took place:

```
<dt>Field of Dreams Game</dt>
<dd>August 13, 2020</dd>
<dd>Game held in Dyersville,
 →Iowa</dd>
<dd>Yankees vs. White Sox</dd>
```

1. After <dt, type `itemscope`.

2. Type `itemtype="https://schema.org/ SportsEvent">`.

3. After the first <dd tag (the one containing the date), type `itemprop="startDate" content="2020-08-13T19:00">`.

   This is a machine-readable version of the date and time.

4. Replace `Dyersville, Iowa` with `<span itemprop="location">Dyersville, Iowa</span>`.

5. Replace `Yankees` with `<span itemprop="awayTeam">Yankees</span>`.

6. Replace `White Sox` with `<span itemprop="homeTeam">White Sox </span>`.

The resulting markup is shown in **CODE 8.4**.

While this doesn't affect the display of your webpage, it gives search engines much more valuable information. You can imagine someone searching "Who is the home team for the Field of Dreams game?" Now search engines can find the answer in our tiny database.

CODE 8.4 Our miniature baseball database, now with Schema.org vocabulary added

```
<dt itemscope itemtype="https://schema.org/SportsEvent">Field of Dreams Game</dt>
    <dd itemprop="startDate" content="2020-08-13T19:00">August 13, 2020</dd>
    <dd>Game held in <span itemprop="location">Dyersville, Iowa</span></dd>
    <dd><span itemprop="awayTeam">Yankees</span> vs. <span itemprop="homeTeam">White Sox
 →</span></dd>
```

Wrapping Up

You covered a lot of ground in this chapter, learning about important structures like tables and description lists. You also have a better understanding of structured data and its importance in creating a better, more user-friendly web.

Web Forms

So far, everything you've learned about webpages and HTML has taught you how to build a one-way street. That is, you can post information to a webpage, but the website visitors have no way of interacting with you. That's where web forms come in.

Web forms are the primary way users interact with websites. From contact forms to Google's search box, forms drive engagement and make the web a more interactive place.

Interacting with Webpages

Forms allow users to submit information to your website. You then have the option to store the data or otherwise do something with it. Some examples of popular web forms:

- Contact forms
- Comments
- Forums
- Login boxes
- Post boxes (on social media websites)
- Search boxes
- Checkout pages, Add To Cart buttons, and payment submissions for online stores
- Chatbots
- Popup opt-in boxes

You've no doubt seen lots of forms (**FIGURES 9.1**, **9.2**, and **9.3**).

▶ **VIDEO 9.1**
Interacting with Forms

There are lots of different forms you can build, as well as many different ways users can interact with those forms. In this video you'll see some unique web forms and learn how they work.

FIGURE 9.1 Google's iconic minimalist home page, with only a search box

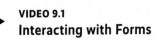

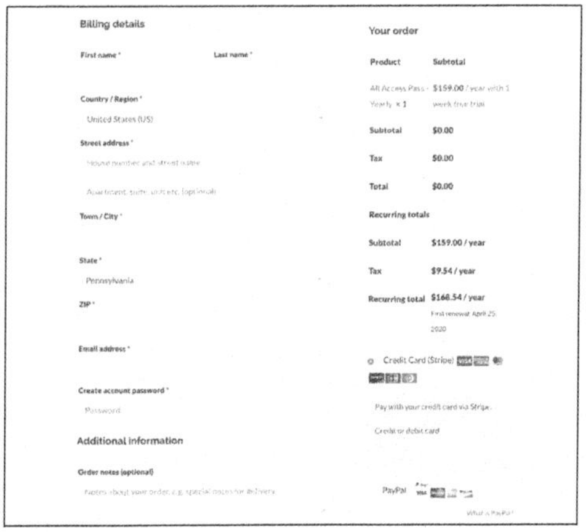

FIGURE 9.2 Checkout form on an ecommerce site

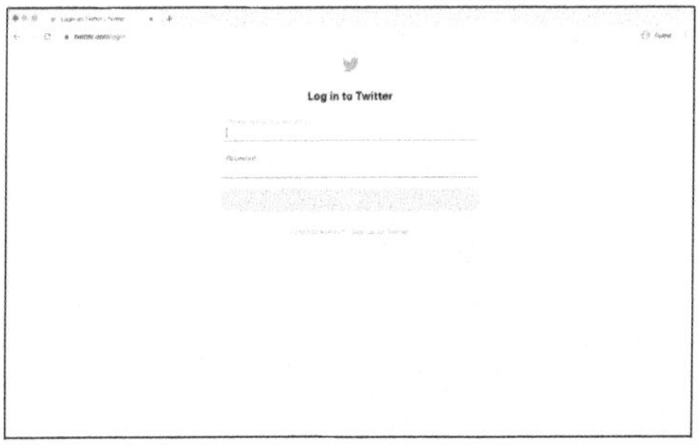

FIGURE 9.3 Twitter's login page

How a Web Form Works

There are several steps to building and processing a web form (**FIGURE 9.4**):

1. Build the form using HTML.

2. Validate the form to make sure all data is submitted properly.

3. Submit and process the form.

   Processing can happen in several ways. You could simply email the contents of the form somewhere, you could store it in a database, you could use it to change your site in real time, and much more.

4. Display confirmation to the user.

Keep this in mind as you read this chapter, though: you're learning how to build the form in HTML, and you're using HTML elements to perform basic validation of the input data.

But with regard to submitting the data, you can't do as much with just HTML. Submission often requires the use of another programming language, which goes beyond the scope of this book. That said, you will learn basic form processing to email the form contents. In Chapter 10, you'll even learn a simple technique for storing the data.

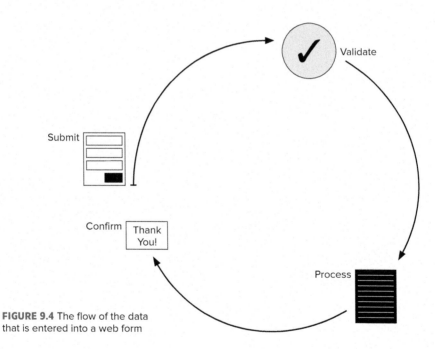

FIGURE 9.4 The flow of the data that is entered into a web form

Components of an HTML Form

Every form is wrapped in a **<form>** element, which consists of the opening **<form>** tag and the closing **</form>** tag.

The bulk of the form itself is made up of *fields* that can accept data from users. Most of these elements are created with **<input>** tags, though there are others you'll also learn about.

TIP Webpages can include more than one form, so placing fields inside the opening and closing **form** tags signals to a browser that all the fields belong to the same form.

The **<form>** Element

Every form needs an opening **<form>** tag and a closing **</form>** tag, which together define a **form** element. The **form** element requires an **action** attribute, and it should have **method** and **name** attributes as well:

```
<form name="search-form"
 method="GET" action="process.php">
```

The **name** attribute is a simple way to uniquely identify the form (each form should have a unique name). Webpages can contain more than one form, and the **name** attribute allows you to easily reference the form in both CSS and JavaScript.

The **method** attribute determines how the form data should be sent, and can take one of two values.

GET is the default value. This method transmits data from one page to another in a URL as *name-value pairs* (**FIGURE 9.5**).

Attributes are a good example of name-value pairs. They have a name (like the **role** attribute) and a value (like "**main**"). In a URL, name-value pairs appear in this format: **role=main**.

When a user fills out your form and clicks Submit, the browser takes all the data from the form and then inserts it into the URL. In the above example, the URL would look something like this: **process.php?name_of _field=value_the_user_input**.

The other **method** value is **POST**. In this method, data is transmitted in the HTTP request and is not shown in the URL. The data is sent, in this instance, to **process.php** via the server.

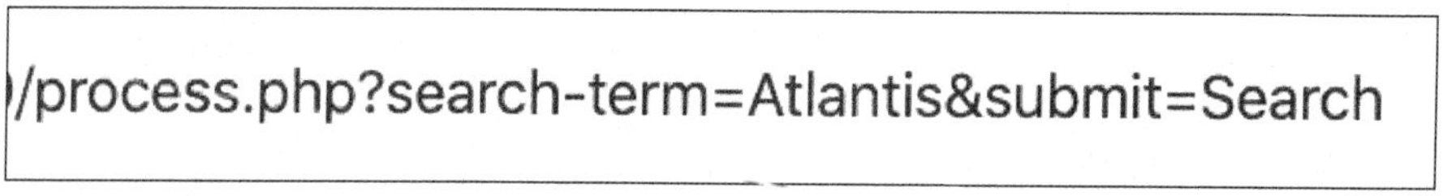

/process.php?search-term=Atlantis&submit=Search

FIGURE 9.5 Using the **GET** method, you can see the results of a form in the URL.

▶ VIDEO 9.2
Comparing the GET and POST Form Submission Methods

To get a better idea of how each action behaves, here you'll see what happens with a GET method compared to a POST method.

The `action` attribute tells the browser *where* to send the form information. It's what does the form processing, whether that's emailing its contents or storing it in a database. If you do not include the `action` attribute, modern browsers will assume the current page will also process the form.

> **TIP** Forms are often processed using a server-side language like PHP, Python, or C#. While that's outside the scope of this book, you can download the `process.php` file from the Github *repo* (short for *repository*, or a place where we can store our code for others to download) for this book (see "Code" in the Introduction).

> **TIP** Privacy and data storage laws are becoming stricter around the world. Depending on where you live, you may need to alert the user to how you're using the data or ask them to explicitly give your website permission to let you store it.

Deciding Between GET and POST

Both GET and POST have pros and cons. With GET, the data entered by the user is visible in the URL, so you should *never* use it to pass sensitive data, like passwords. But using GET (and therefore allowing form data to be visible) is great if you want to make the results shareable or if you want to let the user save them. An example that uses GET is Google search results.

On the other hand, the length of a GET request is limited, ranging from 2000 to 8000 characters, depending on the server and browser configurations.

There is no limit on results when using POST, and it's more secure, but the results pages cannot be shared, nor can the results of a specific form submission be saved.

Form Fields

There are several form fields that you can define in HTML, and each allows the user to interact with the form in a different way.

Input fields

The most common tag you'll find between the opening and closing `<form>` tags is `<input>`. This element creates a field into which users can insert data. It looks something like this:

```
<input type="text" name="search"
 value="" />
```

Let's take each attribute one by one.

The **type** attribute determines the kind of data a user can input. While **text** is the most common (and the default when the **type** attribute is not defined), there are lots of values the **type** attribute can have. You'll see most of them throughout this chapter.

TIP For a complete (and regularly updated) list, check out developer.mozilla.org/en-US/docs/Web/HTML/Element/input.

The **name** attribute assigns a name to the input field. Remember those name-value pairs from earlier? The *name* is derived from the **name** attribute. It should be unique to prevent overriding data.

The *value* part of the name-value pairs is derived from the **value** attribute. Notice that the **value** attribute in the above example is blank. You can add one, but whatever the user inputs will overwrite it (**FIGURE 9.6**).

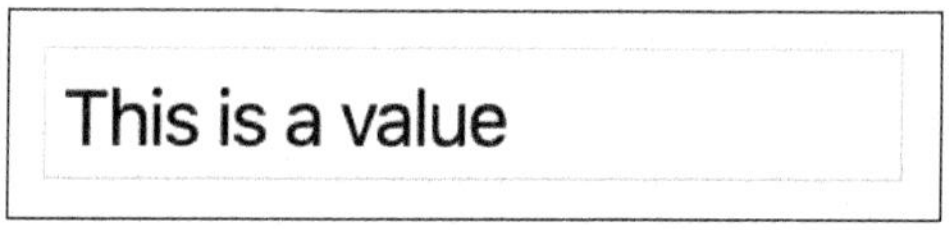

FIGURE 9.6 A text field with the **value** attribute

FIGURE 9.7 A field with the `placeholder` attribute

FIGURE 9.8 A simple search form

With some form fields—namely, those that take on the appearance of a textbox (a single-line white field with gray border, which accepts a limited amount of text)—there is another attribute. Instead of setting the **value** attribute, you can use the **placeholder** attribute. This adds grayed-out text to the field, to suggest the type text that can go in the field.

If the user does not fill out the field, it will have no value (**FIGURE 9.7**).

Each form should also have a **submit** field, which has its own input type. When the browser sees this input type, it will generate a button for the user to click, in order to send the form's data using the **method** and **action** you defined in the opening `<form>` tag.

Although you can set the value of a submit input type, it is immutable outside of markup, so the user cannot change it.

Putting it all together, you get this:

```
<form name="search-form" method="GET"
    action="process.php">
    <input type="text"
        name="search-term" />
    <input type="submit" name="submit"
        value="Search" />
</form>
```

... which looks like **FIGURE 9.8** in the browser.

TIP You can use **type="search"** for input on search forms as well, and a submit button will automatically be included.

If a user were to enter **Atlantis** into the search form, the URL would look like this:

```
yoursite.com/process.php?search-term=
    Atlantis
```

Input types

Text and submit are not the only types of input available. You can submit data using a variety of formats (**FIGURE 9.9**, **CODE 9.1**):

- **text**: A single line of text.

- **password**: A field designed for users to add passwords or other sensitive text. This field obfuscates input, using dots to hide its contents.

- **radio**: A button (typically circular) usually created in groups. Only one of the buttons in a group can be selected at a time, which makes radio buttons the ideal way to offer your user a range of options from which they must choose one.

  Use the **checked** attribute to select a default value.

- **checkbox**: A set of square boxes that present the user with several options. One or more can be selected.

  Use the **checked** attribute to select a default value.

- **email**: This input type tells the browser to make sure the user has entered a properly formatted email address.

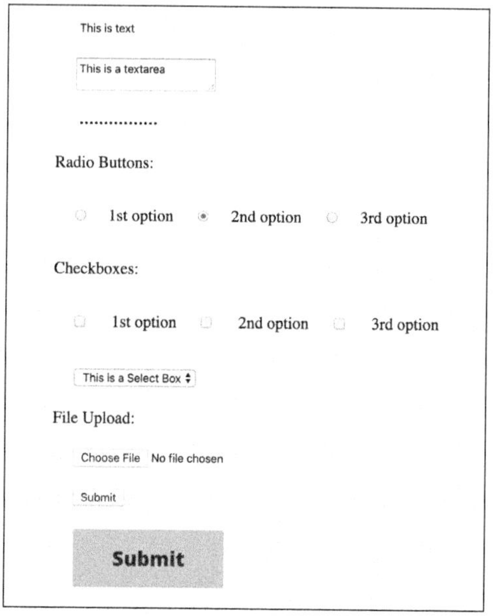

FIGURE 9.9 What each input type looks like

- **file**: A text field with a Choose File button. Clicking the button opens a file navigation dialog box the user can use to find and select a file on their computer for upload to a server.

- **submit**: A button that, when clicked, sends the form for processing.

- **image**: Works just like the submit button, but you can use an image you provide instead of the standard browser-rendered submit button.

  Due to advancements in CSS, you see this used a lot less than it once was.

- **hidden**: Creates a form field that cannot be seen or edited by users. This is often used to capture dynamically generated content, like a timestamp or ID. For example, on a blog post, a comment form would have a hidden field with the ID of the post so that the blog publisher knows which post the comment belongs to.

There are also a few fields that act like text fields but require specific kinds of text. They are **email**, **date**, **search**, **tel**, and **url**. You will learn more about them in the "Validating Forms" section of this chapter.

CODE 9.1 The HTML code used to generate the inputs in Figure 9.9

```
<form name="input-reference" method="get" action="process.php">
<input type="text" name="text" value="This is text"/>
<textarea name="textarea">This is a textarea</textarea>
<input type="password" name="password" value="This is password"/>

<p>Radio Buttons:</p>

<input type="radio" name="radio-option" value="1st option" />1st option
<input type="radio" name="radio-option" value="2nd option" checked />2nd option
<input type="radio" name="radio-option" value="3rd option" />3rd option

<p>Checkboxes:</p>
<input type="checkbox" name="check-option1" value="Atlantis" /> 1st option
<input type="checkbox" name="check-option2" value="Snow White" /> 2nd option
<input type="checkbox" name="check-option3" value="Aladdin" /> 3rd option

        <select name="select">
            <option>This is a Select Box</option>
            <option value="1st option">1st option</option>
            <option value="2nd option">2nd option</option>
            <option value="3rd option">3rd option</option>
        </select>

        <p>File Upload:</p>
        <input type="file" name="file" />

         <input type="submit" name="submit" value="Submit" />

         <input type="image" name="image-submit" src="submit-img.png" alt="Submit" />
    </form>
```

Other field types

Aside from the `<input>` tag, there are two other field elements worth mentioning.

A `<textarea>` field allows users to enter a block or paragraph of text; it also uses a closing `</textarea>` tag. The default text of this field goes in between the opening and closing tags. See Code 9.1 for an example.

The `<select>` element creates a dropdown menu, or list of options. By default, only one option in the list can be selected. You can allow the reader to select more than one option by including the `multiselect` attribute.

To populate a `<select>` field, you'll need to include the `<option>` element between the opening and closing `<select>` tags. In this instance, `<select>` should include the **name** attribute, but each `<option>` tag should have its own **value** attribute.

See Code 9.1 for an example. You'll create your own select box in an upcoming task!

TIP You can also use the `select="selected"` attribute on any `<option>` element to set that as the default option. By default, it will be the first option listed.

Why Use Hidden Fields?

You might be wondering why someone would use a hidden field on their form if a user can't see it. There are several possible reasons, but the main use case is gathering extra information about the user's visit, like the time of day, the URL they were visiting, or the user's IP address.

A hidden field can also be used to defend against spam. If the field is filled out, there's a good chance a spambot did it, not a person. You can then throw out those submissions.

Labeling Fields

Although the `placeholder` attribute does a reasonable job of communicating the kind of information the user should enter into many form fields, there's a better, more semantic way: use a `<label>` element with your `<input>` elements.

```
<div>
    <label for="first_name">First
    → Name:</label>
    <input type="text"
    → name="first_name"
    → id="first_name" placeholder=
    → "Milo" />
</div>
```

In the browser, this code is rendered as a text box labeled with the kind of data the user is expected to enter (**FIGURE 9.10**).

You'll notice that the label has a `for` attribute. That attribute matches the `id` attribute on the input element. This tells the browser, "This label belongs to the `<input>` element whose ID matches the `for` attribute."

Aside from improving user experience, labeling your input fields provides accessibility benefits:

- If a visitor to your site is using a screen reader, it can read the text of the label out loud when the input element has user focus (for example, when the user taps it or clicks it with a mouse).

- Because clicking the label activates the form field, the overall "hit area" for the form element is increased. This can make it easier for users with decreased mobility to activate the input fields.

First Name: Milo

FIGURE 9.10 A form field with label

Setting Up a Basic Form

Before moving on and creating examples of form inputs, you'll write a simple form skeleton, to which you can add the example inputs you create in the rest of the tasks.

TIP Even when labels are applied to inputs throughout a webpage, it's common to omit them for submit buttons.

To create a form skeleton:

1. Type `<form name="example-form"`.

2. Type `method="GET">`.

3. Leave a blank line between the previous line and the next line.

4. On the next line, type `<input type="submit" name="submit" value="Submit" />`.

5. On the next line, type `</form>`.

You should now have this:

```
<form name="example-form"
→ method="GET">

    <input type="submit" name="submit"
    → value="Submit" />
</form>
```

Creating Select Boxes

Select boxes are an intuitive way to allow your users to pick from a list of items. There are two ways a select box can work: as a simple dropdown menu, which allows only one option to be selected, or as a multiselect box, where several items can be selected. The following tasks will show you how to build both. Using the form skeleton you created in the previous task, insert the code you will build in the following task right after the opening `<form>` tag.

To create a select box:

1. First, create the label for the select box. Be sure to include the **for** attribute with the ID for the label. For this example, type `<label for="next-movie">What movie do you want to see next?</label>`.

2. Type the opening tag for the select box: `<select`.

3. Give the box a name and assign its ID by typing `name="next-movie" id="next-movie">`.

   Next, define the `<option>` elements that will be listed on the menu. This example uses movie titles.

4. Type `<option value="Toy Story 4"> Toy Story 4</option>`.

5. Type `<option value="Onward">Onward </option>`.

6. Type `<option value="Fast 9">Fast 9 </option>`.

7. Type `</select>`.

This creates a box that lists three options, from which the user can pick one (**FIGURE 9.11**).

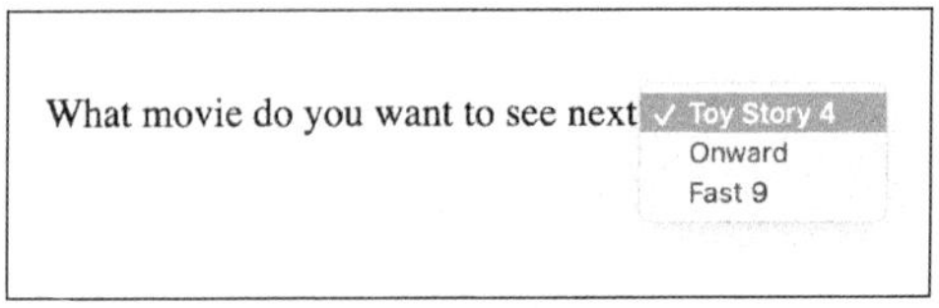

FIGURE 9.11 A select box with all options showing

▶ **VIDEO 9.3**
Converting a Select Box to a Multiselect Box

In this video, you'll see what happens when you convert a select box into a multiselect box, and how each field works.

To create a multiselect box:

1. Type `<label for="seen-movies">What movies have you seen?</label>`.

2. Type `<select name="seen-movies" id="seen-movies"`.

3. Type `multiple>` and press Return/Enter.

   Each of the following `option` elements belongs on its own line.

4. Type `<option value="Atlantis">Atlantis</option>`.

5. Type `<option value="Snow White">Snow White</option>`.

6. Type `<option value="Aladdin">Aladdin</option>`.

7. Type `</select>`.

This creates a box that lists three options. The user can hold the Shift key while clicking to select more than one contiguous option, or they can hold Command (macOS)/Ctrl (Windows) to select multiple noncontiguous options (**FIGURE 9.12**).

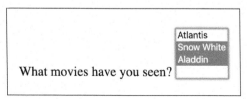

FIGURE 9.12 A multiselect box with two options selected

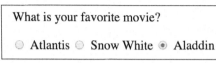

FIGURE 9.13 A set of radio buttons with the default option selected

Creating Radio Buttons

Radio buttons are another way to present a user with options and have them pick one (the select box is the first way). Once a radio button is selected, it cannot be deselected without selecting another radio button.

Using the form skeleton you created in a previous task, place the following code from the task right after the opening `<form>` tag.

To create radio buttons:

1. If you want to provide a title or other introductory text for your buttons, include it in a paragraph element. For this example, type `<p>What is your favorite movie?</p>`.

2. Type `<input type="radio" name="favorite-movie" id="atlantis" value="Atlantis" /> <label for="atlantis">Atlantis</label>`.

3. Type `<input type="radio" name="favorite-movie" id="snow-white" value="Snow White" /> <label for="snow-white">Snow White</label>`.

4. Type `<input type="radio" name="favorite-movie" id="aladdin" value="Aladdin" checked /> <label for="aladdin">Aladdin</label>` (**FIGURE 9.13**).

   Note the **checked** attribute on this input.

   Notice the value of the **name** attribute of all three buttons is the same. That's to tell the browser, "These buttons belong together."

Creating Checkboxes

Checkboxes are a great way to present the user with multiple options and allow them to accept more than one. Unlike radio buttons, where the user can only choose one, there is generally no limit on the number of checkboxes a user can select.

Using the form skeleton you created in a previous task, place the following code from the task right after the opening `<form>` tag.

To create checkboxes:

1. Type the introductory text, if any; in this case, use `<p>What movies do you want to see?</p>`.

2. Type `<input type="checkbox" name="want-to-see-1" id="atlantis" value="Atlantis" checked/> <label for="atlantis">Atlantis</label>`.

   Note the checked attribute.

3. Type `<input type="checkbox" name= "want-to-see-2" id="snow-white" value="Snow White" /> <label for="snow-white">Snow White </label>`.

4. Type `<input type="checkbox" name="want-to-see-3" id="aladdin" value="Aladdin" /> <label for="aladdin">Aladdin</label>` (**FIGURE 9.14**).

   Notice that the names of these checkboxes have a number appended. If they were named the same, they would all effectively represent one option because as we learned earlier, the **name** attribute of each form field on a page must be unique. This rule does not apply to radio buttons, of course.

TIP It's possible to use advanced programming languages like PHP to name a group of checkboxes the same and still keep them as a group, but that's beyond the scope of this book.

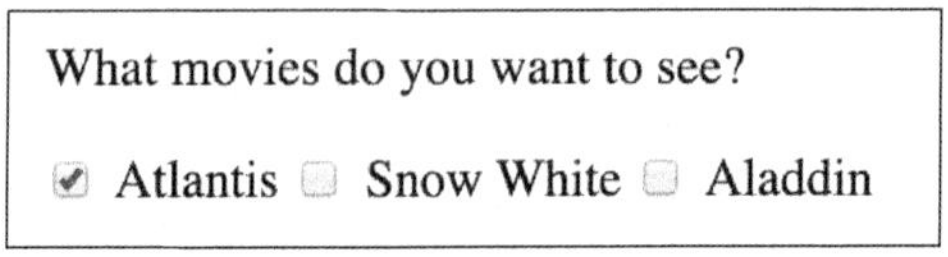

What movies do you want to see?

☑ Atlantis ☐ Snow White ☐ Aladdin

FIGURE 9.14 A set of checkboxes

▶ **VIDEO 9.4**
Creating Checkboxes and Radio Buttons

Checkboxes and radio buttons act a little differently from other input types. In this video you'll learn how to write them, see what their differences are, and learn when to use each.

Creating Email Forms

Email forms are super common online, as are inputs to capture email in general. That's why the `email` input type exists. It will self-validate to make sure the user is entering an email address that's in the proper format (but it won't know whether the email address actually exists).

To create a simple email opt-in form:

1. Type the opening tag for the `form` element, making sure to include the `name` or `id`, `method`, and `action` attributes. For this example, use `<form name="optin" method="GET" action="process.php">`.

   Our example form includes two `<input>` elements, each with a `label`: a `text` input for the user's first name, and the `email` input.

2. Create the label for the user's name: `<label for="first-name">First Name:</label>`.

3. Type `<input type="text" name="first_name" id="first-name" placeholder="First Name" />`.

4. Type `<label for="email-address"> Email Address:</label>`.

5. Type `<input type="email" name="email_address" id="email-address" placeholder="Email Address" />`.

6. Type `<input type="submit" name="submit" value="Join the List!" />`.

7. Type `</form>` (**FIGURE 9.15**).

First Name: First Name   Email Address: Email Address   Join the List!

FIGURE 9.15 A simple email opt-in form

Special Field Types

There is a set of input types that add special controls and selectors. They offer a better way for users to insert properly formatted data. This reduces the need to take separate measures to validate and makes the input more reliable.

TIP You can view a more comprehensive list of these special inputs at www.w3schools.com/html/html_form_input_types.asp.

Date

The **date** input type (**FIGURE 9.16**) brings up a calendar for users to pick a date from (**FIGURE 9.17**). The browser display (what you see in the box) depends on the user's locale (where they are located, based on what the browser knows). The date is always sent in the format YYYY-MM-DD.

```
<input type="date"
  name="release-date" />
```

You can constrain a user's selection to a specific range of dates by using the **min** and **max** attributes:

```
<input type="date" name="release"
  min="1937-12-21" max="1992-11-11" />
```

Note that the **min** and **max** attributes affect the date picker, but a user will be able to manually set any date, even if it's outside the range. This is a good use case for validation with JavaScript.

▶ **VIDEO 9.5**
Building a Rental Application

To get you more familiar with the various input types, in this video you'll build a small application for someone who's looking to rent an apartment.

FIGURE 9.16 The date field, with a locale of "en-US" for English, United States

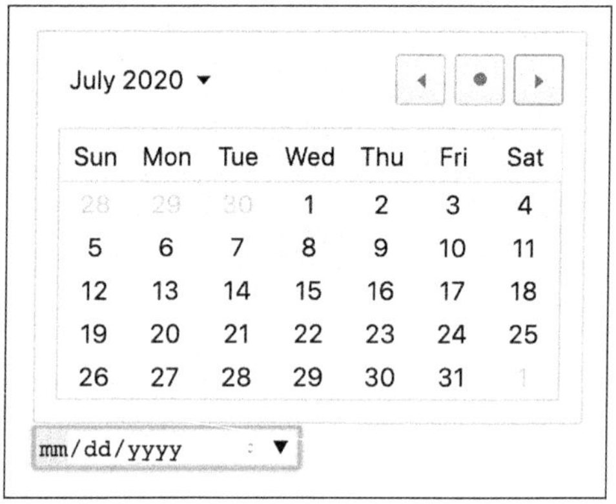

FIGURE 9.17 The date picker, as implemented by Google Chrome

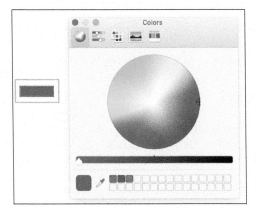

FIGURE 9.18 The color picker, as implemented by Google Chrome

Finally, there are a few other date- and time- related inputs:

- **datetime-local**: This allows the user to select a date and time without including the time zone. That means that even if you're in New York and your user is in London, you'll both see the same date and time inputs.

- **time**: Allows the user to select a time with no time zone included.

- **month**: Allows the user to select a month and year.

- **week**: Allow the user to select a week number and year.

> **TIP** At the time of this writing, **month** and **week** have only partial browser support, but they are supported by all major browsers. They are displayed as text fields if a browser does not support them.

When capturing times in a form, since time zones are not supported, you'll need to capture them a different way. You can use a hidden field for this if you don't want the user to change the time zone (this works best for local events or appointments). If you want them to select their own time zone, you can use a select box.

Color

The **color** input type allows users to select a color through use of a color picker (**FIGURE 9.18**):

```
<input type="color" name="carpet-color"
  value="#FF0000" />
```

The value is a seven-character code in hexadecimal format (which you'll learn all about in Chapter 14). The default value of **color** is black unless you specify a different value.

Range

The **range** input type creates a slide controller that allows users to adjust the value of a parameter by sliding the controller along a scale. You can set **min** and **max** attributes to limit the possible range of values (**FIGURE 9.19**). The default values for **min** and **max** are 0 and 100, respectively.

FIGURE 9.19 The range field, as implemented by Google Chrome

```
<input type="range" name="rating"
  min="0" max="10" />
```

You can also use the **step** attribute, which allows you to set a specific increment by which values can change. The default value is 1. The **step** attribute happens to be supported for **date** inputs as well, but it is best for imprecise values, as in a volume controller.

VIDEO 9.8
Using Range

In this video you'll see how the **range** field is implemented in Chrome. Included is a small bit of JavaScript so you can see the value change in real time.

Grouping Fields Together

If your form is lengthy, you can make it easier for your users to scan it by using two elements for organization: `<fieldset>` and `<legend>`.

You can place any number of form fields and labels into a `<fieldset>` element. By default, they will have a grey border around them.

You can then use the `<legend>` element to caption the `<fieldset>`. The `<legend>`, by default, will appear aligned in the middle of the top border of the `<fieldset>` (**FIGURE 9.20**).

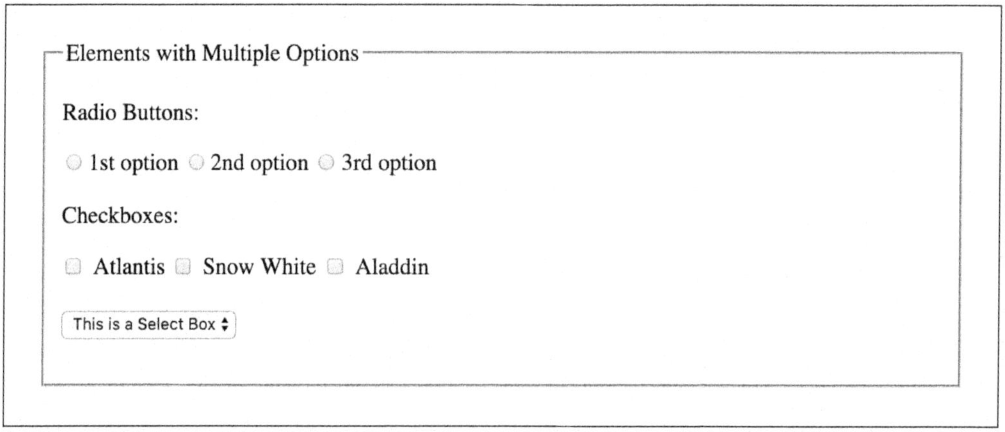

Elements with Multiple Options

Radio Buttons:

○ 1st option ○ 2nd option ○ 3rd option

Checkboxes:

☐ Atlantis ☐ Snow White ☐ Aladdin

This is a Select Box ⇕

FIGURE 9.20 The `<fieldset>` element with `<legend>`

```
<label for="fuel">Fuel level:</label>
<meter id="fuel" value="0.2">
    At 20%
</meter>

<label for="donations">Donations:</label>
<meter id="donations" min="0" max="100000"
 ⇀ value="60000">
    at $60,000
</meter>
```

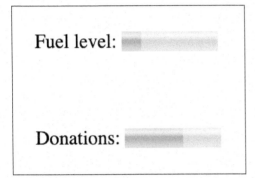

Fuel level:

Donations:

FIGURE 9.21 The two <meter> elements created by
Code 9.2

The <meter> Element

One pretty nifty element is <meter>, which
graphically represents a value over a
range. It accepts several attributes, but
the ones to know about are value, min,
and max. The attributes min and max are
optional. If they are not specified, they
default to 0 and 1, respectively, and value
is a fraction. If min and max are defined,
they determine the scale for value. You
can see <meter> in action in **FIGURE 9.21**,
which is generated by **CODE 9.2**.

Validating Forms

Validation is an incredibly important part of any form. There are three primary ways to validate forms:

- **The built-in HTML5 validation** for specific fields like email, URL, phone number, and more, as well as the validation attributes `required` and, if needed, `pattern`.

- You can use **JavaScript** to validate data when it is input by the user, especially if that data isn't automatically validated by one of the input types. One example in the US is the zip code; they should follow a specific format, but there is no input type defined for them.

- **A server-side script** written in a language like PHP. Validating at this stage makes sure all data is in the right format, and that there are no malicious attempts at hacking before you process it. While you don't need to know server-side validation for the examples in this book, once you start learning how to write server-side code, you will need to keep this in mind as you process forms.

For the purposes of this book, using the built-in HTML validation works well. As you begin to do more advanced form processing, knowing how to validate with both JavaScript and a server-side language is important.

Javascript and PHP are outside the scope of this book, but there are a couple of helpful files in the Github repo for this book.

Instead, here's how to apply some great form validation with HTML5 only.

The most basic validation you can add is to ensure that required fields are filled out. That is as simple as adding the `required` attribute:

```
<div>
<label for=first_name">First Name*:
 </label>
<input type="text" name="first_name"
 id="first_name" placeholder="First
 Name" required/>
</div>
```

TIP It's also a good practice to provide a visual indicator that a field is required. Common methods include adding an asterisk (*) or the word *required* in parentheses next to the label.

Building and Testing a Valid Form

Testing webpages is just as important as building them, and in this video, you'll see how to build a small form using the validation methods, and then you'll test it to make sure it works properly.

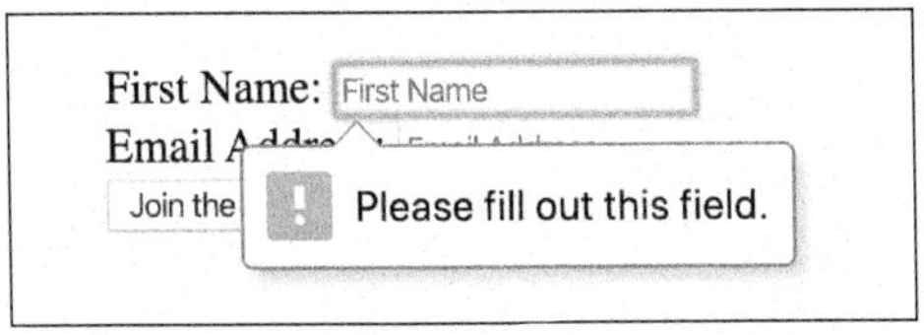

FIGURE 9.22 The error message when a required field is not filled out

If the required field is not filled out, modern browsers will display an error message (**FIGURE 9.22**).

Similarly, there is a set of input types that have automatic validation:

- **email**: Looks for a valid email address (**FIGURE 9.23**).
- **url**: Looks for a valid URL format.
- **number**: Looks for a valid numerical value. Using the **min** and **max** attributes will validate on a specific range:

  ```
  <input type="number" name="age"
    mix="13" max="150" />
  ```

- **tel**: Looks for a telephone number. This requires the **pattern** attribute.

The final piece of validation that can be applied in HTML is the **pattern** attribute. This requires knowledge of *regular expressions* (regex), but it allows you to supply the description of a pattern, which all input can be validated against. Here's an example of a US telephone format:

```
<input type="tel" name="phone_number"
  id="phone_number"
  pattern="[0-9]{3}-[0-9]{3}-[0-9]{4}"/>
```

TIP Regular expressions are a way of performing complex searching of text by describing what they should look like. For example, the regex [0-9]{3} means "any three digits between 0 and 9, inclusive of 0 and 9." A great resource for learning regex is regexone.com/.

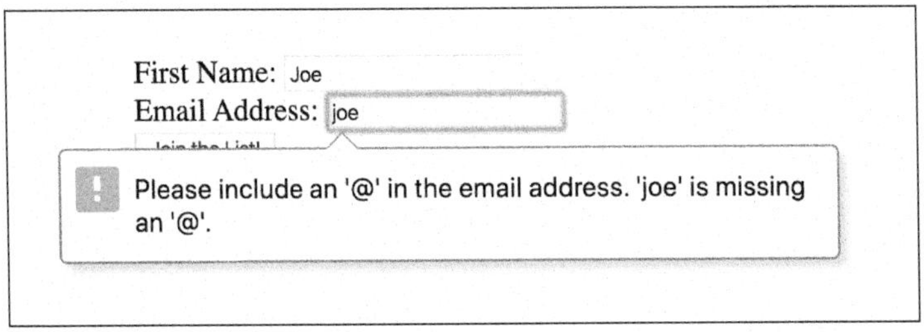

FIGURE 9.23 The error message when a valid email is not entered

Wrapping Up

There's a lot to know about forms, but thanks to HTML5 and advances in browser technology, you can do a lot more with plain HTML today than you could even just a few years ago.

I encourage you to experiment with all the different inputs and data types to learn exactly how they work. You'll find that you can build some pretty impressive, and interactive, webpages.

Advanced and Experimental Features

HTML is constantly changing and evolving to meet the needs of modern web developers, users, and devices. A perfect example of this is the `srcset` attribute, which allows the use of multiple images with the `<img>` and `<source>` elements.

This wasn't part of the original HTML5 spec, but it was added because enough people requested and voted on the proposal. In this chapter, you'll learn about some of the cool advanced features built into HTML5, what's coming down the pike, and how to start using those experimental features today.

It's All About Browser Support

Hopefully it's clear by now that how webpages render and work is highly dependent on the browser on which your end user views them. A page with one set of markup will render differently in two different browsers (**FIGURE 10.1**).

That's a result of the fact that some browsers support new features before others, and the way a new feature is implemented in one browser might be totally different from its implementation in another.

The HTML specification (or spec) is the document that describes new features in HTML and how they should work. Then it's up to browsers to implement that spec. Things have gotten a lot better in recent years, with browser developers working together to make sure there's not a lot of disparity between them.

But you should still be mindful that some browsers might support new features sooner than others, and until a feature is marked as an official part of the HTML spec, its functionality could change from browser to browser.

FIGURE 10.1 A website rendered in Chrome compared to its rendering in Firefox

VIDEO 10.1
Rendering Elements Differently in Different Browsers

To drive home this idea, I'll show you a few live examples of how different browsers implement different HTML elements.

Checking browser support with "Can I Use ..."

The best place to check browser support is the website caniuse.com (**FIGURE 10.2**).

Caniuse.com allows you to look up an HTML or CSS tag or attribute, and it gives you a full report on how it's used and what browsers support it. It will also give you helpful information like global usage statistics, whether some browsers provide partial support, and known issues.

TIP You'll find caniuse.com especially handy when you start to use CSS.

Checking this site is a good idea if you want to implement something (especially for new and experimental features) and you're not sure how widely supported it is.

Fallbacks and polyfills

In the event that you want to use a feature of HTML that might not be supported by all browsers, as a contingency plan you can implement fallbacks or polyfills.

A *fallback* is code or content used in the event that the original code or content isn't supported by the current browser. It's a way of saying to the browser, "If you don't understand the main code, use this other code instead."

HTML is very forgiving, so unsupported markup is just ignored. This is great for you as a web designer, because it means that if you want to use something like srcset, you can. Just make sure to include a standard src attribute as a fallback for browsers that don't yet support srcset.

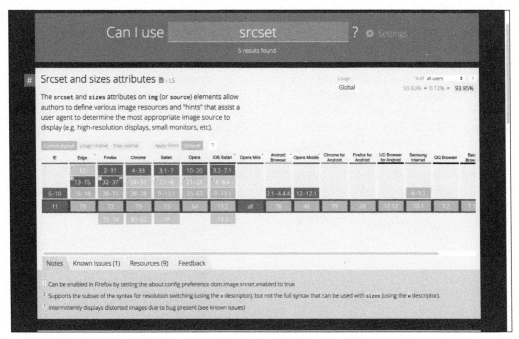

FIGURE 10.2 Caniuse.com

The same goes for most elements. Either there's a default fallback (like unsupported form elements defaulting to the **text** input type) or you can define your own fallback (as in the **srcset/src** example). In features you'll see later in the book, you can even define an error message that users will see if their browser doesn't support the feature. Each of these prevent your website from completely breaking in older browsers.

You can also add a *polyfill*. Mozilla (the creators of the Firefox browser) defines it like this: *A polyfill is a piece of code (usually JavaScript on the Web) used to provide modern functionality on older browsers that do not natively support it.*

Basically, you add code that you can download to older browsers to support newer elements. While writing JavaScript is outside the scope of this book, one example is using a polyfill to add **srcset** support to old browsers. You can download the polyfill, called Picturefill.js, from scottjehl.github.io/picturefill/. Include a reference to the code in the head of your HTML document by using the **<script>** element, which allows you to pull in code that is not HTML or CSS. It's most commonly used for JavaScript, and it works very similarly to the **<style>** element, which you'll learn about when you get to the CSS section of the book. For the examples in this chapter, the **script** element is being used to pull in an external JavaScript file.

Assuming the file **picturefill.js** is in the root directory, add the highlighted code to the <head> element:

```
<head>
    <script  src="picturefill.js">
    </script>
</head>
```

This script will do the heavy lifting of checking the browser to see if **srcset** is supported and, if it's not, creating the attribute for you to use.

What Are Progressive Web Apps (PWAs)?

PWAs are websites written in such a way that they provide on a mobile device an experience that feels like that of a native mobile application.

They use some combination of HTML, CSS, and JavaScript, while also getting help from the browser and operating system.

The Product Feedback app on apple.com, Smashing Magazine, Twitter, and Uber all use PWAs for their mobile sites.

VIDEO 10.2

Examples of the <canvas> Element in Use

The <canvas> element is good at more than just drawing shapes. In this video you'll see fantastic interactive examples of <canvas> being implemented.

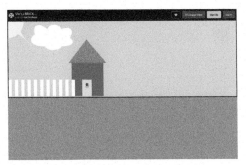

FIGURE 10.3 A house drawn with the <canvas> element

Advanced Elements

So what exactly qualifies as an advanced HTML element? For me, it's any element that is supported by HTML5 but requires something extra (usually JavaScript) to work. Everything you should know about JavaScript would certainly fill more than one book, so there won't be much JavaScript here.

The <canvas> element

The <canvas> element allows you to create drawings by writing JavaScript (**FIGURE 10.3**). In more advanced examples, you can even allow website visitors to use their mouse cursor to draw in real time.

This is an example of an element that requires heavy JavaScript to use. HTML5 basically gives you a way to execute JavaScript in real time to draw things, and then a set of functions to help you draw. This demonstrates how powerful HTML and the browser have become.

Adding support for offline storage

One great feature of HTML5 that has evolved as a result of its use on mobile devices is support for offline storage. This allows you to tap into the browser's local storage and keep content there in case the user's device goes offline (**FIGURE 10.4**).

Designing your website to allow offline storage also lets you store assets on the user's device and helps the site to load faster.

While offline storage does use some JavaScript to store and retrieve data, the code is very readable. This task demonstrates the basic idea. It builds on the example you saw in the Chapter 9 section "Input fields" which gave you the code for building a search box.

To store data offline:

1. In between the opening and closing <head> tags, type **<script>**.

   This tag tells the browser that the following markup is JavaScript and should be processed as such.

2. Type `localStorage.setItem`
   `("lastSearch", "Atlantis");`.

   In Chapter 9, you created a search box and entered the term "Atlantis." You're building on that same code example here.

   `localStorage.setItem` creates a key name-value pair. You'll learn more about variables in a later chapter, but for the purposes of this task, know that we are storing something named "lastSearch" and it has a value of "Atlantis."

3. Type **</script>**.

This produces no visible change on the webpage, but it tells the browser, "Store this, just in case you go offline."

Retrieving information is just as straightforward.

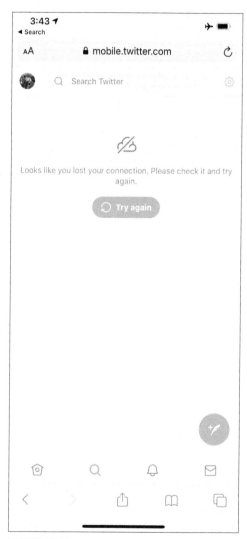

FIGURE 10.4 When viewed with a broken internet connection, the Twitter mobile site uses offline storage to show most of the page.

▶ **VIDEO 10.3**
Store Form Data in Offline Storage

In Chapter 9, you learned how to build web forms. In this video, you will store some of that data using offline storage.

▶ **VIDEO 10.4**
How Twitter Uses Offline Storage

One of the clearest examples of offline storage is the Twitter mobile web app. Once it's loaded, most areas, like the header, logo, and navigation, will not need to refresh, because they're stored on-device. The site will just load new tweets. Here's what that looks like in action.

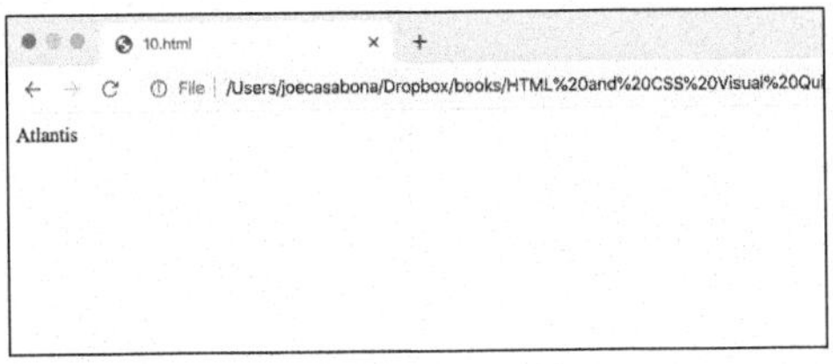

FIGURE 10.5 The data retrieved from offline storage

To retrieve offline storage data:

1. After the opening **<body>** tag, type `<div id="last-search">`.

   You're using the general-purpose **div** here because it's not a specific section of the website. The **id** attribute provides context for what information it contains.

2. Type **<script>**.

3. Type `document.write( localStorage.getItem("lastSearch") );`.

   `document.write` tells JavaScript to display text in the browser for the user to see. Unlike with HTML, which will display anything that isn't a tag, you need to explicitly tell JavaScript when something should be displayed.

   `localStorage.getItem` tells JavaScript to retrieve the item you stored in the last task.

4. `</script>`.

5. `</div>`.

6. Open your HTML file in the browser to view the results (**FIGURE 10.5**).

sessionStorage

If you're looking for a way to store content online or offline that's a bit more temporary than **localStorage**, look at **sessionStorage**, which has been part of HTML much longer.

A page session lasts as long as the browser is open. It can even persist through page reloads. If you visit a site, refresh a page, and see that it remembers certain data you've provided, it might have been stored as session data.

sessionStorage works similarly to **localStorage**, but with **localStorage**, the data is stored on the user's device and survives even if the browser is closed. **sessionStorage** is deleted when the browser is closed or the device is restarted.

Experimental Features

The HTML5 spec is a living document that is constantly changing and being updated based on proposals from developers, companies, and individuals like you.

It's often hard to nail down what new features are being worked on, what's been accepted, and what's going to become official.

Caniuse.com can be a good resource for this, especially the news page: caniuse.com/#info_news.

Many advanced features being developed for HTML today are application programming interfaces (APIs). These APIs, like Canvas and Local Storage, are aided by JavaScript. But there's one fantastic feature that is as easy to implement as an attribute is.

Lazy loading

Lazy loading is a technique used to download and display only the parts of your webpage that a user sees in the browser window. This allows the browser to download only what it needs, making webpages load faster.

Traditionally this has been done with JavaScript or another scripting language. However, native support for the feature is now being added to browsers (**FIGURE 10.6**).

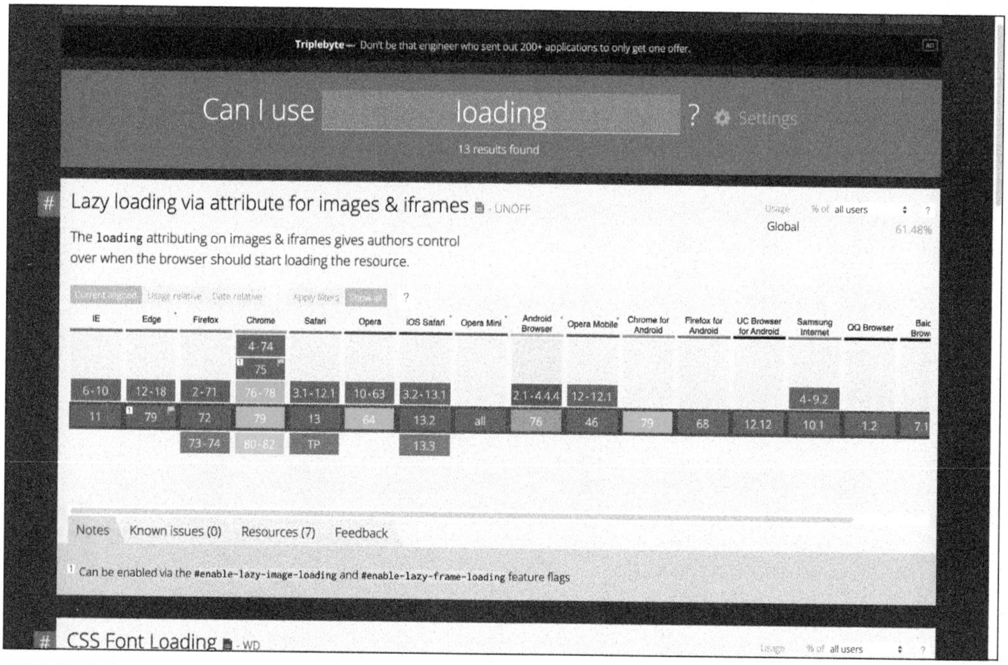

FIGURE 10.6
The caniuse.com page for native lazy loading

To add lazy loading to images:

1. Type `<img src="space.jpg"`.

2. Type `loading="lazy"`.

   This attribute is where the magic happens! You're telling the browser that this image should be lazy-loaded. Since the browser has this information, it checks to see whether the image is showing in the user's viewport (the browser window), and if it is, the image will be loaded.

3. Type `alt="This is outer space."/>`.

   That's it! Now the browser will download and display this image only if the user has scrolled to its vicinity.

Wrapping Up

With that look at some of the more advanced features of HTML, you've come to the end of the HTML section of this book. You can now mark up a page, display text and media, and build forms!

But that's only half the battle. Now that you have the "function" aspect of a website down, it's time to look at the "form" aspect: making websites look good with CSS.

Introduction to CSS

So far, you've learned all about HTML and how to structure a website. But you may have noticed that we haven't talked much about style or design. If HTML provides the function of a webpage, then CSS provides the form.

CSS is used to change the look and feel of webpages by targeting HTML elements and applying different styles. As you'll soon learn, you can change fonts, colors, sizes, and so much more with CSS. But it's also used for positioning elements, layout, and even printed pages.

What Are Styles?

What exactly do we mean when we talk about styles on websites? Back in Chapter 1 you learned how using HTML to structure a web document relates to structuring a document created in Microsoft Word.

If you've ever applied custom formatting to the text in a Word document, like changing the color of the text or picking a new font, you've applied styling to the text. Microsoft Word makes it easy to do this: just select some text and choose a menu command or click a button, and the text changes appearance! You can also style text on webpages, but there are no handy menu commands or buttons.

Word-processing applications also let you save sets of formatting characteristics that you might want to apply to more than one item; these sets are called *styles*. You might want all of your headings to use 20-point boldface font and be bright blue, for example. Rather than choosing those formatting options by hand for each heading, you can define the style you want for headings and apply it very easily.

Much as we write HTML code to give overall structure to a webpage, we write code of a different type to change the styling of text on a webpage. That's where CSS (Cascading Style Sheets) comes in.

CSS uses code to define the styles that should be applied to each element in your webpage. A collection of these code statements is a *style sheet*, and style sheets can be stored in the HTML document they apply to or in separate text files.

CSS styles can be applied to both inline elements and block-level elements. To continue the analogy with word processors, a style applied to an inline element is akin to a character style (which applies only to specific letters or words), and a style applied to a block-level element is similar to a paragraph style (which affects an entire paragraph).

What Does Cascading Mean?

An important concept of CSS is the "cascading" part of the name. One can imagine that "style sheets" are files where the styles are defined. But what exactly does "cascading" mean?

The word might conjure the idea of a waterfall, since that's what it's most commonly associated with. Generally, a cascade is a waterfall that drops in successive steps.

When applied to style sheets or any information, it means that previous information is built upon or successively passed on.

In short, the "cascading" part of CSS means that styles are generally applied in the order in which they're encountered by the browser, from the top of the style sheet to the bottom. If you define on line 1 that paragraphs should have red text, and on line 10 you say they should have green text, the paragraphs will have green text.

▶ **VIDEO 11.1**
Demonstrating the Cascade in CSS

In this video, you'll see the cascade in action when we change the color of text by adding different styles below the original styles. You'll see them update in real time as you edit them in CodePen.

Why is this important?

Understanding how styles cascade is integral to styling websites as well as to troubleshooting. Not only do styles used later in a document take precedence over those used earlier, but styles can also be built upon. This is especially evident while setting font sizes.

TIP "CSS" and "style sheets" are often used interchangeably.

In CSS, you can say something like "I want paragraph text to be two times bigger than the default font size." Without understanding the cascade, you will get unexpected results in your styles (**FIGURE 11.1**).

With that out of the way, it's time to learn how to write some CSS!

TIP Not all web browsers handle cascading styles the same way. See "Browser Support" at the end of Chapter 16 for more information.

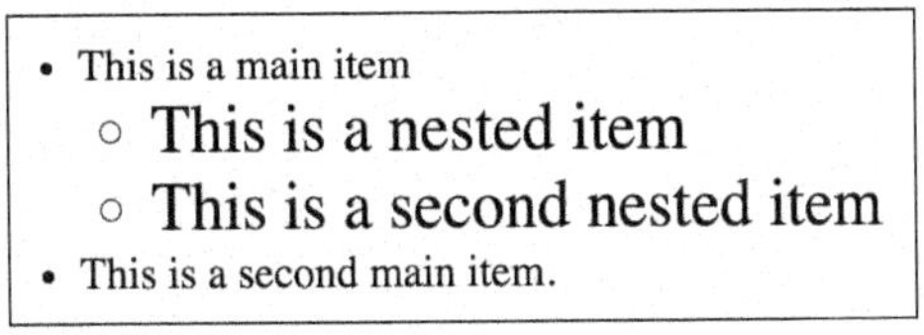

- This is a main item
  - This is a nested item
  - This is a second nested item
- This is a second main item.

FIGURE 11.1 In this example, the nested list uses a bigger font than the main list because of an error in the CSS.

CSS Syntax

A CSS statement, also referred to as a *ruleset*, contains several parts. Here's an example of a ruleset:

```
p {
    font-size: 20px;
    color: red;
}
```

Here you'll find the *selector* followed by an opening curly brace, then the *property*, a colon, and the *value*. Taken together, the property and the value make up a *declaration* (**FIGURE 11.2**). Each declaration ends with a semicolon. A ruleset can have several declarations. It's a good practice, for readability, to have one declaration per line.

After the declarations, you find a closing curly brace. Everything between the opening and closing curly braces is called a *declaration block*.

The selector is the HTML element you want to style with the CSS (this is also referred to as *targeting* an element). There are lots of ways to target elements. For this chapter, you should focus on using the element name (**p**, **h1**, and so on). However, as you'll learn in Chapter 12, you can also target elements based on their attributes—most notably, their class name.

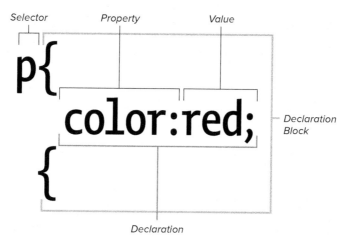

FIGURE 11.2 A simple diagram of a ruleset, with each section labeled

With CSS, you have a ton of flexibility to design pretty much anything you want on a website. And there's no better demonstration of that than CSS Zen Garden (**FIGURE 11.3**).

The idea behind CSS Zen Garden is that several people submitted style sheets for the same HTML markup. The goal was to make the styles as different from each other as possible. If you click through the submissions, you'll see they accomplished that goal! Bounce back to Chapter 1 to see CSS Zen Garden in action in Video 1.2.

TIP To make your rulesets more readable, have only one declaration per line. Most text editors will not do this for you unless you create a custom workflow (which could be complicated), so doing it manually will help form the habit!

TIP In Chapter 12, you'll learn about targeting elements, and in the following chapters you'll learn about a variety of properties and their values.

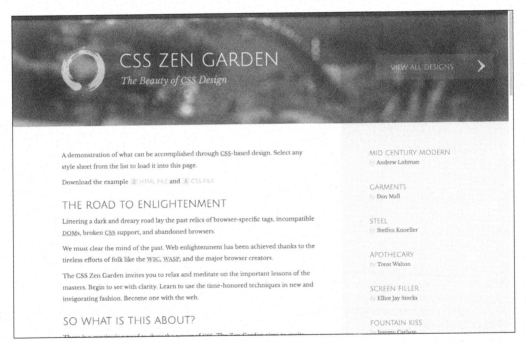

FIGURE 11.3 CSS Zen Garden (csszengarden.com) is a popular website that clearly demonstrates the power of CSS.

Using CSS on Your Webpage

There are two principal ways of adding CSS to any webpage:

- As an *internal style sheet* in the HTML document
- As an *external style sheet* in a separate file

Internal style sheets

To use an internal style sheet (that is, one that's embedded in the page that it applies to), you use the **<style>** tag. This is most commonly placed between the opening and closing **<head>** tags, but it can be referenced anywhere before the **</html>** tag. It will look something like this:

```
<style>
    p {
        font-size: 20px;
        color: red;
    }
</style>
```

You would use this format for one-off references—styles that apply only to the page you're using it on.

> **TIP** Before HTML5, you would use the **type** attribute with the **<style>** tag to explicitly tell the browser you're writing CSS, like this: **<style type="text/css">**. In HTML5, **text/css** is the assumed value.

▶ **VIDEO 11.2**
Using an Internal Style Sheet

In this video, you will use an internal style sheet to add CSS to a webpage and see how the page changes in real time.

```
1    <html>
2        <head>
3            <style>
4                p {
5                    font-size: 20px;
6                    color: □red;
7                }
8            </style>
9        </head>
```

FIGURE 11.4 An internal style sheet CSS added to an HTML file

To add CSS to your webpage using an internal style sheet:

You can use any HTML file you've created for this task. If you'd like a starting point you can use the file found at github.com/jcasabona/html-css-vqs/ch11/starter.html.

1. On the line before the closing </head> tag, type <style>.

2. Type the selector for the element you are styling—in this case, p.

3. Type a left curly bracket ({) to begin the declaration block.

   Next, you'll add the properties for the size of the font and its color. Enter each one on its own line.

4. Type font-size: 20px;.

5. Type color: red;.

6. Type } to close the declaration block and the style rule.

7. Type </style>.

   The resulting markup will look something like **FIGURE 11.4**.

Inline Styles

There is a third method of using CSS, but its use is frowned upon these days. If you want a style to apply only to a single element, you can use an *inline style*. With inline styles you embed the style information directly in the element's tag.

For example, if you want to format just one paragraph to make it stand out from the rest of the page, you could give it a vivid color and super-size the font. The code would look something like this:

```
<p style="color: chartreuse; font-size: 64px;">
```

The syntax is similar to "normal" CSS, but it uses the style HTML attribute right after the element's opening tag, and the value of the attribute is presented as a series of CSS property-value pairs.

Inline styles are not considered good practice, because they mix up the style information with the HTML and the content, making revising or maintaining the code more difficult.

Depending on the contents of the file, the page will look something like **FIGURE 11.5**.

This is great if you are designing a single page or have page-specific styles. But what if you want to use styles across multiple pages? That's what `.css` files are for!

Before

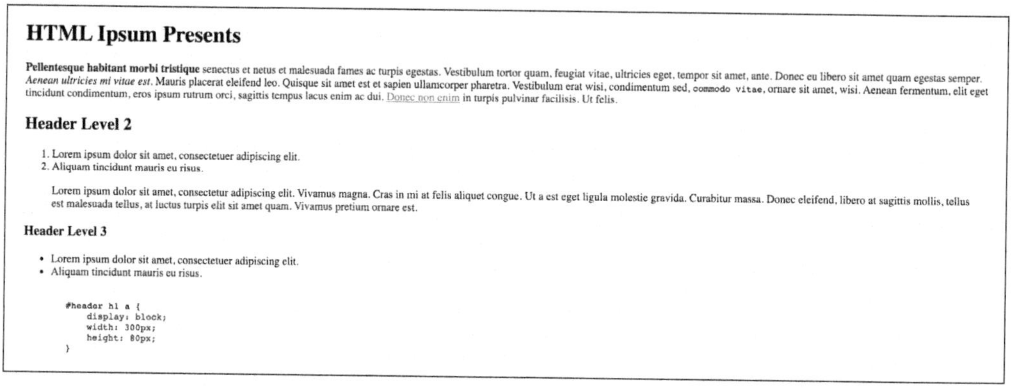

HTML Ipsum Presents

Pellentesque habitant morbi tristique senectus et netus et malesuada fames ac turpis egestas. Vestibulum tortor quam, feugiat vitae, ultricies eget, tempor sit amet, ante. Donec eu libero sit amet quam egestas semper. *Aenean ultricies mi vitae est.* Mauris placerat eleifend leo. Quisque sit amet est et sapien ullamcorper pharetra. Vestibulum erat wisi, condimentum sed, commodo vitae, ornare sit amet, wisi. Aenean fermentum, elit eget tincidunt condimentum, eros ipsum rutrum orci, sagittis tempus lacus enim ac dui. Donec non enim in turpis pulvinar facilisis. Ut felis.

Header Level 2

1. Lorem ipsum dolor sit amet, consectetuer adipiscing elit.
2. Aliquam tincidunt mauris eu risus.

Lorem ipsum dolor sit amet, consectetur adipiscing elit. Vivamus magna. Cras in mi at felis aliquet congue. Ut a est eget ligula molestie gravida. Curabitur massa. Donec eleifend, libero at sagittis mollis, tellus est malesuada tellus, at luctus turpis elit sit amet quam. Vivamus pretium ornare est.

Header Level 3

- Lorem ipsum dolor sit amet, consectetuer adipiscing elit.
- Aliquam tincidunt mauris eu risus.

```
#header h1 a {
    display: block;
    width: 300px;
    height: 80px;
}
```

After

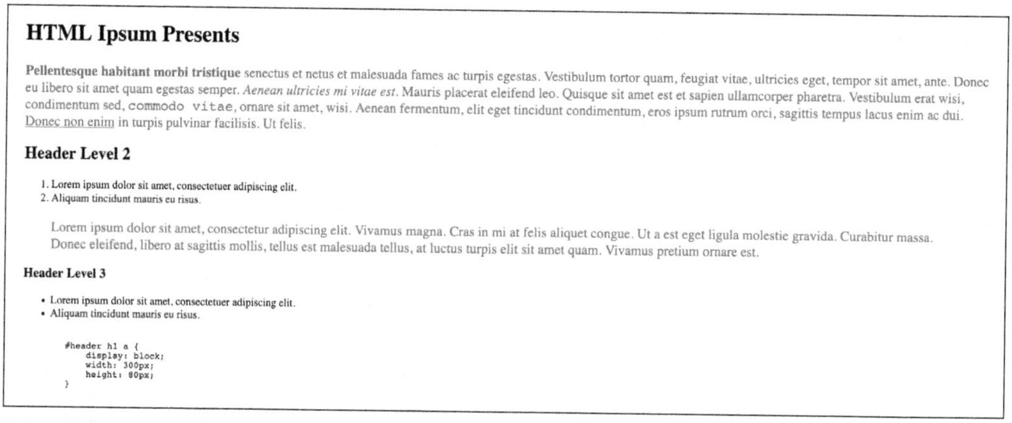

HTML Ipsum Presents

Pellentesque habitant morbi tristique senectus et netus et malesuada fames ac turpis egestas. Vestibulum tortor quam, feugiat vitae, ultricies eget, tempor sit amet, ante. Donec eu libero sit amet quam egestas semper. *Aenean ultricies mi vitae est.* Mauris placerat eleifend leo. Quisque sit amet est et sapien ullamcorper pharetra. Vestibulum erat wisi, condimentum sed, commodo vitae, ornare sit amet, wisi. Aenean fermentum, elit eget tincidunt condimentum, eros ipsum rutrum orci, sagittis tempus lacus enim ac dui. Donec non enim in turpis pulvinar facilisis. Ut felis.

Header Level 2

1. Lorem ipsum dolor sit amet, consectetuer adipiscing elit.
2. Aliquam tincidunt mauris eu risus.

Lorem ipsum dolor sit amet, consectetur adipiscing elit. Vivamus magna. Cras in mi at felis aliquet congue. Ut a est eget ligula molestie gravida. Curabitur massa. Donec eleifend, libero at sagittis mollis, tellus est malesuada tellus, at luctus turpis elit sit amet quam. Vivamus pretium ornare est.

Header Level 3

- Lorem ipsum dolor sit amet, consectetuer adipiscing elit.
- Aliquam tincidunt mauris eu risus.

```
#header h1 a {
    display: block;
    width: 300px;
    height: 80px;
}
```

FIGURE 11.5 The result of adding the above CSS to a webpage, along with what the page looked like before the styles were added

External Style Sheets

You can take all of the CSS in between those `<style>` tags and place it in a separate file with the extension `.css`. You'll then reference that file in the head of your HTML file by using the `<link>` tag.

If you name the file `style.css`, that might look something like this:

```
<link rel="stylesheet"
  href="style.css" />
```

The `<link>` tag is using two attributes here:

- `rel` specifies the relationship between the current document and the linked document. In this case, the link is a style sheet.

- `href` is a relative or absolute URL.

In the actual `style.css` file, you will have only the CSS rulesets—no `<style>` tags required!

TIP There are lots of ways to organize your CSS. Many people create a separate folder for the styles and organize them by section. For the purposes of this book, all CSS goes in one file.

VIDEO 11.3
Moving Internal CSS to an External File

See the previous task in action. You'll create a new file and move internal CSS to it.

To move internal CSS to an external file:

1. In the HTML file, copy all the CSS that's between the `<style>` and `</style>` tags.

    In the above example, it would be:

    ```
    p {
        font-size: 20px;
        color: red;
    }
    ```

2. Create a new file in your text editor called `style.css`. Save it in the same folder as your HTML file.

3. Paste the copied styles into `style.css`.

4. Back in your HTML file, delete everything from `<style>` to `</style>`.

5. Type `<link rel="stylesheet" type="text/css" href="style.css" />`.

That's it! You're now referencing your CSS from an external file. From here on out, that's how all our CSS will be written, unless otherwise specified.

Commenting Your CSS Code

Just as with HTML, you can include non-functional text inside your CSS (whether it's internal or external). This allows you to make notes and document your styles. Here's a CSS comment:

```
/* This is a CSS Comment */
```

Each comment starts with a forward slash (/) and asterisk (*), followed by the comment text, and closes with another asterisk and forward slash. What you see above is a single line comment, but you can also add multiple-line comments:

```
/* This is
a comment that spans
multiple lines. */
```

You can use CSS comments to add descriptions of the styles, note the specific purpose of the css file, credit the file's author, or create sections in your CSS file (this can be helpful if your style sheet is especially long).

▶ **VIDEO 11.4**
Review of the new File System

Before moving on, we review how the website directory is organized.

Wrapping Up

CSS opens up a whole world of opportunity for you to take a website and make it your own through design.

In the next several chapters, you'll see how to customize everything, create stunning layouts, and even learn a few shortcuts to save you some time.

But first, you need to learn how to target all the elements.

Targeting Elements

The crux of styling websites is understanding which elements to target and how targeting them affects the rest of your style sheet.

At face value, you can target any HTML element and apply a set of styles to it. However, you can also target elements *within* other elements, elements with specific attributes, and much more.

As you'll see, you can get incredibly specific with how you target elements on a webpage.

Targeting Elements by Tag

The clearest way to target any element in HTML is by its tag—namely, **p**, **h1**, **ul**, or any other HTML tag. The example you saw in Chapter 11 worked this way, and doing this will target every instance of that element. So if you target the **<p>** tag and have seven paragraphs, all of them will adopt the styles you have defined for the paragraph element.

TIP This is also referred to as a *type selector*.

To target an element by its tag:

1. In your **style.css** file, type the tag for the element you want to target, without the < and > characters. For this example, use **p**.

2. Type **{** to open the style declaration block.

   Every ruleset is contained between **{** and **}**.

3. Type **color:** (the property you wish to define).

4. Type **green;** (the value of the **color** property).

5. Type **}** to close the style declaration.

   This turns all paragraph text green (**FIGURE 12.1**).

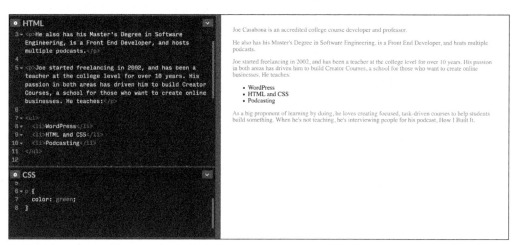

FIGURE 12.1 All the paragraphs on the page adopt the style of green text.

Targeting multiple elements

You can also target multiple elements, as long as they're separated by commas. So if you want all paragraphs, unordered lists, and ordered lists to have green text, the CSS code in Figure 12.1 would look like this:

```
p, ul, ol {
    color: green;
}
```

This would change the page to look like **FIGURE 12.2**.

> ▶ **VIDEO 12.1**
> ### Setting Basic Styles on HTML Elements
>
> In this video, you'll learn some of the most common CSS properties you'll use for styling elements, and you'll set baseline styles for your website.

Targeting Elements by Class

The best way to target some instances of an element without targeting all of them is to use a descriptor on all the elements you want to target. The **class** attribute is used for this:

```
<p class="standout">
```

I chose the value (or name) **standout** for the **class** attribute because I'm going to style any elements with this class to make them stand out more. Your class names can be anything, but web developers increasingly argue that they should be semantically descriptive, not stylistically descriptive. For example, don't set **class="green"** merely because the text is green. If the text needs to be red sometime in the future, the class name will no longer make sense.

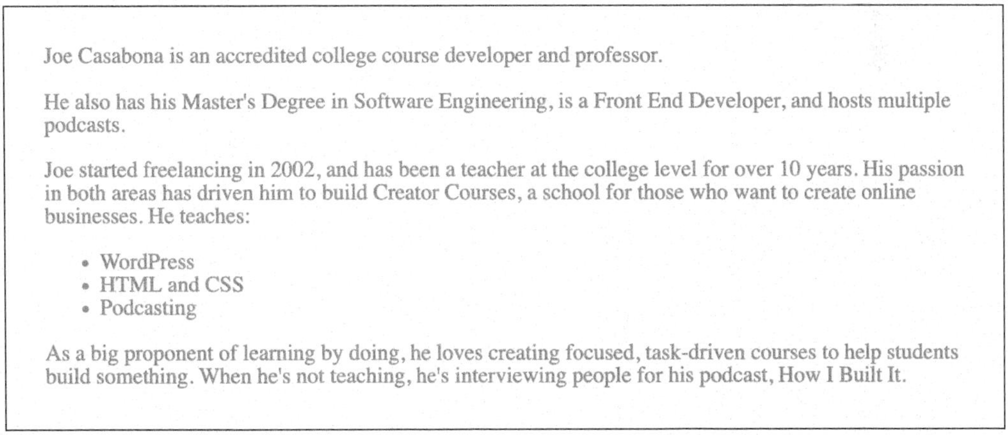

Joe Casabona is an accredited college course developer and professor.

He also has his Master's Degree in Software Engineering, is a Front End Developer, and hosts multiple podcasts.

Joe started freelancing in 2002, and has been a teacher at the college level for over 10 years. His passion in both areas has driven him to build Creator Courses, a school for those who want to create online businesses. He teaches:

- WordPress
- HTML and CSS
- Podcasting

As a big proponent of learning by doing, he loves creating focused, task-driven courses to help students build something. When he's not teaching, he's interviewing people for his podcast, How I Built It.

FIGURE 12.2 Now all paragraphs and lists (ordered and unordered) have green text.

Then in your style sheet, you can target any class by preceding the value with a period (.), like this:

```css
.standout {
    color: green;
}
```

This says, "For any element with the class **standout**, make the text color green."

You can also get more specific by combining element and class to say, "Only paragraphs with the class **standout** should be targeted":

```css
p.standout {
    color: green;
}
```

To make the first paragraph of a page bigger:

1. In your HTML file, find the first paragraph and add to it a **class** attribute with a value of "intro" by typing **\<p class="intro">**.

   Assigning the **intro** class to the first paragraph of each page allows you to style it differently from the other paragraph elements.

2. In your CSS file, on the next blank line, type **p.intro {**.

   This limits the style declaration to paragraphs of class **intro**.

3. Type **font-size: 24px;**.

   The default font-size for most browsers is 16px, so the text in any **\<p>** element with the class **intro** will be larger than the default size for the page.

4. Type **}**.

5. Save the files and open the HTML file in the browser to see the result (**FIGURE 12.3**).

Classes are a powerful way to add extra specificity to your styles and to highlight certain text.

▶ **VIDEO 12.2**
Targeting Specific Classes

In this video you'll create an HTML page with various classes on it, then write CSS to target those classes.

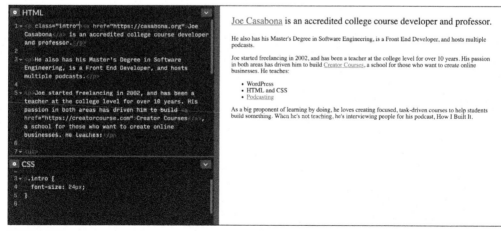

FIGURE 12.3 With the new class and style, the first paragraph on the page is now bigger than the others.

▶ VIDEO 12.3
Creating a Set of Alert Elements

In this video you'll create a set of alert classes to use throughout your website.

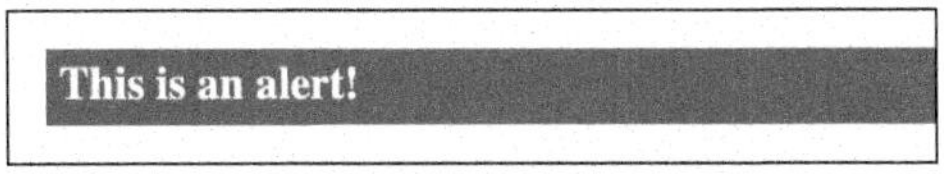

This is an alert!

FIGURE 12.4 Here's the simple `alert` class, applied to a paragraph.

This is a blue alert!

FIGURE 12.5 The `alert` element, now with a blue background

About Naming Classes

Naming conventions for CSS classes have been hotly debated. The schools of thought move between "the class name should describe the content of the element" and "the class name should describe the styles being applied." As more semantic HTML has emerged, along with more CSS frameworks, a strong argument exists for style-descriptive names.

You'll notice that the examples in this chapter use both. The truth is, it depends. If you're working on rule-sets that can be applied specifically to achieve a certain style, then they should be named appropriately (`.green-text` is a good example of this). But if you're making a ruleset to create a specific type of element and the style can change, a more descriptive class is appropriate (`.button` and `.alert` are good examples).

Targeting multiple classes

Just like with elements, you can target multiple classes with a single style by using a comma-separated list:

`.intro, .outro {...}`

And you can target elements if, and only if, they have multiple classes by "daisy-chaining" them, like this:

`.class-one.class-two {...}`

A good example of why you might want to do this is if you have a base style but want to alter a single instance of that style. Say we have a class called `alert`, with these properties (**FIGURE 12.4**):

```
.alert {
    background: red;
    color: white;
    font-weight: bold;
    padding: 5px;
}
```

Assume that you've defined this as the default style for alerts on the site. But perhaps there is a single instance where you want to use a background color of blue. To achieve that, start by creating a new class whose background color is styled blue:

```
.alert.blue-background {
    background: blue;
}
```

Then combine the two styles. In the HTML file it will look like this: **<p class="alert blue-background">** (**FIGURE 12.5**).

This technique can also work without combining the styles in the CSS. So if you wanted more than just alerts to have blue backgrounds, you could target the rule like this:

```
.blue-background {
    background: blue;
}
```

In this case, you don't have to change the HTML, and everything will still work as expected!

TIP There is one caveat to the less specific method: you need to make sure the generic class (in this case, `.blue-background`) comes after the class you want to change in the CSS (in this case, `.alert`). Otherwise, the less specific class will override the generic class, thanks to the cascade.

The Cascade, Inheritance, and Parent-Child Relationships

In Chapter 11, you were introduced to the idea of the cascade, the principle that the lower on a CSS style sheet a ruleset is, the more likely it is that it will be used to style the element it's targeting. But that's only part of the story.

Throughout this chapter, you get the other part of the story: styles are applied depending on how you target elements. You've learned how to target elements and classes, and soon you'll see how to be really specific with your targeting. But before we get to that, you need to understand inheritance and the family tree of HTML elements (**FIGURE 12.6**).

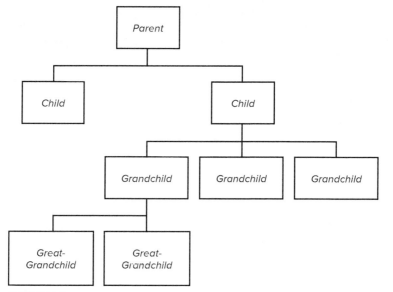

FIGURE 12.6 A simple family tree. Descending elements fall "under" their parent elements, inheriting styles that aren't specifically overridden by a declaration.

Just about any set of HTML markup will include elements in parent-child relationships. In fact, all the HTML markup on a given page is a descendant of the **<html>** element, which is considered the *root* of the document—the topmost level, or the start of the family tree.

FIGURE 12.7 will help you visualize the family tree structure. In this example, **<article>** is the parent element of the elements between its opening and closing tags. It has three children: **<h1>**, **<p>**, and **<p>**. The first **<p>** contains one child element, which is **<a>**. The second **<p>** has two children: **<span>** and **<b>**. And **<a>**, **<span>**, and **<b>** are also grandchildren, or descendants, of **<article>**. **CODE 12.1** shows how these relationships might appear in HTML.

Another way to think of children and descendants is that they exist *within* another element. Siblings exist next to each other. So in Figure 12.7, **<h1>**, **<p>**, and **<p>** are siblings. So are **<span>** and **<b>**.

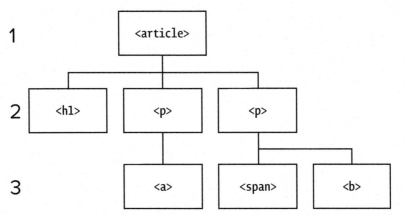

FIGURE 12.7 This chart should help you visualize the "family" terms that are applied to HTML elements.

CODE 12.1 A sample of HTML demonstrating the family relationships shown in Figure 12.7.

```
<article>
    <h1>Welcome to Joe's Website!</h1>
    <p><a href="https://casabona.org">Joe Casabona</a> is an accredited college course
    → developer and professor.</p>
    <p>He also has his <span>Master's Degree in Software Engineering</span>, is a <b>Front End
    → Developer</b>, and hosts multiple podcasts.</p>
</article>
```

Selecting Elements by their Relationships

You can select elements according to their relationships with other elements in the same family tree. For example, you can choose to target only the descendants of a particular parent element.

To target only the descendant of a particular element:

1. Type the selector of the ancestor element. For example, to target only links inside paragraphs, you would first type **p**.

2. Type a space (this is very important).

3. Type the name of the descendant element, which in our example is **a**.

4. Type the declaration block for the style.

Our complete example looks like this:

```
p a {
    background: lightgrey;
    color: darkblue;
}
```

This turns gray the backgrounds of all anchor tags inside paragraphs (**FIGURE 12.8**).

Targeting specific types of elements works well if you want to apply styles uniformly across those elements, and it's often used to define what are referred to as "base" styles. Those can include:

- Site-wide text colors
- Font face/typography
- Font sizes
- Spacing between elements
- Heading sizes

... and anything else you want to define on a global level.

But what happens when you only want to target certain elements? There are a few ways to do that.

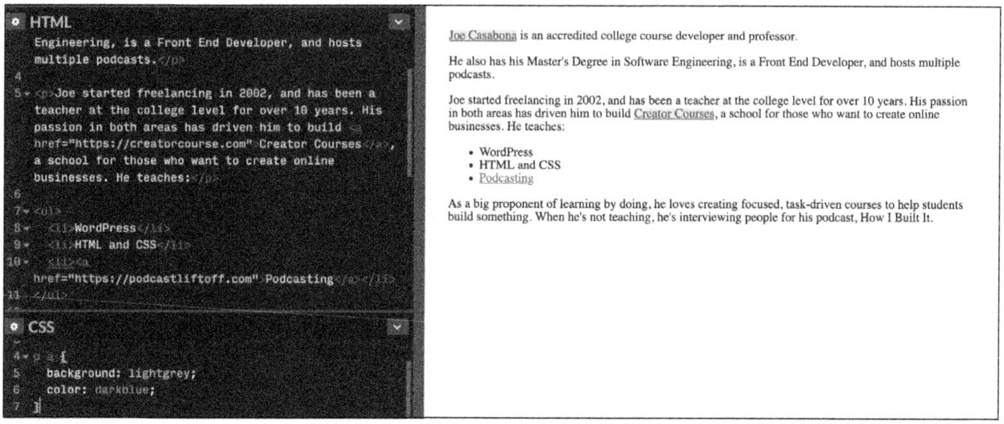

FIGURE 12.8 Notice that links in paragraphs have a gray background, but links in unordered lists (`<ul>`) do not.

```
<footer>
    <p>This is the footer with a
    → <a href="#">link in it</a></p>
    <a href="#">Click here to learn more</a>
</footer>
```

Selecting a child element (>)

Using a child selector says, "Target any elements that are direct children of a specific element." This is slightly different from the descendant selector because with child selectors, there can be no other element between the element on the left side of the child selector and the right side. In **CODE 12.2**, <p> and the second <a> are children of <footer>, but the first <a> is a child only of <p>.

To target only the direct child of a particular element:

1. Type the selector of the parent element. Building on the example in Code 12.2, use **footer**.

2. Type a greater-than symbol >.

3. Type the selector of the element that is the immediate child of the parent. In this case, use **a**.

4. Type the declaration block for the style.

This is how you would style only links that are direct children of the **footer** element (in our example, the second **a** element):

footer > a {...}

But **footer a** {...} would not work. It is not specific enough, and all links inside the <footer> tag would be styled.

Selecting an adjacent sibling (+)

To target an element that immediately follows another, use the adjacent sibling selector. For example, you would use an adjacent sibling selector to apply a style to the first paragraph after the heading in the following HTML, but not to the second:

```
<h1>Here's the Scoop!</h1>
<p>...</p>
<p>...</p>
```

To target an adjacent sibling element:

1. Type the selector for the first element—in this case, **h1**.

2. Type a plus sign +.

3. Type the selector for the sibling to which you want the style to apply. In our example, that's **p**.

4. Type the declaration block for the style.

> **TIP** This is a more succinct way to style a single paragraph than using the custom **intro** class style, as we did earlier in the chapter.

Using a general sibling selector (~)

Similarly, if you *do* want to target all paragraphs that are siblings of the **h1**, rather than just the first one, use the general sibling selector, like so: **h1~p {...}**.

> **TIP** As of CSS3, child and descendant selectors are officially called *child combinator* and *descendant combinator*, but many people still use the old terminology.

VIDEO 12.4
Putting Child and Sibling Selectors to Work

The best way to understand these selectors is to see them in action, and in this video, you'll get a single HTML example to see how the different selectors affect it.

Specificity and Precedence in the Cascade

Throughout this chapter, the topics of specificity and precedence have been unavoidable. CSS relies heavily on both to apply the appropriate styles to elements. Precedence of a style is based on two criteria:

- The order of styles in the style sheet
- Specificity of the selector

If a ruleset comes later in the style sheet, it takes precedence over earlier styles that target the same element, unless the earlier style is more specific. Things can get a little confusing at this point, but in general, here are some reasons a ruleset is more specific:

- It has more selectors (**p a** is more specific than **a**).
- A class is applied (**p.alert** is more specific than **p**).
- Multiple classes are applied (**.alert.blue-background** is more specific than **.alert**).

Whenever you're troubleshooting CSS, always check to make sure another style isn't taking precedence over the style you expect to be applied.

Note that elements will inherit any styles that aren't explicitly changed with a more specific or more recent selector. For example, text (in most browsers) defaults to **color: black;** and **font-size: 16px;** until you change it in CSS.

VIDEO 12.5
A Look at Styles and Precedence

In this video you'll see how changing specificity and order affect precedence, demonstrated by applying styles to elements and changing them in real time on CodePen.io.

!important: Proceed with Caution

In your travels, you might come across the value !important at the end of CSS declarations, like this:

```
p {
    color: blue !important;
}
```

The !important tag says, "Never override this style, even if another ruleset takes precedence." In this example it means your paragraph text will always be blue.

This may seem like an easy fix when you can't figure out why your CSS isn't working, but it is often unnecessary and makes your CSS unmanageable. My rule is that if you use !important, you need to add a comment to the style sheet explaining why you used it.

Styling with IDs

In the early days of CSS, there was another way to target elements for CSS, and that was with the **id** (*identifier*, or ID) attribute:

```
<p id="intro">
```

To use an ID in your CSS, instead of prepending the value with a . (period), as you do with classes, you'd use **#**:

```
#intro {
    font-size: 24px;
}
```

While this method works, you should not use IDs in your CSS unless you have a rock-solid reason (if I were to use the word *never* in programming/computing, I'd use it here).

That's because when it comes to precedence, ID trumps pretty much everything.

Instead, classes should always be used for styles. Today, IDs are more often used to target elements in JavaScript.

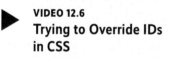

VIDEO 12.6
Trying to Override IDs in CSS

To demonstrate why you shouldn't use IDs in CSS, this video demonstrates what happens when one is used, and how hard it is to override.

Targeting Elements with Specific Attributes

So far you've learned how to use type and class selectors to target elements, and how to get more specific by targeting descendants and multiple classes. But even more options are available.

Classes aren't the only attributes you can target. In fact, you can target any attribute with this syntax: $element[attr]$, where **attr** represents the name of an attribute. The name of the attribute is enclosed in square brackets. So to target all images with an **alt** attribute, use this:

```
img[alt] {
    background: blue;
}
```

The Difference Between ID and Class

There's a semantically significant difference between classes and IDs that give some insight into why IDs take so much precedence.

Classes can be assigned to multiple elements on a page. You might find the class **alert** or **button** several times on a webpage.

IDs, on the other hand, should be completely unique to a single element on the page. You should only find an ID once on a webpage.

You can even target attributes with specific values; the value is also inside the square brackets and follows the attribute. So to apply a specific color to links that go to a specific URL, you would use something like this example:

```
a[href="https://google.com"] {
    color: green;
}
```

Lastly, a few selectors let you search on attribute values by inserting a special character before the equals sign (=). For example, adding an asterisk (*) to the attribute tells CSS to find any attribute whose value contains the text after the equals sign. So to highlight all images with the word *dog* in the alt tag, you would use the following:

```
img[alt*="dog"] {
    background: red;
}
```

To highlight links that go to sites in the .org domain, use the dollar sign ($) attribute selector to search for URLs that end in .org:

```
a[href$=".org"] {
    background: yellow;
}
```

TIP There's a lot more you can do with attribute selectors. Check out **MDN** for a comprehensive guide: **developer.mozilla.org /en-US/docs/Web/CSS/Attribute_selectors.**

Advanced Targeting

In addition to targeting specific elements and classes, you can use a set of advanced selectors known as *pseudo-selectors*. Right now, we'll focus on a specific subset of these selectors known as *pseudo-classes*. There are two types of pseudo-classes: those that focus on state and those that focus on order.

The pseudo-classes that are based on a particular state of an element allow us to target elements based on how a user is interacting, or has interacted, with the element. They are always preceded by a colon (:). Here's an example:

```
a:link
```

TIP There are a lot of pseudo-classes! This chapter introduces the idea and points out some popular ones, but you can see a comprehensive list at **developer.mozilla.org/ en-US/docs/Web/CSS/Pseudo-classes.**

User interaction states

Likely the most common pseudo-classes you'll use are those for link states. They allow us to give the user a visual cue as to how they are interacting with an element. For example, these states tell the user if they have or have not clicked a link:

- `:link` for links that have not been clicked or visited
- `:visited` for links that have been clicked or visited

The following states, which allow us to tell a user if they are *currently* interacting with an element, are most often associated with links but can be applied to any element:

- `:hover` for when a visitor's pointer is hovering over the target element.
- `:active` is used when an element is "activated" by a user. A good example of this is a button click.
- `:focus` is used when a user clicks, taps, or uses the keyboard to select an element. This is known as giving the element focus, and it's often used with form elements.

To style link states:

1. Type `a, a:link {`.
2. Type `color: green;`.
3. Type `font-weight: bold;`.
4. Type `}`.
5. Type `a:visited {`.
6. Type `color: grey;`.
7. Type `}`.
8. Type `a:focus, a:hover, a:active {`.
9. Type `color: red;`.
10. Type `}`.

This creates link states in which non-visited links are green, visited links are grayed out, and active/hovered-on links are red (**FIGURE 12.9**).

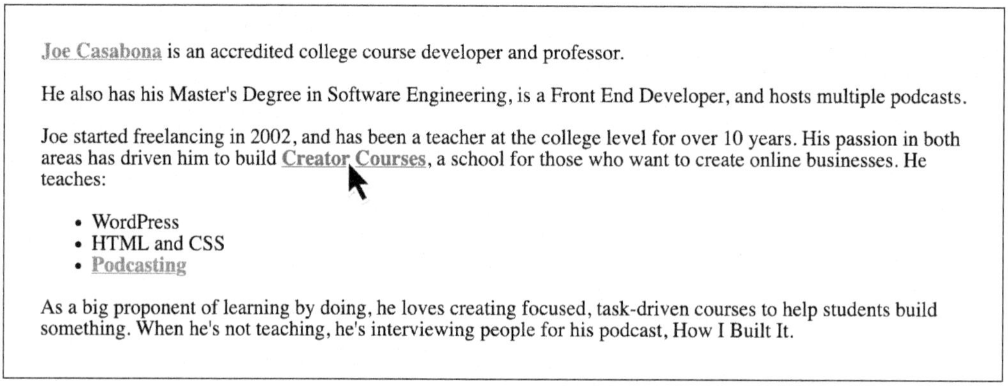

Joe Casabona is an accredited college course developer and professor.

He also has his Master's Degree in Software Engineering, is a Front End Developer, and hosts multiple podcasts.

Joe started freelancing in 2002, and has been a teacher at the college level for over 10 years. His passion in both areas has driven him to build Creator Courses, a school for those who want to create online businesses. He teaches:

- WordPress
- HTML and CSS
- Podcasting

As a big proponent of learning by doing, he loves creating focused, task-driven courses to help students build something. When he's not teaching, he's interviewing people for his podcast, How I Built It.

FIGURE 12.9 The user has already visited the first link on the page (now colored gray) and is hovering over the "Creator Courses" link, giving it focus. They have not visited the Podcasting link, so it is green.

Order-based selectors

Another common set of pseudo-classes is based on the order of the elements. There can be a lot of combinations for these, but here are the ones you'll see most:

- `:first-child` for the first child of a specific element within the parent.

- `:last-child` for the last child of a specific element within the parent.

- `:nth-child(even)` or `:nth-child(odd)` for the even or odd child of a specific element within a parent.

- `:nth-child(x)`, where *x* is an integer, targets the number *x* child on a specific element within a parent.

- `:first-of-type` for the first type of a specific element within a parent.

TIP The difference between `:first-child` and `:first-of-type` can be confusing, but it boils down to this, using `p:first-child` and `p:first-of-type` as an example: if the first child of some element—say, <article>—is a <p>, `first-child` and `first-of-type` will be the same. However, if the first child is <h1>, first-child styles won't apply to the p, only `first-of-type` styles will.

 VIDEO 12.7
Reimagining the `p.intro` Class with Advanced Selectors

Now that you have a few more tools in your selector kit, you'll see where you can remove classes and instead target by using pseudo-selectors.

To create a list with alternating background colors:

1. Type `ul li:nth-child(even) {`.

   This targets instances of <li> that are descendants of <ul>.

2. Type `background: lightgrey;`.

3. Type `}`.

4. Type `ul li:nth-child(odd) {`.

5. Type `background: lightblue;`.

6. Type `}`.

   Even-numbered list items now have a light gray background, and odd-numbered items have a light blue background (**FIGURE 12.10**).

This is a great way to style tables!

- WordPress
- HTML and CSS
- Podcasting

FIGURE 12.10 Using `nth-child`, you can create a list with alternating background colors.

The universal/wildcard selector (*)

There's one more selector you should know about it, but use it with caution—the universal selector:

```
* { ... }
```

This targets all elements on the page, and it could have unexpected results. You can also get slightly more specific with it and target everything within a certain element:

```
article * { ... }
```

This is often used to set site-wide styles for font face, size, or other items that need to be the same.

Wrapping Up

You got a lot of information in this chapter, and it's okay if some of it hasn't sunk in yet! I suspect you'll regularly refer to this chapter. I know I will!

But it provides important groundwork for the chapters to come. Now that you know what's possible in terms of targeting, it will be easier to envision how the styles you're about to learn can transform your websites.

CSS Resets

A common practice is to use a *CSS reset*. Because each browser has its own default style sheet applied, you can get mixed results after applying your styles. A CSS reset makes sure every browser starts at the same point with regard to styles.

It might be tempting to use the * selector to reset everything in one fell swoop. But then you'll also reset important default styles like bold and italic text, or possibly link colors, padding, and more.

You should be more surgical with CSS resets. A great and very popular reset is Eric Meyer's, which you can get at meyerweb.com/eric/tools/css/reset/.

Styling Text

When it comes to styling text, you have a ton of freedom to make it look however you like. But understanding the effect it makes is important. How you style your text can have the biggest impact on the general design of your site.

Typography is a huge part of design, and getting it right can take your site to the next level. While this book doesn't go into a full study of typography, you will get everything you need to customize the text on your site with CSS.

In This Chapter

Choosing Fonts

When you're thinking about which font (or typeface) to use on your website, first consider which fonts are actually available to you.

Today, the world is your oyster when it comes to fonts. But there used to be only a small number of cross-platform fonts that you could be confident the user would see correctly. They are still called *web-safe fonts*. The following are fonts that have traditionally been considered web-safe:

- Arial
- Courier New
- Georgia
- Verdana
- Trebuchet MS
- Times New Roman

TIP By default, browsers use Times New Roman as the font for text. This is a very safe font that comes on pretty much every device.

That's why we have the syntax for font handling that we do today—you list the main font you want to use, and then provide one or two fallback choices. This is also called a *font stack*.

In CSS, the property used to specify the font used for an element is `font-family`. The value of `font-family` is a comma-separated list of fonts you want to use, from highest to lowest priority. The font you want to use is listed first, followed by the fallbacks in the order in which you want to use them.

TIP While it might seem like `font-family` refers to the overall list of the individual fonts you want to use, that's not the case. A font, also known as a *typeface*, should include several styles, such as roman, bold, italic, and so on. The entire set of styles taken together is the font family.

Here's an example:

```
p {
    font-family: Cambria, "Times New
     Roman", serif;
}
```

This says, "Use the font Cambria. If that's not available, use Times New Roman. If that's not available, use the system's default serif font."

TIP You'll learn about popular sources for fonts later in the chapter. But first, you should know about what types of fonts are available to you.

TIP Nowadays, "font" and "typeface" are generally used interchangeably. In earlier times, though, when typesetting was done with metal or wood, they had distinct meanings. A *typeface* was the overall design of a set of letterforms (Garamond), but a *font* was subset of that collection of a specific style and size (Garamond Italic 14-point).

Types of fonts

Always try to group a font with fallbacks that look similar. That's because in the event that a fallback is used, you want your site to look as close as possible to what you originally intended.

Fonts used with CSS are broken down into a few categories, based on their style (**FIGURE 13.1**):

- Serif, which is a font that has extra strokes on the ends of each letter.
- Sans serif, which lacks the extra strokes.
- Monospace, or fonts where every character has exactly the same width. These fonts are often reminiscent of classic typewriter text. They're also commonly used to represent computer code.

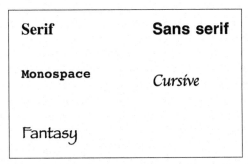

Serif	**Sans serif**
`Monospace`	*Cursive*
Fantasy	

FIGURE 13.1 An example of each major font style

▶ **VIDEO 13.1**
Using Distinct Styles for Heading and Body Elements

In this video, you apply different fonts to different sections of your site. A common practice is to have different fonts for the headings and the body copy.

- Cursive, which are fonts designed to look like handwriting.

- Fantasy, which are highly decorative fonts.

To set the default font for a whole website:

1. At the top of your **style.css** file, type **body {**.

   This targets the **<body>** tag. All the elements within this tag will inherit the font styles that we assign to it.

2. Type `font-family:`.

3. Type `Futura, Helvetica, Arial, sans-serif;`.

   Futura is a great sans serif font but is installed by default only on macOS, so this font stack provides fallbacks that are more widely available.

4. Type **}**, save the file, and open it in your browser.

   The text on the page is now displayed in a sans serif font (**FIGURE 13.2**).

A Case of Identity

by Sir Arthur Conan Doyle

"My dear fellow," said Sherlock Holmes as we sat on either side of the fire in his lodgings at Baker Street, "life is infinitely stranger than anything which the mind of man could invent. We would not dare to conceive the things which are really mere commonplaces of existence. If we could fly out of that window hand in hand, hover over this great city, gently remove the roofs, and peep in at the queer things which are going on, the strange coincidences, the plannings, the cross-purposes, the wonderful chains of events, working through generations, and leading to the most outré results, it would make all fiction with its conventionalities and foreseen conclusions most stale and unprofitable."

"And yet I am not convinced of it," I answered. "The cases which come to light in the papers are, as a rule, bald enough, and vulgar enough. We have in our police reports realism pushed to its extreme limits, and yet the result is, it must be confessed, neither fascinating nor artistic."

"A certain selection and discretion must be used in producing a realistic effect," remarked Holmes. "This is wanting in the police report, where more stress is laid, perhaps, upon the platitudes of the magistrate than upon the details, which to an observer contain the vital essence of the whole matter. Depend upon it, there is nothing so unnatural as the commonplace."

FIGURE 13.2 Viewed in macOS, the page now uses Futura, with a fallback to more common fonts on other systems.

Pairing Fonts

When pairing fonts (choosing multiple fonts to display on a page), try to find ones that complement each other.

Your goal is to provide visual distinction between different types of text, such as headings and body copy. Here are some tips:

- Pair a serif font with a sans serif font.
- Differentiate using size and weight.
- Don't pick fonts within the same classification (fonts that look similar).
- Give each font its own role. If you're using one for the heading (say, Futura bold), don't also use it for the body.

There's a lot to know around typography and font theory—more than this book can cover. But one really great resource is *On Web Typography,* by Jason Santa Maria (abookapart.com/products/on-web-typography).

Google Fonts

While the main source for fonts is the user's device, there are also many ways to use fonts from other sources. It's now possible to use basically any font you like.

A common source of fonts is Google Fonts, a library of free open source fonts that anyone can include on their website (**FIGURE 13.3**). There are *tons* of fonts to choose from, as well as recommended pairings and more!

TIP There are other services that work similarly to Google Fonts, like Adobe Fonts (fonts.adobe.com) and H&Co for the web (www.typography.com/webfonts), but most of them cost money.

▶ **VIDEO 13.2**
Browsing Google Fonts

A crash course on how to use Google Fonts, from finding the fonts and creating collections to getting the embed link.

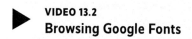

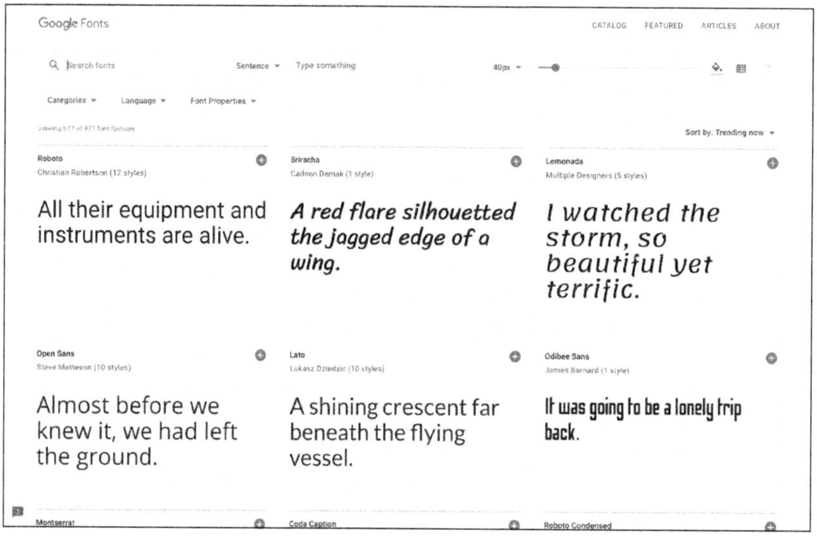

FIGURE 13.3
The Google Fonts (fonts.google.com) homepage

Roboto   12 styles

Christian Robertson

Almost before we knew it, we had left the ground.

FIGURE 13.4 The Roboto font option on fonts. google.com. Clicking this takes you to a list of all the styles you can select.

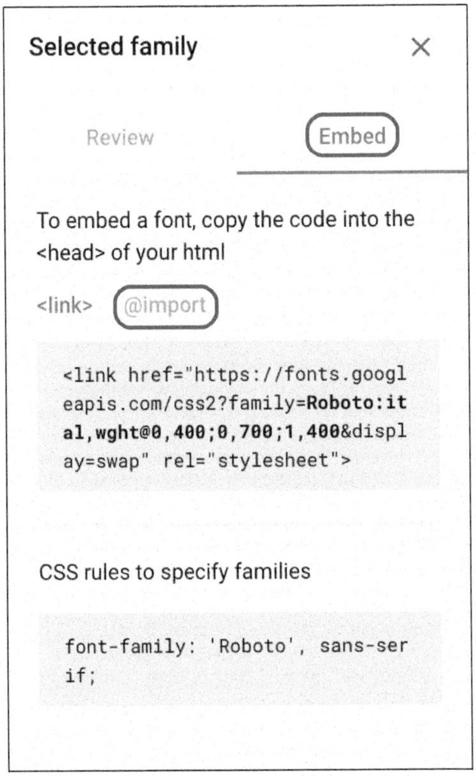

Selected family   ✕

Review   (Embed)

To embed a font, copy the code into the <head> of your html

<link>   (@import)

```
<link href="https://fonts.googl
eapis.com/css2?family=Roboto:it
al,wght@0,400;0,700;1,400&displ
ay=swap" rel="stylesheet">
```

CSS rules to specify families

```
font-family: 'Roboto', sans-ser
if;
```

FIGURE 13.5 The Embed tab on Google Fonts. This is where you will find the CSS code to copy.

To add Google Fonts to your website:

1. Visit fonts.google.com.

2. Find a font you like and click it.

   For this task, I'll use Roboto (**FIGURE 13.4**).

3. Click Select This Style for each style you want to include (+ Select this style).

   I'll select Regular 400, Regular 400 Italic, and Bold 700.

4. In the Selected Family box that appears, click Embed (**FIGURE 13.5**).

5. Click @import.

6. Copy the text between the <style> tags, without including the tags themselves.

7. Paste the copied text into your style.css file, at the top.

8. Below that, type body {.

9. Type `font-family: Roboto, sans-serif;`.

10. Type `}`, save the file, and open it in your browser.

Your webpages now use Roboto as the default font for body text (**FIGURE 13.6**).

TIP Google Fonts is a great way to include a nice-looking font for free, but be aware that using too many fonts in your design increases the number of files the browser needs to download, and it will slow down your site for users.

▶ **VIDEO 13.3**
Embedding Fonts from Google Fonts

In this video, you'll explore even more options for using Google Fonts on your website, plus some pitfalls to look out for.

Including External Fonts with @font-face

If you don't find a font you want in one of the online services, you can download and use an external font by linking to it using the @font-face at-rule.

An *at-rule* is a CSS statement that tells CSS how to perform or behave. All at-rules start with an at sign: @. You'll see several at-rules throughout the rest of the book. The @font-face at-rule tells CSS to use the provided files as a font.

The statement begins with the at-rule, followed by an opening curly brace. That's followed by the `font-family` property, which tells the browser how to reference the font by creating a new font family to use. Since it's a declaration, it ends in a semicolon.

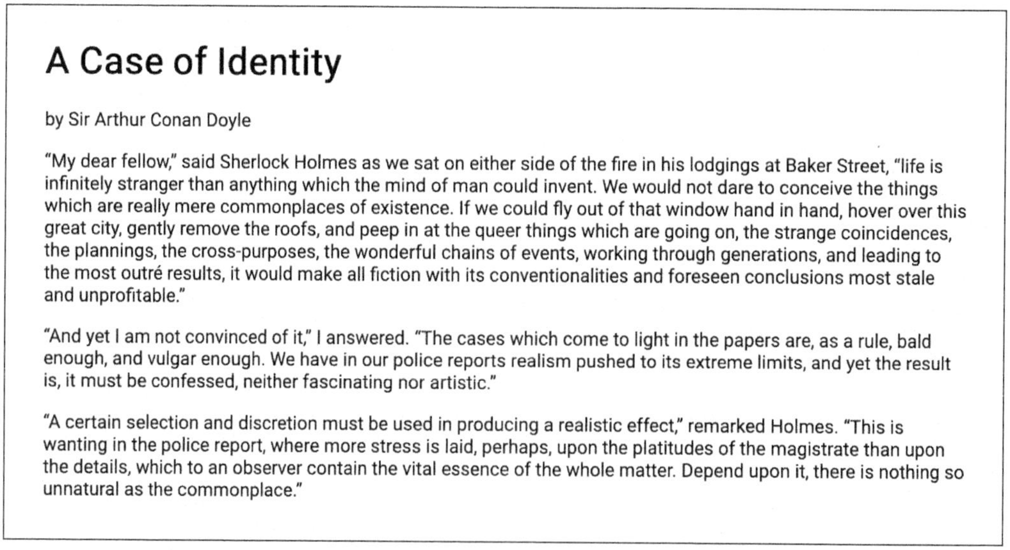

A Case of Identity

by Sir Arthur Conan Doyle

"My dear fellow," said Sherlock Holmes as we sat on either side of the fire in his lodgings at Baker Street, "life is infinitely stranger than anything which the mind of man could invent. We would not dare to conceive the things which are really mere commonplaces of existence. If we could fly out of that window hand in hand, hover over this great city, gently remove the roofs, and peep in at the queer things which are going on, the strange coincidences, the plannings, the cross-purposes, the wonderful chains of events, working through generations, and leading to the most outré results, it would make all fiction with its conventionalities and foreseen conclusions most stale and unprofitable."

"And yet I am not convinced of it," I answered. "The cases which come to light in the papers are, as a rule, bald enough, and vulgar enough. We have in our police reports realism pushed to its extreme limits, and yet the result is, it must be confessed, neither fascinating nor artistic."

"A certain selection and discretion must be used in producing a realistic effect," remarked Holmes. "This is wanting in the police report, where more stress is laid, perhaps, upon the platitudes of the magistrate than upon the details, which to an observer contain the vital essence of the whole matter. Depend upon it, there is nothing so unnatural as the commonplace."

FIGURE 13.6 An HTML page using the Roboto font

The `font-family` declaration is followed by another property, `src`. It behaves much like the `<srcset>` implementation of `src`. In this syntax, `src` is followed by a colon and two values: `url`, encapsulated by parentheses and single quotes, and `format`, also encapsulated by parentheses and single quotes. The URL can be relative or absolute. The `format` is the file format, which will most likely match the font file's extension. More on font formats later in the chapter.

`src` can accept multiple sources separated by commas, and the last source ends in a semicolon. Here's an example:

```
@font-face {
    font-family: 'Best Font';
    src: url('bestfont.woff')
format('woff'),
        url('bestfont.ttf')
format('ttf') ;
}
```

Reference the font like this in your CSS:

```
font-family: 'Best Font', sans-serif;
```

In this instance, you'll likely pay for a font, and they can range from a few dollars to hundreds. However, you can download free fonts from websites like Font Squirrel (**FIGURE 13.7**).

TIP Be aware of licensing issues! Even though you can technically upload any font to your server for your website doesn't mean you can *legally*. If you're using this technique, make sure you have a license to use the font on the web.

There are two caveats to using this method. The first is that different browsers support different font file formats.

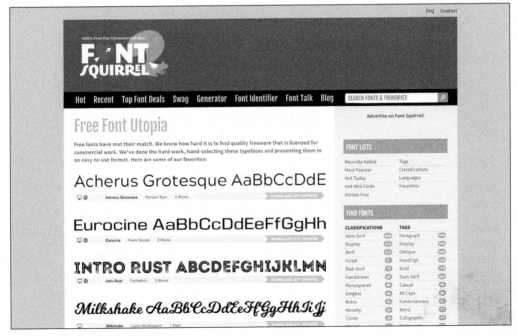

FIGURE 13.7 The Font Squirrel (fontsquirrel.com) homepage

Luckily, it can pretty much be boiled down to two: WOFF (Web Open Font Format) and WOFF2. Most modern websites use WOFF2 because it offers 30 percent compression gain over WOFF, making it faster for browsers to download. Optionally, you can use TTF (True Type Font).

In either case, you might have to convert your font into one of the above formats. To do so, you can use a webfont generator called Transfonter (**FIGURE 13.8**).

▶ VIDEO 13.4
Converting a Font with Transfonter

In this video, you'll download a font and then process it using the webfont generator at transfonter.org to output the font in the formats you need.

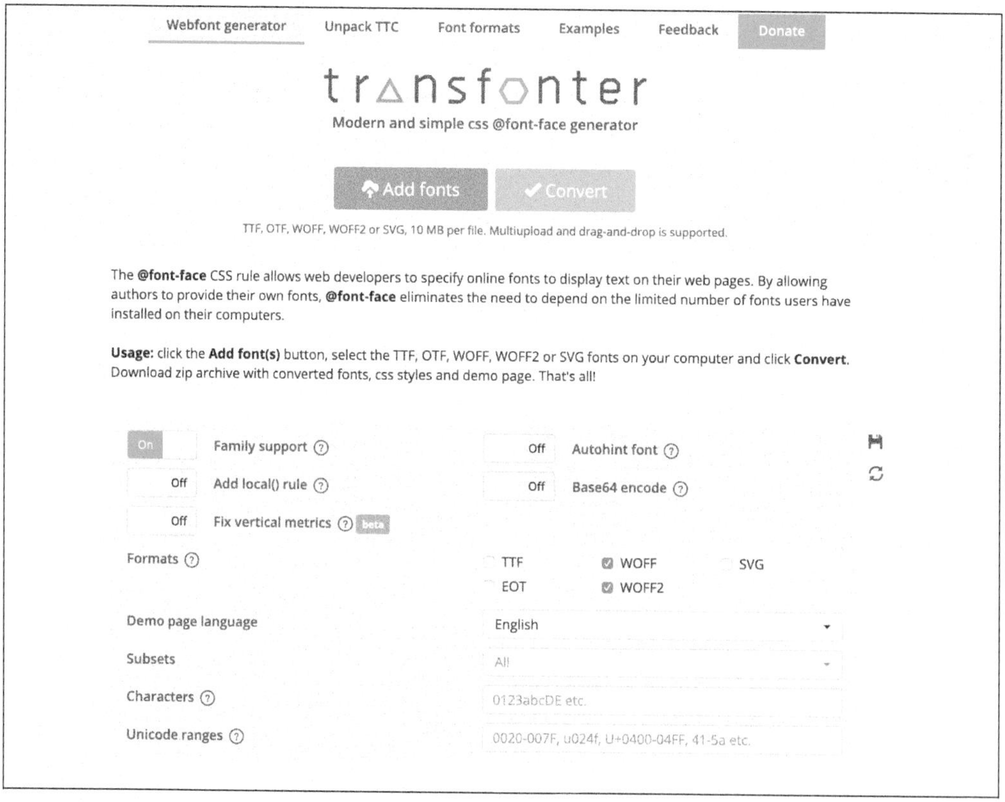

FIGURE 13.8 The Transfonter webfont generator (transfonter.org)

The other caveat is that you'll need to include each style of the font as a separate @font-face directive in your style.css file. So regular, bold, and italic (as well as other variations) all have their own files that need to be included (**FIGURE 13.9**). This can make your style file lengthy, but it might be worth it to get that perfect font.

TIP The browser can fake certain styles, like bold and italic, but the text can end up looking warped. It's best to use the specifically designed style instead.

TIP If you want to see this in action, open the Google Fonts import file to see lots of @font-face inclusions. Do that by copying the URL in your @import statement and pasting it into your browser.

To add a custom font to your CSS with @font-face:

1. At the top of the file style.css, type @font-face { to begin the @font-face rule.

   It's assumed all fonts for this task are in the same folder as style.css.

2. Type font-family:.

3. Type the name of the font family you want to include—for example, 'JetBrains Mono';.

   Use any font you like, and name the font family whatever you like.

4. Type src: url('jetbrains-mono.woff2') format('woff2'),.

5. Type url('jetbrains-mono.woff') format('woff'),.

6. Type src: url('jetbrains-mono.woff') format('woff');.

7. Type }.

8. Type body {.

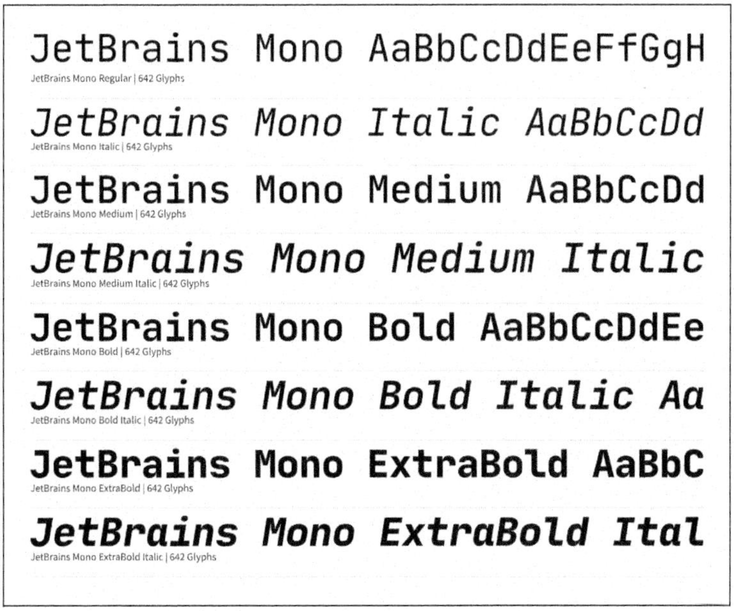

JetBrains Mono AaBbCcDdEeFfGgH
JetBrains Mono Regular | 642 Glyphs

JetBrains Mono Italic AaBbCcDd
JetBrains Mono Italic | 542 Glyphs

JetBrains Mono Medium AaBbCcDd
JetBrains Mono Medium | 642 Glyphs

JetBrains Mono Medium Italic
JetBrains Mono Medium Italic | 642 Glyphs

JetBrains Mono Bold AaBbCcDdEe
JetBrains Mono Bold | 642 Glyphs

JetBrains Mono Bold Italic Aa
JetBrains Mono Bold Italic | 642 Glyphs

JetBrains Mono ExtraBold AaBbC
JetBrains Mono ExtraBold | 642 Glyphs

JetBrains Mono ExtraBold Ital
JetBrains Mono ExtraBold Italic | 642 Glyphs

FIGURE 13.9 JetBrains Mono is a font with many styles.

9. Type `font-family: 'Jetbrains Mono', Courier, monospace;`.

10. Type `}`.

Now you're ready to use a custom font on your website (**FIGURE 13.10**)!

Now that you know how to choose the font, it's time to look at what else you do to style your text.

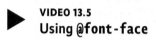

VIDEO 13.5
Using @font-face

In this video, you'll get an in-depth look at using `@font-face`, as well as at including (versus excluding) multiple styles.

Sizing Text

You resize text using the **font-size** property, like this:

```
p {
    font-size: 18px;
}
```

Several different units of measurement can be used for **font-size**:

- Pixels (**px**): This is a fixed measurement, which means 18px will always be 18px. Designers like this because it gives them the most control over the font size.

- Percentage (**%**): This is a percentage of the parent element's font. In most browsers, the default size is 16px, so if we want headings to be 32px, we could specify a font size of **200%**.

- Em (**em**): Traditionally in typography, this has meant "the size of a capital *M*." Today, it's a way of measuring **font-size** as a multiplier relative to the parent. So using the example above, if we want a 32px heading, we could specify **2em** (or two times the parent's font size).

A Case of Identity

by Sir Arthur Conan Doyle

"My dear fellow," said Sherlock Holmes as we sat on either side of the fire in his lodgings at Baker Street, "life is infinitely stranger than anything which the mind of man could invent. We would not dare to conceive the things which are really mere commonplaces of existence. If we could fly out of that window hand in hand, hover over this great city, gently remove the roofs, and peep in at the queer things which are going on, the strange coincidences, the plannings, the cross-purposes, the wonderful chains of events, working through generations, and leading to the most outré results, it would make all fiction with its conventionalities and foreseen conclusions most stale and unprofitable."

"And yet I am not convinced of it," I answered. "The cases which come to light in the papers are, as a rule, bald enough, and vulgar enough. We have in our police reports realism pushed to its extreme limits, and yet the result is, it must be confessed, neither fascinating nor artistic."

"A certain selection and discretion must be used in producing a realistic effect," remarked Holmes. "This is wanting in the police report, where more stress is laid, perhaps, upon the platitudes of the magistrate than upon the details, which to an observer contain the vital essence of the whole matter. Depend upon it, there is nothing so unnatural as the commonplace."

FIGURE 13.10 JetBrains Mono is now being used on this page.

- Root em (**rem**): This behaves just like em, except it is always based on the root (or default) size. In this case, it is based on the **font-size** applied to the **body** selector. This makes the relative font sizes much easier to keep track of, because you don't have to worry about multipliers on children or grandchildren.

TIP Many people use a CSS reset (see Chapter 12) to make the default **font-size** value 10px, which makes for much easier font size arithmetic.

TIP Relative font sizes (%, em, rem) were often favored by web designers because they take custom user settings into account. This was an accessibility and inclusion benefit for those who have trouble seeing. But now, modern browsers zoom the entire page when a user increases the size of the visuals on a page.

One way to use **font-size** is to establish a harmonious relationship between the sizes of heading and body text (**FIGURE 13.11**).

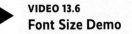

VIDEO 13.6
Font Size Demo

In this video, you'll see how each measurement unit affects font size.

To set the size of headings relative to the size of body text:

1. In style.css, type **h1 {**.
2. Type **font-size: 2em;**.
3. Type **}**.

Size isn't the only thing you can change. In fact, there's a whole set of text formatting properties available to you.

VIDEO 13.7
Creating a Heading Hierarchy with Font Sizes

Using **em** or **rem** can make it easy to create a nice visual hierarchy for your text and headings—something called a type scale. In this video, you'll do just that.

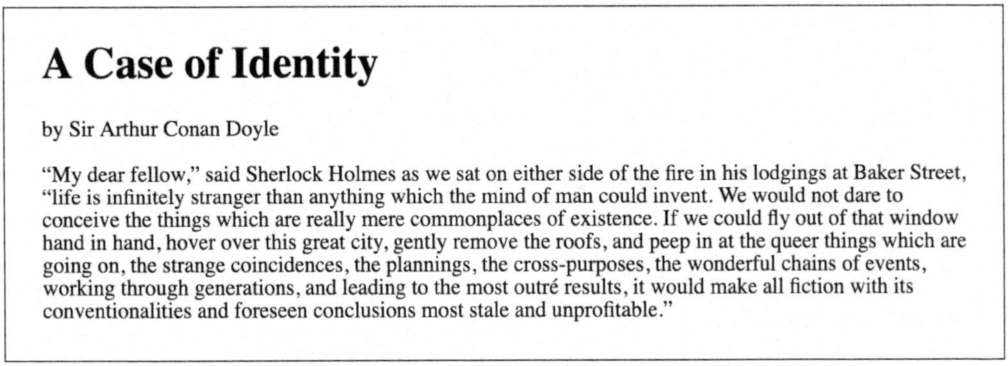

A Case of Identity

by Sir Arthur Conan Doyle

"My dear fellow," said Sherlock Holmes as we sat on either side of the fire in his lodgings at Baker Street, "life is infinitely stranger than anything which the mind of man could invent. We would not dare to conceive the things which are really mere commonplaces of existence. If we could fly out of that window hand in hand, hover over this great city, gently remove the roofs, and peep in at the queer things which are going on, the strange coincidences, the plannings, the cross-purposes, the wonderful chains of events, working through generations, and leading to the most outré results, it would make all fiction with its conventionalities and foreseen conclusions most stale and unprofitable."

FIGURE 13.11 Notice that the **h1** is double the size of the body copy.

Formatting Text

There are lots of properties for formatting text, but here are the most common ones.

font-weight

The `font-weight` property allows you to apply a different boldness to text. There are two primary values:

- `normal`, which is unbolded text
- `bold`, which creates bold, darker text

But as CSS has evolved, there are now some other values to consider:

- `lighter` makes text thinner than the normal weight.
- `bolder` makes text thicker than the bold weight.
- Numbered values: You can define a weight at `100`, `200`, `300`, `400`, `500`, `600`, `700`, `800`, or `900`. `400` is akin to `normal`; `700` is akin to `bold` (**FIGURE 13.12**).

TIP Depending on the font, many of these may depend on the style. If you don't have a font's style for a **900** weight, the browser will default to the highest weight you have.

For example, to make all your links bold, you would define the style for the anchor element this way:

```
a {
    font-weight: bold;
}
```

font-style

Next up is the `font-style` property, which italicizes text (**FIGURE 13.13**). There are three values:

- `normal`, which is normal, straight text.
- `italic`, which uses the italic style to show italic text.

- `oblique`, which uses the oblique style if it exists. If there is no such style, the browser tilts normal text slightly to make it look oblique.

TIP Often italic and oblique look the same. If there is no italic style supplied, the browser defaults to oblique. If neither is supplied, the browser simulates the style.

Here's an example:

```
h3 {
    font-style: italic;
}
```

text-decoration

The `text-decoration` property allows you to add emphasis lines to your text. There are several values (**FIGURE 13.14**):

- `none`: There is no change to the text.
- `underline` adds a line under the text. Use this to force links to be underlined (most modern browsers display link underlines when the user hovers over them).
- `overline` adds a line over the text.
- `line-through` adds a line through the text (like a strike).

If you have an article or story with a byline, you can use `text-decoration` to make the byline stand out a little bit.

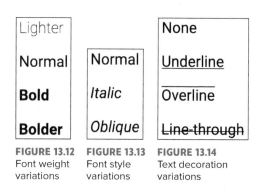

FIGURE 13.12
Font weight variations

FIGURE 13.13
Font style variations

FIGURE 13.14
Text decoration variations

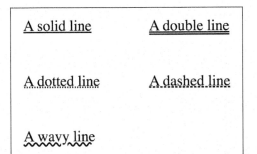

FIGURE 13.15 Text decoration style variations

by Sir Arthur Conan Doyle

FIGURE 13.16 The byline class with a wavy blue line instead of the standard solid black line

As an example, here's one way to style a byline class:

```
.byline {
        text-decoration: underline;
}
```

You can make **text-decoration** accept multiple values by listing them separated by spaces. So if you want to have an over-line and an underline, for example, you can do the following:

```
.byline {
    text-decoration: underline
    → overline;
}
```

Finally, **text-decoration** is actually short-hand for three other properties. Include them in this order, separated by spaces:

- **text-decoration-line**, which uses the values you've seen above.
- **text-decoration-style**, which changes what the line looks like. The default value is **solid**; the other options are **double** (two solid lines), **dotted** (a line made out of dots), **dashed** (a line made out of dashes), and **wavy** (a squiggly line) (**FIGURE 13.15**).
- **text-decoration-color**, which accepts any color.

This allows you to add more personality to the line (**FIGURE 13.16**):

```
.byline {
        text-decoration: underline
        → wavy blue;
}
```

You can take this example a little further and apply some of the other properties you've learned as well.

To format a byline class:

1. In `style.css`, type `.byline` to target the `byline` class.

2. Type `{` to begin the style declaration.

3. Type `font-style: italic;`.

4. Type `font-weight: bold;`.

5. Type `text-decoration: underline;`.

6. Type `}` to close the style declaration.

   Now, text assigned the **byline** class is styled bold, italic, and underlined (**FIGURE 13.17**).

Formatting for Readability

The styles in the previous section are mostly used to apply emphasis or draw attention to text. But there are also styles that improve text readability—things like line and text spacing, alignment, and more. Here are the common ones.

Alignment and justification

Using CSS, you can align text both horizontally and vertically.

With the **text-align** property, you can align the edge of the text to the left or right margin, center the text, or even justify it.

Justified text expands every line (except the last line) so that it takes up the full width of the container (**FIGURE 13.18**).

A Case of Identity

by Sir Arthur Conan Doyle

"My dear fellow," said Sherlock Holmes as we sat on either side of the fire in his lodgings at Baker Street, "life is infinitely stranger than anything which the mind of man could invent. We would not dare to conceive the things which are really mere commonplaces of existence. If we could fly out of that window hand in hand, hover over this great city, gently remove the roofs, and peep in at the queer things which are going on, the strange coincidences, the plannings, the cross-purposes, the wonderful chains of events, working through generations, and leading to the most outré results, it would make all fiction with its conventionalities and foreseen conclusions most stale and unprofitable."

FIGURE 13.17 The `byline` class applied to the author credit paragraph

---

"My dear fellow," said Sherlock Holmes as we sat on either side of the fire in his lodgings at Baker Street, "life is infinitely stranger than anything which the mind of man could invent. We would not dare to conceive the things which are really mere commonplaces of existence. If we could fly out of that window hand in hand, hover over this great city, gently remove the roofs, and peep in at the queer things which are going on, the strange coincidences, the plannings, the cross-purposes, the wonderful chains of events, working through generations, and leading to the most outré results, it would make all fiction with its conventionalities and foreseen conclusions most stale and unprofitable."

FIGURE 13.18 Justified text

With **vertical-align**, you can move elements vertically as they line up next to each other. So when you have two elements next to each other and one is taller than the other (for example, an image next to text), you can use **vertical-align** to line up their top edges. It's also useful for vertically aligning text in tables.

TIP Don't use **vertical-align** to set text in the middle or bottom of a container. Other features of CSS, like **flexbox** (which you'll learn about later), serve that purpose.

vertical-align values include the following:

- **baseline** aligns the element with the baseline of the parent (the baseline is the line on which most letters of a font sit).
- **sub** aligns the element with the subscript baseline of the parent (about 50 percent below the baseline).
- **super** aligns the element with the superscript baseline of the parent (about 50 percent above the baseline).
- **text-top** aligns the top of the element with the top of its parent's font.
- **text-bottom** aligns the bottom of the element with the top of its parent's font.

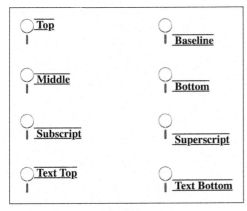

FIGURE 13.19 vertical-align values demonstrated

Along with the above, you can use the following values for table cells:

- **top** aligns the text in the cell with the top of the cell.
- **middle** aligns the text in the cell into the middle of the cell.
- **bottom** aligns the text in the cell with the bottom of the cell.
- You can see them in **FIGURE 13.19**.

Text spacing

Finally, there are several properties for spacing text, all using the same unit measurements as **font-size** (though **em** is popular for these properties):

- **line-height**: The amount of space a line takes up, including font size and leading (the whitespace between lines). For most fonts, this is around 1.2em (or 1.2 times the font size).
- **letter-spacing**: The amount of space between each letter (also known as kerning).
- **word-spacing**: The amount of space between each word.
- **text-indent**: Indents the first line by some amount. Most often, **px** is used here.

TIP To figure out the line height, subtract the **font-size** value from the **line-height** value. So if **line-height** is 20px and **font-size** is 16px, the space between lines is **4px**.

TIP If you want to move text completely off canvas, you can apply a negative **text-indent** value (like -9999px). This gives you the element to work with, without the text. You might do this if you want to make text animate on a hover state (you'll learn more about animations in Chapter 18).

To set the internal spacing for paragraphs:

1. Type p {.
2. Type line-height: 1.5em;.
3. Type letter-spacing: 0.1em;.
4. Type word-spacing: 0.2em;.
5. Type }.

You can see in **FIGURE 13.20** that this gives the text a completely different feel.

▶ **VIDEO 13.8**
Using text-indent to Hide Text

Using the **text-indent** property, you'll learn how to hide written text and replace it with a background image.

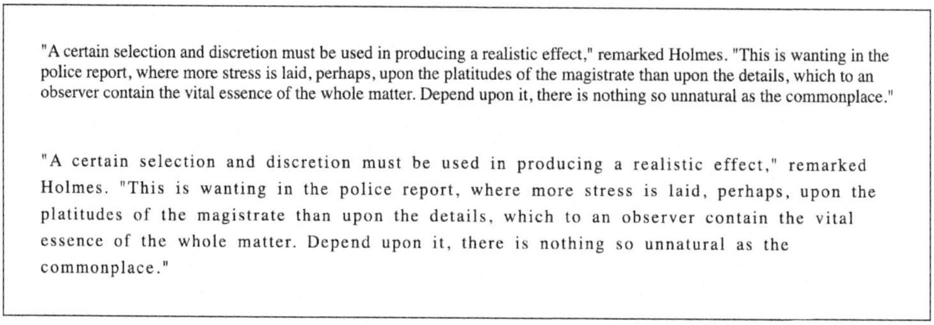

Before | "A certain selection and discretion must be used in producing a realistic effect," remarked Holmes. "This is wanting in the police report, where more stress is laid, perhaps, upon the platitudes of the magistrate than upon the details, which to an observer contain the vital essence of the whole matter. Depend upon it, there is nothing so unnatural as the commonplace."

After | "A certain selection and discretion must be used in producing a realistic effect," remarked Holmes. "This is wanting in the police report, where more stress is laid, perhaps, upon the platitudes of the magistrate than upon the details, which to an observer contain the vital essence of the whole matter. Depend upon it, there is nothing so unnatural as the commonplace."

FIGURE 13.20 Before and after adjusting line, letter, and word spacing

More Text-Related Properties

Even with all the ground this chapter covers, there are still more text-related properties. Here's a quick list of other helpful properties:

- **text-transform** allows you to change the capitalization of an element's text.
- **hyphens** specifies whether text should be hyphenated at line breaks.
- **overflow-wrap** specifies whether the browser should insert line breaks into otherwise unbreakable text (like long words).
- **white-space** specifies how to handle whitespace inside an element.
- **word-break** specifies whether to insert a line break when a word would flow outside an element.
- **text-shadow** allows you to apply drop shadows to text and adjust their styling.

To learn more about these properties, check out developer.mozilla.org/en-US/docs/Learn/CSS/Styling_text/Fundamentals.

▶ **VIDEO 13.9**
**Building the Page from
Figure 13.21**

In this video, you'll see how the page from Figure 13.21 was put together using primarily typographic parameters.

Wrapping Up

Using these properties, you can completely transform the look and feel of your site without doing much else. **FIGURE 13.21** shows a great-looking page that is 99 percent powered by the techniques you learned in this chapter.

But still, typography is only a small part of the vast toolset you have in CSS. Another great way to customize your site is with color, the subject of the next chapter.

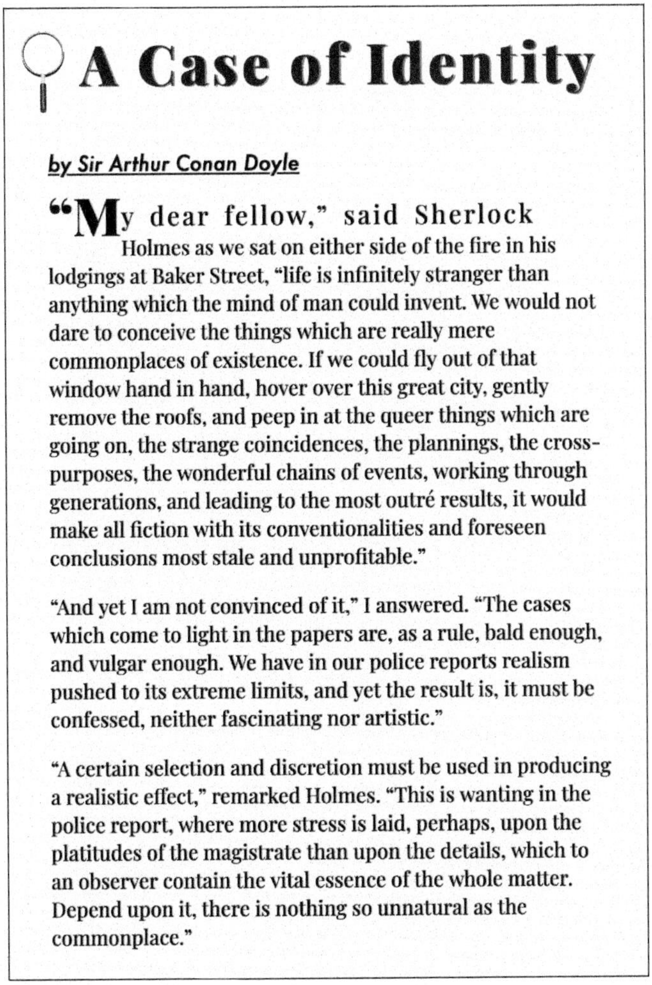

♀ A Case of Identity

by Sir Arthur Conan Doyle

"My dear fellow," said Sherlock Holmes as we sat on either side of the fire in his lodgings at Baker Street, "life is infinitely stranger than anything which the mind of man could invent. We would not dare to conceive the things which are really mere commonplaces of existence. If we could fly out of that window hand in hand, hover over this great city, gently remove the roofs, and peep in at the queer things which are going on, the strange coincidences, the plannings, the cross-purposes, the wonderful chains of events, working through generations, and leading to the most outré results, it would make all fiction with its conventionalities and foreseen conclusions most stale and unprofitable."

"And yet I am not convinced of it," I answered. "The cases which come to light in the papers are, as a rule, bald enough, and vulgar enough. We have in our police reports realism pushed to its extreme limits, and yet the result is, it must be confessed, neither fascinating nor artistic."

"A certain selection and discretion must be used in producing a realistic effect," remarked Holmes. "This is wanting in the police report, where more stress is laid, perhaps, upon the platitudes of the magistrate than upon the details, which to an observer contain the vital essence of the whole matter. Depend upon it, there is nothing so unnatural as the commonplace."

FIGURE 13.21 A beautiful website whose design is created by text styles

Color in CSS

The web has come a long way since its beginning. It used to be that the only way to get fun colors or complex graphics into a webpage was by incorporating images. But now that the web supports a wide range of colors—along with gradients, patterns, and more—you can use CSS to add a lot of color.

Finding the right color scheme for a website is key to good design. In this chapter, you'll learn all the CSS you need to know in order to customize the colors of elements, sections, and states.

How Computer Monitors Work

Before jumping into choosing colors, you should know a little bit about how computers represent colors. The screens of computer monitors are made up of millions of tiny squares called *pixels*.

When you turn a screen on, light shines through those pixels to illuminate them, and each pixel colors the light with a combination of red, green, and blue. A Venn diagram (**FIGURE 14.1**) is a good way to show the three *primary* colors—red, green, and blue—and the colors they produce when combined.

You can see that as they overlap, they begin to form other, *secondary* colors:

- Combining red and green produces yellow.
- Combining green and blue produces cyan.
- Combining blue and red produces magenta.
- Combining all three colors produces white.
- A lack of color produces black.

Armed with that information, you can generate a numerical code for any color.

Representing Color in CSS

In CSS, there are four ways you can define colors:

- **RGB:** A comma-separated list of the amount of red, green, and blue in a color, from 0–255.
- **Hexadecimal (or hex) values:** A six-character code that defines the amount of red, green, and blue in a color preceded by a hashtag (#).
- **Color names:** There is a set of predefined names for colors, like `blue`, `aquamarine`, and `rebeccapurple`. You can see the full list of names, and their colors, at htmlcolorcodes.com/color-names/.
- **HSL:** This defines the color in terms of hue (as an angle on the color wheel), saturation (as a percentage), and lightness (as a percentage). This is an uncommon method.

Both RBG and HSL can also accept an *alpha* value, which defines the opacity of the color.

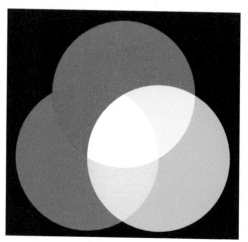

FIGURE 14.1 A Venn diagram for combining red, green, and blue

Hexadecimal colors

FIGURE 14.2 is a pretty basic table. In the top row, the letters *R*, *G*, and *B* (representing red, green, and blue) are at the heads of the columns. Underneath it, you have six *F*s, two in each column. This second row shows how you represent colors in CSS.

The three pairs of *F*s represent hexadecimal values, which are numbers in base 16. They include the standard digits from base 10 (0–9) and continue up the scale using the letters A–F to represent 10–15. A two-character hexadecimal number can range from 00–FF, or from 0–255 in decimal (base 10) notation.

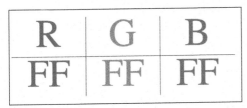

FIGURE 14.2 Red, green, and blue divided into columns

FIGURE 14.3 Using a CSS style rule to define the background and text colors with hex values

Because these numbers cover a huge range of values (over 16 million), you can use them to create almost any color you'd like. The first two characters state how much red goes into a color, the middle two how much green, and the last two how much blue. A value of all *F*s is white, and all 0s is black. You can think of all 0s as the complete lack of any color, and all *F*s as the maximum amount of any color.

For example, "pure" red is **#FF0000** (it has the most red there can be, no green at all, and no blue at all). Purple in this instance would be **#FF00FF** (maximum red, no green, maximum blue).

To set a color for a style:

1. In `style.css`, type the name of the selector you want the style rule to apply to—in this case, **body**.

2. Type **{** to begin the declaration block.

3. Type the name of the property you want to define and the value of that property. In this example, to turn the page black, type **background: #000000;**.

4. Type the next property you want to define and its value. Here, to make the body text white, type **color: #FFFFFF;**.

5. Type **}** to close the declaration block and the style rule.

FIGURE 14.3 shows the result.

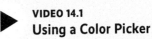

VIDEO 14.1
Using a Color Picker

Aside from getting the color code, a good color picker will recommend complementary colors to use in color schemes. You'll learn about two tools that help you do that.

Color Contrast

Color contrast is an important concept to understand because bad contrast makes your website harder to read. It can also negatively affect those who have color blindness. That's why most books are white pages with black text—in most cases, it's easiest to read.

You want to get the right contrast between background and text colors to enhance the legibility of the page. Make sure your text stands out on the page, as far as color, font size, and line height go. Dark text on a light background is generally pretty safe. If you want a dark background, darker grays work best, along with increasing the line height.

Of course, you're not expected to know every color's hex code (or RGB/HSL value) off the top of your head. Lots of tools can help you find the values for the colors you want to use. The website htmlcolorcodes.com has a fantastic one (**FIGURE 14.4**).

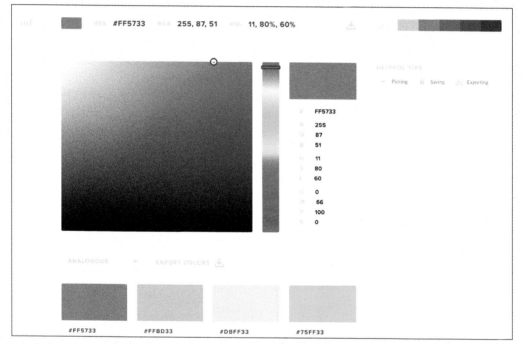

FIGURE 14.4 The color picker at htmlcolorcodes.com/color-picker/

Using RGB and RGBA to set color

Using RGB to set color is very much like using hex: you specify numerical values for red, blue, and green, but in decimal notation, not hexadecimal notation. For example, to specify pure red, type `rgb(255, 0, 0)`. To specify purple (a mixture of red and blue), type `rgb(255, 0, 255)`.

Both hex and RGB share one big problem: there's no way to change the opacity of a color. Luckily, there's a variant of RGB that does allow you to set the opacity level: RGBA.

The *A* in RGBA stands for alpha channel. It adds to the color specification a component that lets you set the opacity value from 0 (completely transparent) to 1 (completely opaque, the default value) (**FIGURE 14.5**).

For example, to define a semitransparent red background, you would type `rgba(255, 0, 0, 0.5)`.

To define background color using RGBA:

1. Type `body {`.
2. Type `background: rbga(0, 0, 0, 0.25);`.
3. Type `}`.

That gives you a page that looks like **FIGURE 14.6**.

You can also use the `opacity` property to change the transparency of an element. This property accepts values between 0 and 1, but that applies to the entire element—including text, images, and anything else—and not just its background.

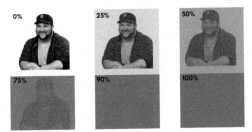

FIGURE 14.5 A photo with a red overlay at different stages of opacity

VIDEO 14.2
Using Transparency to Make Text Stand Out

To demonstrate how transparency can make a section stand out, in this video you'll learn how to create a semitransparent white box on a darker background.

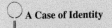

FIGURE 14.6 A page with a semitransparent black background

Using HSL and HSLA

HSL is a relatively new way to define colors based on the color wheel (**FIGURE 14.7**).

The value of hue, or *H*, is its position on the color wheel, which is measured in degrees from 0 to 360. This makes it a little easier to figure out the color as you increment or decrement the H value. Especially with hex, it might be hard to look at a value and figure out what color it will translate to. With HSL, thanks to the hue, beginners have a better understanding of what color they'll see based on the value.

Saturation, or *S*, is the amount of gray in a color (or conversely, how pure the color is). This is represented as a percentage, where 0 percent is gray and 100 percent is full saturation of the hue.

Lightness, or *L*, is the amount of white or black in the color, again as a percentage:

0 percent is no light (black), and 100 percent is full light (white). This is true no matter what the hue or saturation. Using HSL, red would be `hsl(0, 100%, 50%)`.

Like RGB, HSL can also accept an alpha value for opacity. So a semitransparent red would be `hsla(0, 100%, 50%, 0.5)`.

With that, you've seen the most common properties for controlling color in CSS: **background** (which changes the background color) and `color` (which changes the text or foreground color). But there are a few other ways you can use color in CSS.

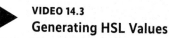

VIDEO 14.3
Generating HSL Values

Since HSL is a little different from hex and RGB, in this video you'll see how HSL values are generated, and how they can be more intuitive to use than the former methods.

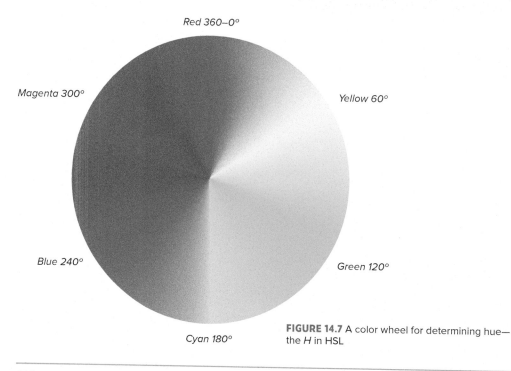

FIGURE 14.7 A color wheel for determining hue—the *H* in HSL

Gradients

Using CSS you can generate a gradient to smoothly transition between two or more colors, or *color stops*. There are two types of gradients: `linear-gradient()` (which transitions in a straight line) and `radial-gradient()` (which transitions outward from the center).

TIP CSS also includes the `conic-gradient()` type, but at the time of this writing it isn't supported by all the major browsers.

Gradients in CSS are actually functions that generate a background image. Because of that, there is a lot of information you can send to them.

In their most basic form, you just need the type of gradient you want to use and two colors. Each function has built-in defaults to take care of the rest:

`background: linear-gradient(red, orange);`
`background: radial-gradient(red, orange);`

The first line generates a red-to-orange linear gradient (**FIGURE 14.8**). If direction isn't assigned, top to bottom is assumed.

The second line generates a red-to-orange radial gradient. By default, the first color listed is at the center (**FIGURE 14.9**).

You have lots of other options when designing gradients:

- More than one color
- Direction
- Color stops (as in, stop red at 10 percent and begin the transition to orange)
- Size

Let's take a look at the functions and the information you can send to them.

FIGURE 14.8 A simple red-to-orange linear gradient

FIGURE 14.9 A simple red-to-orange radial gradient

Linear gradients

The `linear-gradient()` function accepts two types of values: those for direction and those for a color list.

Here's how to define direction with `linear-gradient`:

- **angle:** The starting angle of the gradient. It defaults to 180 degrees.

  Angles can be defined using four units: **deg**, **grad**, **rad**, and **turn**. You can learn more about each unit at developer.mozilla.org/en-US/docs/Web/CSS/angle.

- **side-or-corner:** This is a set of keywords that correspond to specific angles. This value starts with the word **to** and then contains up to two keywords: one for the horizonal line (**left** or **right**) and one for the vertical (**top** or **bottom**).

  to bottom, **to top**, **to right**, and **to left** correspond to, respectively, **180deg**, **0deg**, **90deg**, and **270deg**.

To create a full two-color background using `linear-gradient()`:

1. Type **body {**.
2. Type **background:**.
3. Type **linear-gradient(** to open the function.
4. Type **to right**.

   This specifies the direction the gradient should go. "From left" is implied.
5. Type **rgba(0,0,0,0.25) 68%,**.

   This defines the first color as black at 25 percent opacity. The color stops at 68 percent of the width of the container.
6. Type **rgb(0,0,0) 69%**.

   Stopping the second color 1 percent later gives a definitive border.

7. Type **)** ; to close the function.
8. Type **}** to close the style declaration.

The result is a background that serves as a content area, with a black background for a sidebar (**FIGURE 14.10**).

And here's the code:

```
body {
    background: linear-gradient
    (to right, rgba(0,0,0,0.25)
    68%, rgb(0,0,0) 69% );
}
```

Radial gradients

With radial gradients, you define the color stop list in the same way, but defining the gradient is a bit different. You can use these values to define `radial-gradient()`:

- **<position>:** This is relative to the top left of the container, and can be **top**, **bottom**, **left**, **right**, or **center**. It can also be a numeric offset (two numbers, on the *x* and *y* axes).

- **<shape>:** This is how the gradient will be drawn. You can use **ellipses** (the default) or **circle**.

TIP You can define how big a radial gradient is with **<extent-keyword>**, which is a bit advanced. Read about it at developer.mozilla.org/en-US/docs/Web/CSS/radial-gradient.

FIGURE 14.10 Creating a background with sidebar using `linear-gradient`

FIGURE 14.11 Creating a radial gradient

To create a radial gradient:

1. Type body {.
2. Type background:.
3. Type radial-gradient(.
4. Type circle at center,.
5. Type red, blue.
6. Type);.
7. Type }.

The result is a background that looks like a long circle in the middle, transitioning to blue around the edges (**FIGURE 14.11**).

TIP CSS Tricks has a very comprehensive writeup on gradients: css-tricks.com/css3 -gradients/.

Just as with colors, there are helpful tools with which you can generate the CSS code for gradients. One good tool is cssgradient.io/ (**FIGURE 14.12**).

▶ VIDEO 14.4
Experimenting with Gradients

There are many different properties you can assign to gradients. In this video, you'll learn more about them and see what they do.

FIGURE 14.12 cssgradient.io

Background Images

Gradients are treated as background images in CSS (using the **background-image** property). The **background** property is shorthand, and the browser is smart enough to figure out what you mean.

But that means you can set images as backgrounds in CSS. Here's the syntax for that:

```
background: url('url/of/image');
```

You can also set parameters for other values. One is **position**, which is measured relative to the upper-left corner of the screen by default. You can provide *x* or *y* coordinates or keywords, like **top**, **bottom left**, **right**, and **center**.

You can also state whether you want the background to repeat, and more.

▶ **VIDEO 14.5**
Background Images

Gradients are one implementation of background images, but there are several more background-related properties. These include **background-position**, **background-repeat**, and **background-size**.

In this video you'll learn more about how to use images for backgrounds.

The border Property

The other (much less complicated) CSS property that uses color is **border**, which is shorthand for three properties: **border-width**, **border-style** (from a set of options; see **FIGURE 14.13**), and **border-color**. The styles are as follows:

- **solid**
- **dashed**
- **dotted**
- **double**
- **groove**
- **ridge**
- **inset**
- **outset**
- **hidden**
- **none**

A definition looks like this:

```
border: 1px solid #000000;
```

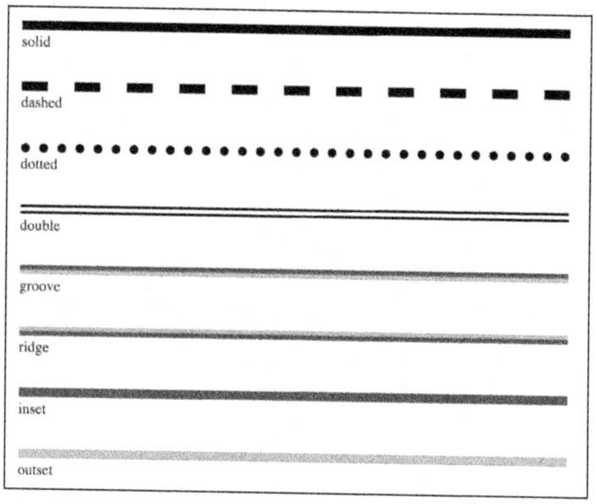

FIGURE 14.13 Border styles

To define a border around paragraph elements:

1. Type p {.
2. Type border:.
3. Type 1px.
4. Type solid.
5. Type red;.
6. Type }.

You end up with something like **FIGURE 14.14**.

You can also use each of these properties, and the same declarations, for each individual border, the top, bottom, left, and right. Use the following syntax:

```
border-[side]
border-[side]-[property]
```

So if you want to style just the top border:

```
p {
    border-top: 1px solid red;
}
```

or

```
p {
    border-top-style: solid;
}
```

TIP The main reason to use **border** instead of a text decoration like **underline** or **overline** is that those apply only to the text; **border** includes the whole container.

There's a lot more you can do regarding borders or box decorations in general.

VIDEO 14.6
Doing More with Borders

Aside from changing border style, width, and color, you could change **border-radius**, giving elements a nice rounded/button effect. You could also add a **box-shadow**. See those CSS border properties and more in action.

VIDEO 14.7
Creating a Stylized Aside Section

With all of these nifty new things you can do with colors, it's time to see it all come together. In this video, you'll style <aside> to stand out in a body of text.

"And yet I am not convinced of it," I answered. "The cases which come to light in the papers are, as a rule, bald enough, and vulgar enough. We have in our police reports realism pushed to its extreme limits, and yet the result is, it must be confessed, neither fascinating nor artistic."

FIGURE 14.14 A red border around a paragraph

Wrapping Up

Understanding color is a fundamental part of creating websites. Luckily, there are a lot of online resources dedicated to making it easier.

With your color schemes, you can design pages that come to life or even evoke an emotional response. With this fundamental concept down, it's time for you to start manipulating the elements and laying them out just the way you like them.

Using CSS for
Page Layout

You've learned how to use CSS to change
the appearance of text and manipulate
colors. Those are likely the most common
actions you'll take with CSS, but it is much
more powerful than that.

You can place elements wherever you
want on a page without changing the
underlying CSS. In Chapter 6 you learned
about using HTML to structure a page.
Now it's time to learn how CSS can
change the layout.

The Box Model

In Chapter 6, you were briefly introduced to the box model. The simplest way to put it is that CSS treats every HTML element as if it's in its own box. By default, when a browser renders a webpage, the boxes flow onto the page in sequence as it encounters them in the code. This is sometimes called *normal flow*.

FIGURE 15.1 shows an example from the *New York Times*.

For each element, you can control a number of parameters:

- The width and height of its box
- Border color and thickness around the box
- Whether or not the border is visible
- Whether the box itself is visible

- Where the box fits in the flow of elements on the page
- How much space is around the box (margins), and around the content within the box (padding)

You can also change the position of an element in the flow of a page by choosing whether to make it an inline element or a block element. This can have an effect on how much space is (or can be defined) around the box.

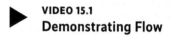

VIDEO 15.1
Demonstrating Flow

In this video, you'll see the different ways an element can be arranged, and how changing the CSS affects the flow of a page.

FIGURE 15.1 Elements outlined on the *New York Times* homepage, illustrating the box model

The CSS display property

Using the **display** property, you can change the flow of an element. These are the most common values:

- **block** makes an element start on a new line and take up the full width of the container (forming a block of content, if you will).

- **inline** leaves an element in its position in the flow of content. It will not start on a new line, and it will take up only the horizontal space it needs. Certain properties, like **height** and **width**, have no effect on inline elements.

- **inline-block** is a hybrid of **inline** and **block**. The element will display inline but take on the properties of a block, like height, width, and spacing.

- **none** completely hides the element and removes it from the flow. It will only be viewable in source code.

> **TIP** There's another property, called **visibility**. If it's set to **hidden**, users will not be able to see the element, but it will still take up the same amount of space on the page. It will not be removed from the flow.

> **TIP** There are several other display properties that are less common. Two you'll learn about in depth in Chapter 16 are **flex** and **grid**.

To set a link to display as a block-level element:

1. In your style sheet, type the selector you want to change. In this example, use **a**.

2. If you want the style to apply to a specific class, type a period followed immediately by the class name, then add a left curly brace. Here, use **.button {**.

3. Type the property you want to assign to the selector. In this case, use **display: block;**.

4. Type **}** to close the style declaration.

This moves any link (**<a>** tag) of the class **button** from inline to its own block (**FIGURE 15.2**).

Height and width

Unless you specifically define a height and width, they'll default to a size big enough to hold the content (with the caveat that block-level elements are the full width of their parent container). To define a specific size, you can use the **height** and **width** properties. They accept the same units you would use to measure text size: **px**, **em**, **rem**, and **%**.

> **TIP** Using % will cause the targeted element to take up that percentage of the parent container. So if the container is 100px and you define, say, a **width** of 50%, the target element will be 50px wide.

We would not dare to conceive the things which are really mere commonplaces of existence. If we could fly out of that window hand in hand, hover over this great city, gently remove the roofs, and peep in at the queer things which are going on,
Click the Button
to read more!

FIGURE 15.2 This <a> tag of the class **button** now sits on its own line.

To set a specific height and width for an element:

1. In your style sheet, define the element to which you want to apply the rule, followed by a left brace. In this example, use **aside {**.

2. Type **width:** followed by the desired width. In this case, **400px;**.

3. Type **height:** followed by the desired height. In this case, **200px;**.

4. Type **}** to end the style declaration.

This gives you a 400x200 box for all **aside** elements (**FIGURE 15.3**).

TIP You can also use the value **auto** for either **height** or **width**. This is especially useful when resizing images. If you want images to be **600px** wide, using a height of **auto** will make sure the image maintains the correct aspect ratio.

Finally, you can set minimum and maximum values for both height and width.

The minimum properties are **min-width** and **min-height**. They say, "Do not drop the container's size below this value." If you set **min-width: 300px;** the container will always be at least 300px wide but can be wider, depending on the content.

And **max-width** and **max-height** say, "Do not let a container go beyond this size." So **max-height: 500px** means the container can be shorter than, but will never be taller than, 500px.

Each of these can make sense depending on the context. But the main thing to remember is that the **height** and **width** properties are fixed. They will always be exactly the size you define, no matter the size of the browser window or parent container (**FIGURE 15.4**).

This is one of 56 short stories written about Sherlock Holmes by Sir Arthur Conan Doyle. It was published in 1891.

FIGURE 15.3 An **aside** element with a set width and height. A border has been added to show the full container.

A Case of Identity

Arthur Conan Doyle

s one of 56 short stories written about Sherlock Holmes by Sir Arthur Conan Doyl

dear fellow," said Sherlock Holmes as we sat on
r side of the fire in his lodgings at Baker Street,
is infinitely stranger than anything which the
of man could invent. We would not dare to
ive the things which are really mere
nonplaces of existence. If we could fly out of that
ow hand in hand, hover over this great city,
y remove the roofs, and peep in at the queer
s which are going on, the strange coincidences,
lannings, the cross-purposes, the wonderful chains
ents working through generations and leading to

FIGURE 15.4 This element's width has been set bigger than the browser's width, causing the content to go beyond the user's viewable window.

 VIDEO 15.2
Adjusting Heights and Widths in Layout

Now that you know all about managing height and width, it's time to put that knowledge to the test. In this video, you'll set and adjust the widths and heights of various elements to make everything line up nicely.

Using overflow

You may find yourself in situations where setting a specific height or width causes the box to break and text to flow outside of that box.

Luckily, the `overflow` property is there to help you. The two values that can help you out here are:

- `hidden`: Hides any content that goes beyond the container.
- `scroll`: Adds scroll bars to the container.

Padding and Margins

In Chapter 14, you learned how to adjust spacing for text to make it more readable and how to add whitespace when necessary. You can do the same thing with entire elements and everything they contain—text, images, and otherwise.

As stated earlier, there are two ways to add spacing to an element: around the outside of the whole box, which is `margin`, and around the content inside the box, which is `padding`. That, taken with `height`, `width`, and `border`, creates the complete amount of space a block-level element takes up (**FIGURE 15.5**).

You can define `padding` and `margin` values using the same units as those for `height` and `width`. Using a single value for either property applies the same value to all four sides of the element.

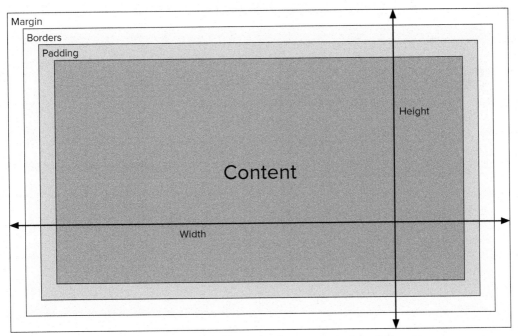

FIGURE 15.5 How `padding`, `margin`, `height`, `width`, and `border` affect a block-level element

To add padding and margin to a paragraph:

1. In your style sheet, type the selector you wish to target, followed by a left curly brace. In this case, use **p {**.

2. Type **padding:** followed by the value; this example uses **20px;**.

3. Type **margin:** and the value; here, use **20px;**.

4. Type **}** to close the declaration.

This adds a little extra spacing to your paragraphs (**FIGURE 15.6**).

VIDEO 15.3
Building a Completely Styled Button

Now that you know how to turn links into blocks and add spacing, you can create a real-looking button using only CSS. You'll learn how in this video.

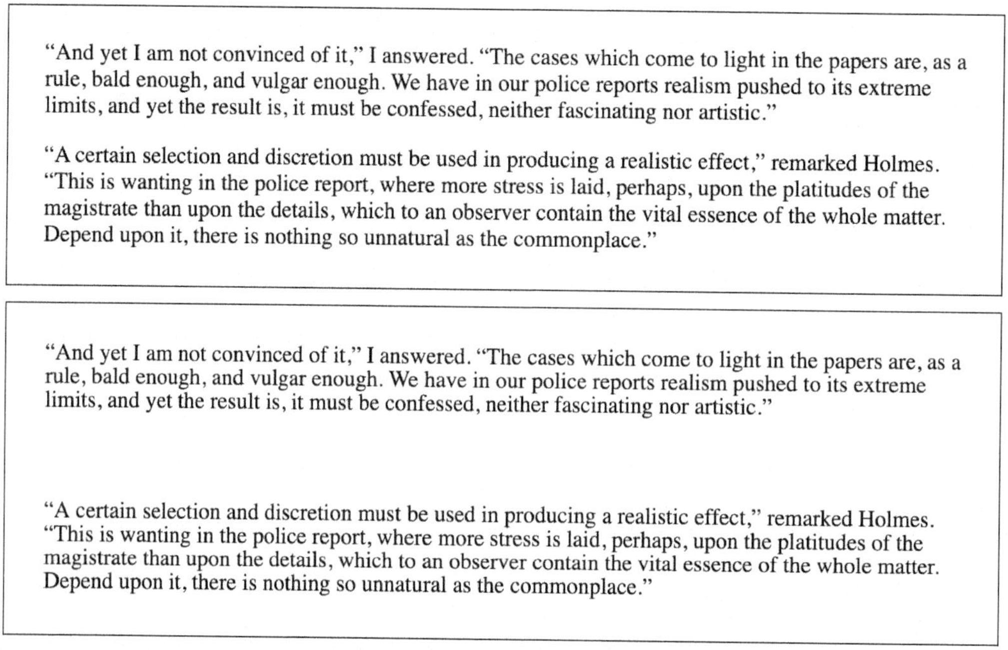

"And yet I am not convinced of it," I answered. "The cases which come to light in the papers are, as a rule, bald enough, and vulgar enough. We have in our police reports realism pushed to its extreme limits, and yet the result is, it must be confessed, neither fascinating nor artistic."

"A certain selection and discretion must be used in producing a realistic effect," remarked Holmes. "This is wanting in the police report, where more stress is laid, perhaps, upon the platitudes of the magistrate than upon the details, which to an observer contain the vital essence of the whole matter. Depend upon it, there is nothing so unnatural as the commonplace."

"And yet I am not convinced of it," I answered. "The cases which come to light in the papers are, as a rule, bald enough, and vulgar enough. We have in our police reports realism pushed to its extreme limits, and yet the result is, it must be confessed, neither fascinating nor artistic."

"A certain selection and discretion must be used in producing a realistic effect," remarked Holmes. "This is wanting in the police report, where more stress is laid, perhaps, upon the platitudes of the magistrate than upon the details, which to an observer contain the vital essence of the whole matter. Depend upon it, there is nothing so unnatural as the commonplace."

FIGURE 15.6 The first image shows two paragraph elements with neither **padding** nor **spacing**. The second has both.

Finer control over values

With both **padding** and **margin**, you're not locked into assigning a single value to the attribute for the entire element. You can define a different value for the left, top, right, and bottom of each box. There are a few ways to do it.

You can explicitly define each side, as shown in **TABLE 15.1**.

You can also use a shorthand version, in which you set the values for each of the four sides individually in a single declaration:

padding: *[top] [right] [bottom] [left]*;
margin: *[top] [right] [bottom] [left]*;

For each property the values are applied in clockwise order around the element, starting from the top. Slightly shorter would be:

padding: *[top/bottom] [left/right]*;
margin: *[top/bottom] [left/right]*;

Here, you have two values instead of four, where the first value sets the top and bottom spacing, and the second value sets the left and right spacing.

Finally, there's also a three-value declaration:

padding: *[top left/right bottom]*;
margin: *[top left/right bottom]*;

Here, the first value is for the top spacing, the middle value is for the left *and* right, and the last is for the bottom.

TABLE 15.1 Padding and Margin Side Properties

Padding	Margin
padding-left	margin-left
padding-top	margin-top
padding-right	margin-right
padding-bottom	margin-bottom

Shorthand Properties

Shorthand properties are properties in CSS that combine several different properties into one. You've seen some, like **border** (which combines **border-width**, **border-style**, and **border-color**), and **padding** and **margin** in this chapter.

They are a convenient and generally cleaner way to write CSS when you want uniformity (for example, when you want all borders to be the same color).

On the other hand, there are factors you need to keep in mind when using shorthand properties, particularly default values of properties and issues of inheritance.

To learn more about shorthand properties, check out this page at MDN: developer.mozilla.org/en-US/docs/Web/CSS/Shorthand_properties.

Using `margin: auto`

Sometimes when you set a width, you might want to center the container on the page. That's very easy to do using the `margin` property. You can set `margin` to the value `auto`, and it will calculate the width of the parent container, subtract the width of your target element, and distribute the leftover value evenly on both sides.

Say you have a `wrapper` class that has a `width` of 800px:

```
.wrapper {
    width: 800px;
}
```

On most tablets and desktop devices, the width of the window (and therefore, the entire website) will be more than 800px, and your content will look like what you see in **FIGURE 15.7**, where there is a lot of space to the right of the container.

Using the keyword `auto` with `margin` allows you to automatically center that content in the middle of the window.

You can use the `auto` keyword in two ways: as the only value for `margin` (`margin: auto`) or in conjunction with a set top and bottom (`margin: 30px auto`). Both cases result in horizontal centering. The latter also includes a 30px margin before and after the container.

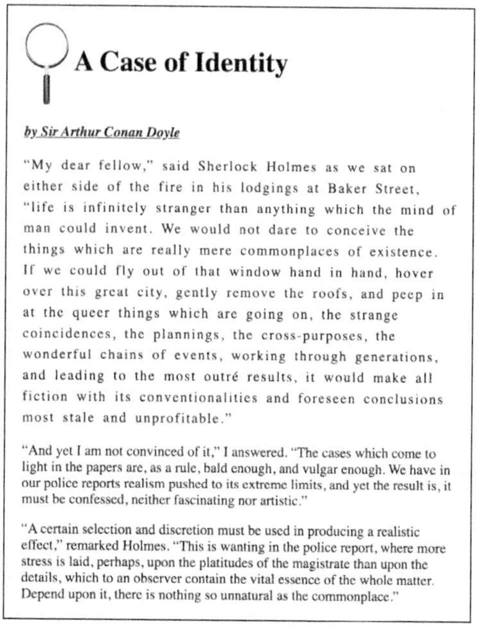

A Case of Identity

by Sir Arthur Conan Doyle

"My dear fellow," said Sherlock Holmes as we sat on either side of the fire in his lodgings at Baker Street, "life is infinitely stranger than anything which the mind of man could invent. We would not dare to conceive the things which are really mere commonplaces of existence. If we could fly out of that window hand in hand, hover over this great city, gently remove the roofs, and peep in at the queer things which are going on, the strange coincidences, the plannings, the cross-purposes, the wonderful chains of events, working through generations, and leading to the most outré results, it would make all fiction with its conventionalities and foreseen conclusions most stale and unprofitable."

"And yet I am not convinced of it," I answered. "The cases which come to light in the papers are, as a rule, bald enough, and vulgar enough. We have in our police reports realism pushed to its extreme limits, and yet the result is, it must be confessed, neither fascinating nor artistic."

"A certain selection and discretion must be used in producing a realistic effect," remarked Holmes. "This is wanting in the police report, where more stress is laid, perhaps, upon the platitudes of the magistrate than upon the details, which to an observer contain the vital essence of the whole matter. Depend upon it, there is nothing so unnatural as the commonplace."

FIGURE 15.7 A fixed-width container (`.wrapper`) without using `margin: auto` aligns the content all the way to the left of the window.

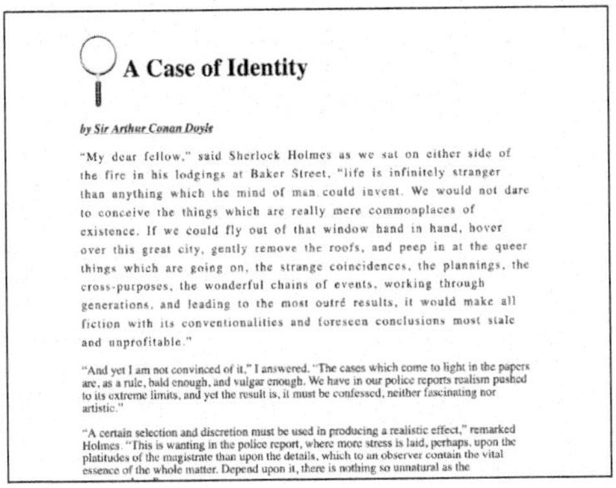

FIGURE 15.8 Centering a container using margin: auto

To center an element automatically with `margin: auto`:

1. In your style sheet, type the selector you wish to target, followed by a left curly brace. In this case, use `.wrapper {`.

2. On a new line, type `width:`, followed by the value. In this case, `800px;`.

   Setting a width for the container isn't strictly necessary, but without it you will not see the results of using the `auto` keyword.

3. On a new line, type `margin:`, then the values, including values for options like top or bottom margins. In this case, type `30px auto;`.

4. On a new line, type `}`.

Your full ruleset looks like this:

```
.wrapper {
    width: 800px;
    margin: 30px auto;
}
```

That results in a **div** with the class **wrapper** being center aligned on a page (**FIGURE 15.8**).

Element Flow

By default, elements flow onto the page in the order they appear in the HTML, depending on whether they are a block or inline element. **FIGURE 15.9** shows how the elements on a page naturally flow, with block-level elements outlined. You can see that block-level elements take up the entire width of the page and dictate most of the natural flow. Links and other text formatting fall in line with those blocks (like the links in the unordered list).

However, there are a few ways to change the flow of elements. You might want to do this to pull out certain content (like a quote or an aside), draw attention to an image, or even reorder elements when viewing the site on a smaller device.

The most common way to change the flow of HTML elements is to use the `float` property.

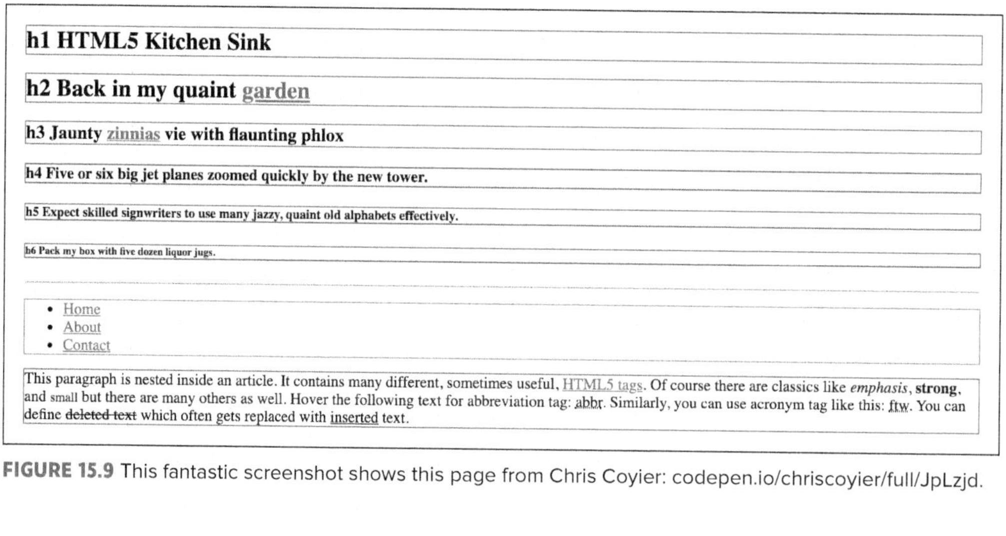

---

h1 HTML5 Kitchen Sink

h2 Back in my quaint garden

h3 Jaunty zinnias vie with flaunting phlox

h4 Five or six big jet planes zoomed quickly by the new tower.

h5 Expect skilled signwriters to use many jazzy, quaint old alphabets effectively.

h6 Pack my box with five dozen liquor jugs.

- Home
- About
- Contact

This paragraph is nested inside an article. It contains many different, sometimes useful, HTML5 tags. Of course there are classics like *emphasis*, **strong**, and small but there are many others as well. Hover the following text for abbreviation tag: abbr. Similarly, you can use acronym tag like this: ftw. You can define ~~deleted text~~ which often gets replaced with inserted text.

FIGURE 15.9 This fantastic screenshot shows this page from Chris Coyier: codepen.io/chriscoyier/full/JpLzjd.

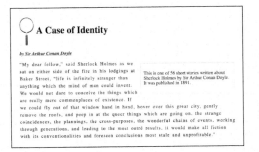

FIGURE 15.10 An aside that floats to the right of the rest of the content

CODE 15.1 The CSS used to style the page in Figure 15.10

```
main {
    width: 800px;
    margin: 0 auto;
}

aside {
    border: 1px solid #333333;
    padding: 30px;
    width: 200px;
    float: right;
}
```

Using floats

The **float** property takes an element out of its normal flow and places it to the right or left inside the container:

```
aside {
        float: right;
}
```

This moves the **aside** element to the right and lets everything else flow around it (**FIGURE 15.10**). You can see the code in **CODE 15.1**.

Note that the floated element will be surrounded by any elements below it, so if you want it to appear in the top of a container, it will have to be the first element.

You can even use **float** to create a grid of elements. Floating all elements of a particular type takes them out of the normal flow and lines them up next to each other. Before the creation of the layout modules Flexbox and CSS Grid (which you'll learn about in Chapter 16), this is how many web designers created column-based layouts.

Making a Simple Two-column Layout with Floats

While there are newer ways to create layouts in CSS, using floats is still pretty popular. In this video, you'll learn how to do that, and all the nuances of doing it correctly.

To create a grid layout with floats:

1. In your style sheet, type the selector you wish to target, followed by a left curly brace. This example targets paragraphs, so use **p {**.

2. Type **float:**.

3. Type **left;** to force the element to float on the left side of its container.

   To force the element to float on the right side, you would use the value **right**.

4. Type **margin:** to set the spacing between the elements. For this example, use **15px;**.

5. Type **width:** to set the width of each element. This example uses **300px;**.

6. Type **}** to close the style declaration.

This makes the paragraphs flow onto the page in a grid (**FIGURE 15.11**).

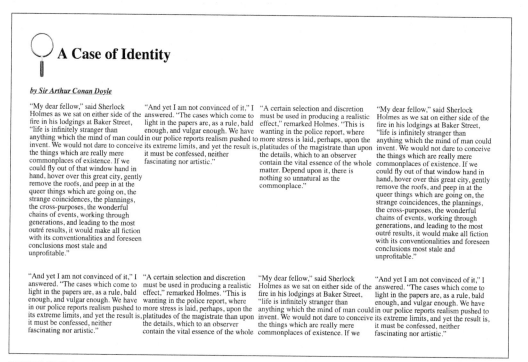

FIGURE 15.11 A grid of paragraphs achieved using the **float** property

Clearing floats

While this can work, it can also cause havoc for any elements in the normal flow. Elements can end up in unexpected places to work their way around floated elements. And although there are better ways to achieve a grid (as you'll see in Chapter 16), you could always use the clear property, which tells the element to place itself below any floated content:

```
.next-section {
        clear: left;
}
```

Other values for this property include right and both.

> **TIP** Using the **clear** property for layout is sometimes referred to as the *clearfix*. You might even see a class named **clearfix** that's designed for this very purpose.

Using the position property

Another way to place elements and containers precisely is by using the **position** property. It accepts several values, which I'll list in a moment.

This property is often accompanied by a set of properties that position elements in specific areas of the window or container: left, right, top, and bottom. These all accept the normal units (px, em, rem, %), and they all have slightly different meanings depending on the value of position. Here are the values for position, and positioning properties:

- static: This is the default value. There is no special positioning.

- relative: Places the container based on its normal position. The directional properties will move the container away from its normal position.

    So left: 50px moves the container to the right by 50 pixels, similar to margin.

- fixed: The container is in a fixed position on the page, so no matter what part of the page is being displayed to the user, the container will be in the same spot.

    The directional properties in this instance are exact coordinates; left: 0; top: 0; means the container will be at the left edge at the very top of the window.

- absolute: The container is positioned in a fixed position in its parent container.

    Directional properties work the same way as those for the fixed position.

- sticky: The container is positioned relatively (as in the normal flow) until the user reaches a specific scroll position. Then it sticks in place on the screen.

    For example, top: 0 positions the element relatively in the normal flow until the page is scrolled and there are zero pixels between the element's top edge and the visible area of the webpage. Beyond that threshold, the element behaves as if it used fixed positioning and will be fixed to zero pixels from the top.

To get a better idea of how each of these work, check out Video 15.5.

▶ **VIDEO 15.5**
Demonstrating the position Property

Visualizing how the position property works, even with the help of screenshots, can be tough. This video goes through all the properties and values and shows how they work.

To make a sticky sidebar:

The starting markup for this task is listed below. Since there's no HTML5 element specifically for "wrapping" other elements (from a semantic meaning standpoint), it's common practice to use the **<div>** element with a **wrapper** class:

```
<div class="wrapper">
    <aside>
        ...
    </aside>
    <main>
        ...
    </main>
</div>
```

1. In your style sheet, type `.wrapper {`.
2. Type `width: 800px;`.
3. Type `margin: 30px auto;`.
4. Type `}`.
5. Type `main {`.
6. Type `width: 500px;`.
7. Type `}`.
8. Type `aside {`.
9. Type `width: 260px;`.
10. Type `padding: 15px;`.
11. Type `float: right;`.
12. Type `position: sticky;`.
13. Type `top: 0;`.
14. Type `}`.

This code produces a two-column layout with a sticky sidebar. You can also add a background and border to **aside** to distinguish it a bit (**FIGURE 15.12**). You can see the code in **CODE 15.2** and **15.3**.

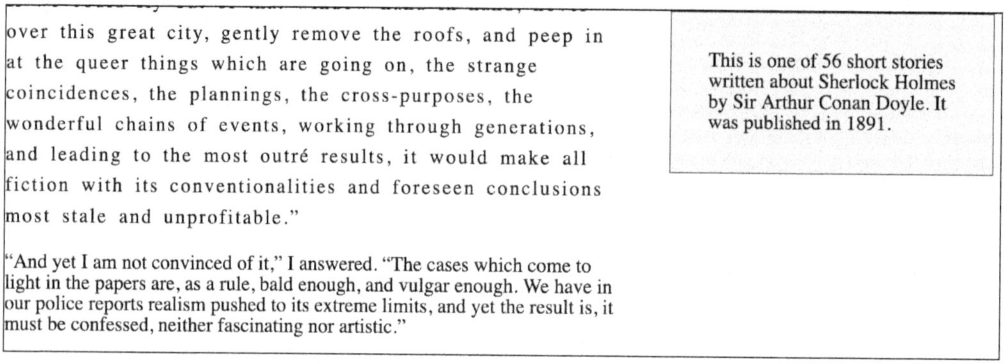

over this great city, gently remove the roofs, and peep in at the queer things which are going on, the strange coincidences, the plannings, the cross-purposes, the wonderful chains of events, working through generations, and leading to the most outré results, it would make all fiction with its conventionalities and foreseen conclusions most stale and unprofitable."

"And yet I am not convinced of it," I answered. "The cases which come to light in the papers are, as a rule, bald enough, and vulgar enough. We have in our police reports realism pushed to its extreme limits, and yet the result is, it must be confessed, neither fascinating nor artistic."

This is one of 56 short stories written about Sherlock Holmes by Sir Arthur Conan Doyle. It was published in 1891.

FIGURE 15.12 A two-column layout with a sticky sidebar

CODE 15.2 The HTML code used in Figure 15.12

```
<div class="wrapper">
    <aside>
        This is one of 56 short stories
        ↦ written about Sherlock Holmes by
        ↦ Sir Arthur Conan Doyle. It was
        ↦ published in 1891.
    </aside>
    <main>
        <p>"My dear fellow," said Sherlock
        ↦ Holmes as we sat on either
        ↦ side of the fire in his lodgings
        ↦ at Baker Street, "life is
        ↦ infinitely stranger than
        ↦ anything which the mind of
        ↦ man could invent. We would not
        ↦ dare to conceive the things
        ↦ which are really mere
        ↦ commonplaces of existence.
        ↦ If we could fly out of that
        ↦ window hand in hand, hover
        ↦ over this great city, gently
        ↦ remove the roofs, and peep in
        ↦ at the queer things which
        ↦ are going on, the strange
        ↦ coincidences, the plannings,
        ↦ the cross-purposes, the
        ↦ wonderful chains of events,
        ↦ working through generations,
        ↦ and leading to the most outré
        ↦ results, it would make
        ↦ all with its conventionalities
        ↦ and foreseen conclusions most
        ↦ stale and unprofitable."</p>

<p>"And yet I am not convinced of it," I
↦ answered. "The cases which come to
↦ light in the papers are, as a rule,
↦ bald enough, and vulgar enough. We have
↦ in our police reports realism pushed to
↦ its extreme limits, and yet the
↦ result is, it must be confessed, neither
↦ fascinating nor artistic."</p>
    </main>
</div>
```

CODE 15.3 The CSS code used in Figure 15.12

```
.wrapper {
    width: 800px;
    margin: 30px auto;
}

main {
    width: 500px;
}

aside {
    width: 260px;
    padding: 15px;
    float: right;
    position: sticky;
    top: 0;
    background:rgba(0,0,0,0.085);
    border: 1px solid #333333;
}

p:nth-of-type(1) {
    line-height: 1.5em;
    letter-spacing: 0.1em;
    word-spacing: 0.2em;
}
```

Creating Layers and Overlapping Elements

Although taking elements out of the natural flow can create interesting layouts for your content, you can run into situations where content overlaps and becomes unreadable. For example, if you had not set the `width` property on the main `div` in the previous task, your users would have run into a problem (**FIGURE 15.13**). Because we've fixed the position of the aside, the browser is essentially saying, "Keep the aside in this spot, no matter what the rest of the flow looks like." That means when the user scrolls, the main text overlaps the aside.

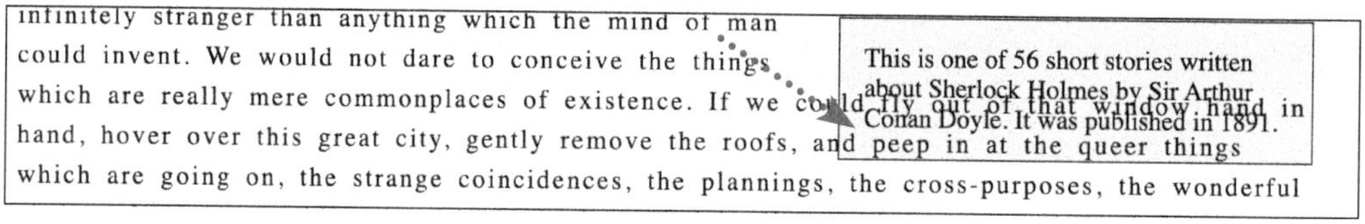

infinitely stranger than anything which the mind of man could invent. We would not dare to conceive the things which are really mere commonplaces of existence. If we could fly out of that window hand in hand, hover over this great city, gently remove the roofs, and peep in at the queer things which are going on, the strange coincidences, the plannings, the cross-purposes, the wonderful

This is one of 56 short stories written about Sherlock Holmes by Sir Arthur Conan Doyle. It was published in 1891.

FIGURE 15.13 Overlapping elements as a result of positioning

CSS has a fix for that: the z-index property. You can think of z-index as a layer or stacking property, where the value is an integer. The closer the integer is to 0, the "lower" on the page the element is (**FIGURE 15.14**). You can also think of elements with a lower z-index as being "behind" elements with a higher z-index.

A ruleset that uses z-index looks something like this:

```
aside {
        position: fixed;
        top: 0;
        z-index: 10;
}
```

TIP z-index works only if the element has a position other than static.

TIP Choosing z-index values in multiples of 10 or 100 is a good convention to follow. That gives you some wiggle room on bigger projects, where you might later realize you need to add an in-between value to existing values.

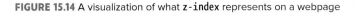

FIGURE 15.14 A visualization of what z-index represents on a webpage

Creating an Overlay Using `z-index`

One practical example of using `z-index` is to create a piece of content that should be shown in front of the rest of the content. You see this with popups asking you to join mailing lists, for example.

In this task, you will learn the basics of how to do that. In the real world, you might make the overlay dismissible with a bit of JavaScript, but you will clearly see how `z-index` works.

To create an overlay using `z-index`:

The markup being styled will be the following:

```
<div class="overlay">
    <h3>This is an important alert!
    </h3>
</div>
<header>
    <h1>A Case of Identity</h1>
</header>
<main>
    (content goes here)
</main>
```

1. In your stylesheet, first type the element you want to apply the styles to, followed by a left curly brace. In this case, `.overlay {`.

2. Now set the position of the element to absolute by typing, on a new line, `position: absolute;`.

3. Since the element is absolute, you can now use positional properties to move it. Move it down the page a little bit. On a new line, type `top: 10%;`.

4. Move the element in front of all other elements using `z-index`. Since the default `z-index` is 0, on a new line type `z-index: 1000;`.

   This will make sure the overlay is above the rest of the content—as long as nothing has a `z-index` over 1000.

5. Strictly so you can more easily see the result, apply a background color to the element. On a new line, type `background: #cfcfcf;`.

6. You can also center the text. On a new line type `text-align: center;`.

7. Finally, adding some padding so it stands out a bit more. On a new line, type `padding: 40px;`.

8. On a new line, type `}`.

This results in a block of text that is layered on top of the main page (**FIGURE 15.15**).

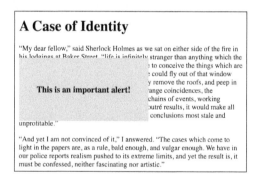

FIGURE 15.15 An overlay created using `position: absolute` and `z-index`.

▶ **VIDEO 15.6**
Creating a Pricing Table

In this video, you make a three-column pricing table using the methods you've learned in this chapter.

A Note About Creating Layouts

In recent years, great strides have been made in creating layouts with CSS. The practice of laying out elements on a webpage moved from tables, in HTML, to floating elements and clearing them using CSS. There are many frameworks designed to help you to create beautiful grid layouts. A *framework* is a set of structured files (HTML, CSS, and maybe JavaScript) that give you a head start on creating websites. See the sidebar "Using CSS Frameworks" to learn more.

But now, CSS Grid and Flexbox (two suites of layout properties you'll see in Chapter 16) have much wider browser support, so they should be used instead of floating and clearing elements. They allow for code that is semantic, much cleaner, and easier to support. The techniques you saw in this chapter—floats, positioning, and changing the default flow—still have their place in web design, though.

At this point, you have enough tools in your toolbox to create nice-looking layouts. In Video 15.6, you put most of that to the test by creating a pricing table.

Using CSS Frameworks

CSS frameworks—sets of prefabricated styles that help you fast-track development—are hugely helpful because streamlining the web design workflow is not just about layout but also about using a set of common elements.

Plus, the best frameworks continue to be updated to support new methods. Bootstrap, a very popular CSS framework, supports Flexbox for layouts now.

In this article, Rachel Andrews weighs the pros and cons of using a framework: www.smashingmagazine.com/2018/11/css-frameworks-css-grid/.

Two popular frameworks I recommend are Bootstrap (getbootstrap.com) and Foundation (get.foundation).

Wrapping Up

You know all about how to change the default flow of a page and the elements/containers on it. You've learned about common methods like floating (and clearing those floats), changing the position of elements, and `z-index`.

You can probably imagine that you'll run into a lot of fringe cases when you try to make these properties work for complex layouts—which is why frameworks became popular in the first place. But CSS has solved that with two important new systems: CSS Grid and Flexbox.

Layouts with CSS Grid and Flexbox

In the last chapter, you learned the finer points of how the box model can be styled, and some of the longer-standing methods for manipulating layout.

But new tools have been introduced in CSS to give you better control over your markup and to give it more semantic meaning. Those tools are the CSS Grid Layout Module and the CSS Flexible Box Layout Module, known more familiarly as CSS Grid and Flexbox. In this chapter, you'll learn what they are, how they work, and when to use each.

In This Chapter

Modern Solutions for an Important Problem

Part of the reason Flexbox and CSS Grid (or simply Grid) have emerged is because they are a modern solution to an important problem: creating flexible layouts that work properly on different screen sizes.

With the advent of *responsive web design* (RWD), floating elements to create column layouts revealed a critical bug that also affected SEO: you could not control the stacking order.

That means if you float the `aside` element, as in Chapter 15, that element needs to go above the main content. Search engines will prioritize the aside, and if you stack the content, the aside will always be first (Video 16.1).

CSS Grid vs. Flexbox: Which should you use?

This chapter shows you both CSS Grid and Flexbox, but it's good to know what the difference is so that you can keep it in mind moving forward.

The most common answer to this question is that Flexbox organizes content in one dimension—by rows *or* columns. CSS Grid organizes content in two dimensions—rows *and* columns.

Both are well supported by browsers at this point, as these tables at caniuse.com demonstrate (**FIGURES 16.1** and **16.2**).

VIDEO 16.1
Stacking Order

In this video, you'll see the stacking order of a multicolumn layout as the screen gets smaller, using simple floats for layouts.

Responsive Web Design

With the emergence and increasing popularity of mobile devices, the importance for making websites work on small screens was a catalyst for the responsive web design (RWD) movement. Among other things, RWD ensures that your website looks good no matter what device it's being viewed on.

With a feature of CSS called *media queries*, which you'll learn about in Chapter 17, you can create CSS rules for your layout based on the size of the screen.

RWD provides a bevy of benefits, chief among which are:

- You don't need a separate site for mobile devices.
- Your site loads faster.
- Your layouts are optimized.

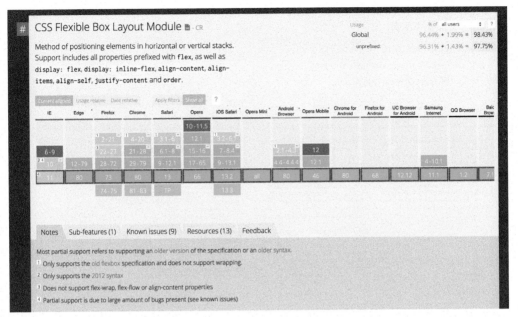

FIGURE 16.1 Browser support for Flexbox

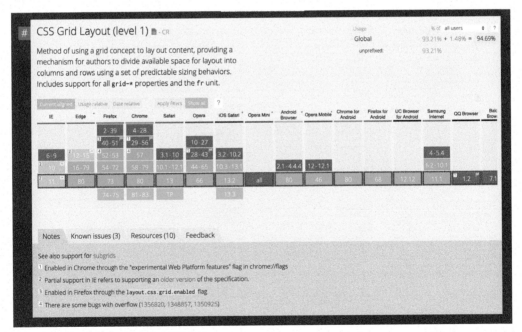

FIGURE 16.2 Browser support for CSS Grid

And both give you similar results quickly (**FIGURES 16.3** and **16.4**).

What you'll quickly find is that CSS Grid is a bit more granular. Before we dig into that, let's take a look at Flexbox.

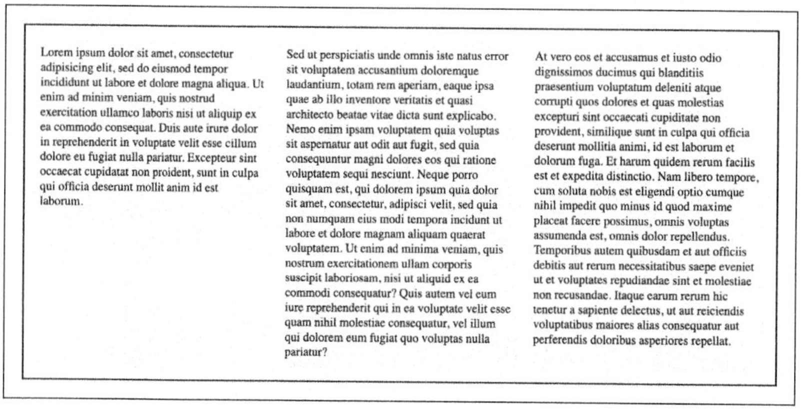

FIGURE 16.3
A simple Flexbox example

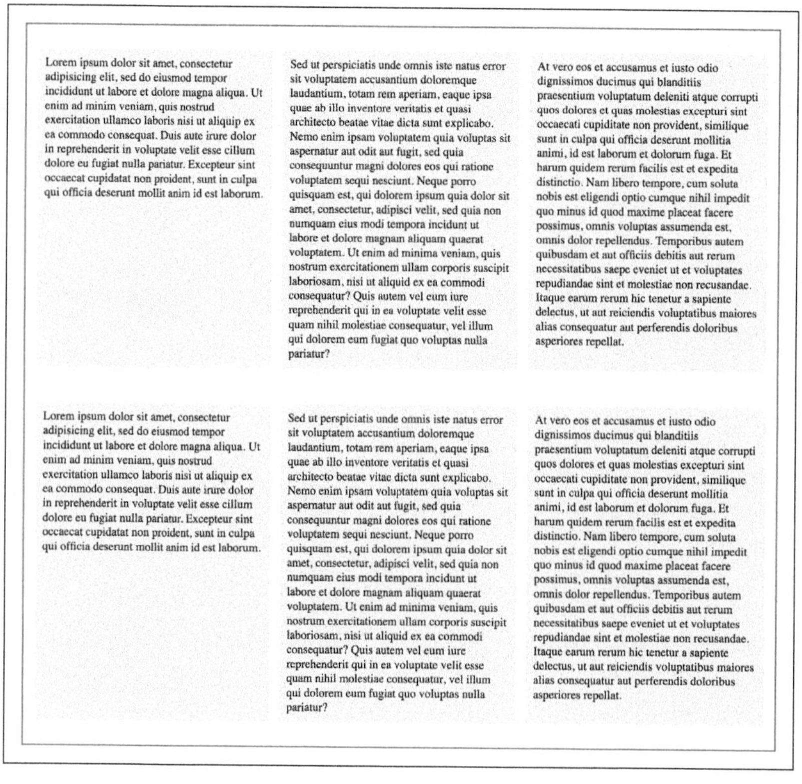

FIGURE 16.4
A simple CSS Grid example

Resources Galore!

This chapter introduces you to both Flexbox and CSS Grid, but there is a lot to know, so it is not comprehensive. Here are some fantastic resources and even some interactive guides to help you though:

- CSS-Tricks's A Complete Guide to Flexbox: css-tricks.com/snippets/css/a-guide-to-flexbox

- CSS Tricks's A Complete Guide to Grid: css-tricks.com/snippets/css/complete-guide-grid

- Grid by Example: gridbyexample.com

- Flexbox Froggy: flexboxfroggy.com

- Grid Garden: cssgridgarden.com

Using Flexbox

We start by setting the `display` property to the value `flex`, which will lay out the element and its children according to the CSS Flexible Box Layout Module, known by its close friends as Flexbox.

It essentially enables you to use a set of properties that also use the word `flex` in the parent and child elements.

All of these properties have default values, so you will see results as soon as you use the `display` property to enable Flexbox. Let's say you have a set of paragraphs inside a `div` container (**FIGURE 16.5**).

> **TIP** *Flexbox* **commonly refers to the feature in CSS. There is no property called "flexbox."**

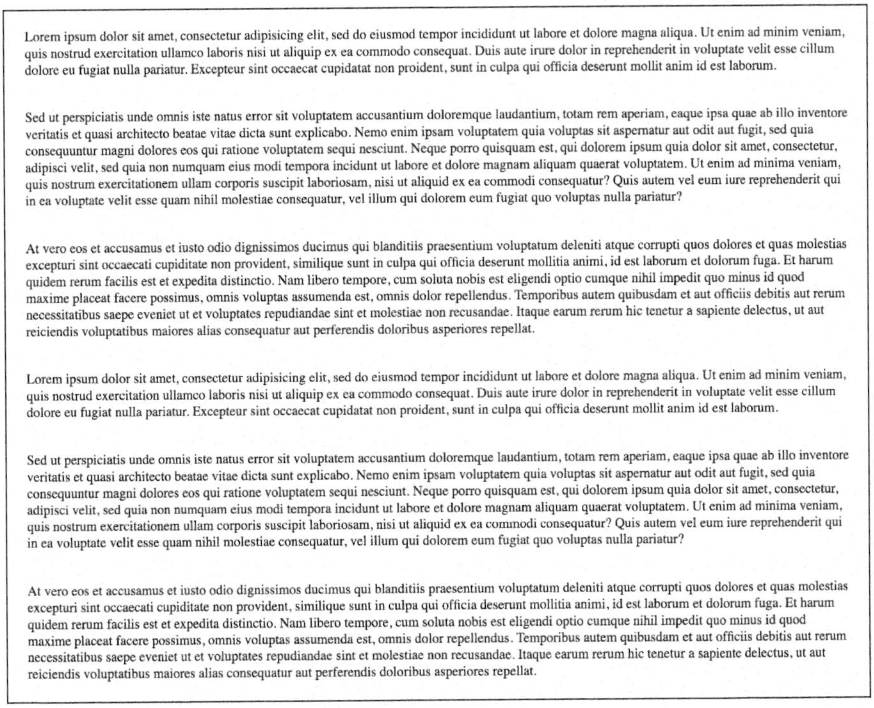

Lorem ipsum dolor sit amet, consectetur adipisicing elit, sed do eiusmod tempor incididunt ut labore et dolore magna aliqua. Ut enim ad minim veniam, quis nostrud exercitation ullamco laboris nisi ut aliquip ex ea commodo consequat. Duis aute irure dolor in reprehenderit in voluptate velit esse cillum dolore eu fugiat nulla pariatur. Excepteur sint occaecat cupidatat non proident, sunt in culpa qui officia deserunt mollit anim id est laborum.

Sed ut perspiciatis unde omnis iste natus error sit voluptatem accusantium doloremque laudantium, totam rem aperiam, eaque ipsa quae ab illo inventore veritatis et quasi architecto beatae vitae dicta sunt explicabo. Nemo enim ipsam voluptatem quia voluptas sit aspernatur aut odit aut fugit, sed quia consequuntur magni dolores eos qui ratione voluptatem sequi nesciunt. Neque porro quisquam est, qui dolorem ipsum quia dolor sit amet, consectetur, adipisci velit, sed quia non numquam eius modi tempora incidunt ut labore et dolore magnam aliquam quaerat voluptatem. Ut enim ad minima veniam, quis nostrum exercitationem ullam corporis suscipit laboriosam, nisi ut aliquid ex ea commodi consequatur? Quis autem vel eum iure reprehenderit qui in ea voluptate velit esse quam nihil molestiae consequatur, vel illum qui dolorem eum fugiat quo voluptas nulla pariatur?

At vero eos et accusamus et iusto odio dignissimos ducimus qui blanditiis praesentium voluptatum deleniti atque corrupti quos dolores et quas molestias excepturi sint occaecati cupiditate non provident, similique sunt in culpa qui officia deserunt mollitia animi, id est laborum et dolorum fuga. Et harum quidem rerum facilis est et expedita distinctio. Nam libero tempore, cum soluta nobis est eligendi optio cumque nihil impedit quo minus id quod maxime placeat facere possimus, omnis voluptas assumenda est, omnis dolor repellendus. Temporibus autem quibusdam et aut officiis debitis aut rerum necessitatibus saepe eveniet ut et voluptates repudiandae sint et molestiae non recusandae. Itaque earum rerum hic tenetur a sapiente delectus, ut aut reiciendis voluptatibus maiores alias consequatur aut perferendis doloribus asperiores repellat.

Lorem ipsum dolor sit amet, consectetur adipisicing elit, sed do eiusmod tempor incididunt ut labore et dolore magna aliqua. Ut enim ad minim veniam, quis nostrud exercitation ullamco laboris nisi ut aliquip ex ea commodo consequat. Duis aute irure dolor in reprehenderit in voluptate velit esse cillum dolore eu fugiat nulla pariatur. Excepteur sint occaecat cupidatat non proident, sunt in culpa qui officia deserunt mollit anim id est laborum.

Sed ut perspiciatis unde omnis iste natus error sit voluptatem accusantium doloremque laudantium, totam rem aperiam, eaque ipsa quae ab illo inventore veritatis et quasi architecto beatae vitae dicta sunt explicabo. Nemo enim ipsam voluptatem quia voluptas sit aspernatur aut odit aut fugit, sed quia consequuntur magni dolores eos qui ratione voluptatem sequi nesciunt. Neque porro quisquam est, qui dolorem ipsum quia dolor sit amet, consectetur, adipisci velit, sed quia non numquam eius modi tempora incidunt ut labore et dolore magnam aliquam quaerat voluptatem. Ut enim ad minima veniam, quis nostrum exercitationem ullam corporis suscipit laboriosam, nisi ut aliquid ex ea commodi consequatur? Quis autem vel eum iure reprehenderit qui in ea voluptate velit esse quam nihil molestiae consequatur, vel illum qui dolorem eum fugiat quo voluptas nulla pariatur?

At vero eos et accusamus et iusto odio dignissimos ducimus qui blanditiis praesentium voluptatum deleniti atque corrupti quos dolores et quas molestias excepturi sint occaecati cupiditate non provident, similique sunt in culpa qui officia deserunt mollitia animi, id est laborum et dolorum fuga. Et harum quidem rerum facilis est et expedita distinctio. Nam libero tempore, cum soluta nobis est eligendi optio cumque nihil impedit quo minus id quod maxime placeat facere possimus, omnis voluptas assumenda est, omnis dolor repellendus. Temporibus autem quibusdam et aut officiis debitis aut rerum necessitatibus saepe eveniet ut et voluptates repudiandae sint et molestiae non recusandae. Itaque earum rerum hic tenetur a sapiente delectus, ut aut reiciendis voluptatibus maiores alias consequatur aut perferendis doloribus asperiores repellat.

FIGURE 16.5
Paragraphs
pre-Flexbox

To enable Flexbox on an element:

1. Type the element or selector you want to target. In this case, it's `div {`.

2. On the next line, type `display: flex;`.

3. On the next line, type `}` to close the style declaration.

This gives you **FIGURE 16.6** (some styling has been added so that you can better see the effects).

You might notice that the paragraphs are not equal width and that they're very cramped, with all six on the same line/row.

That's because `display: flex` takes all the child elements and converts them into columns of content. In fact, they don't even need to be the same type of element. Here's another example, with more than just paragraph elements (**FIGURE 16.7**).

Luckily, this doesn't extend to all descendants, just children. So without much fuss, you can get a pretty good two- or three-column layout working.

How width works in Flexbox

By default, `display: flex` takes all child elements and evenly distributes them into columns. But there are a few ways to define column widths, which Flexbox will take into account.

FIGURE 16.6 Paragraphs with Flexbox applied

FIGURE 16.7 Flexbox applied to all children

The first is simply by defining the `width` property. Flexbox will respect a defined width (meaning it will use the defined width instead of overriding it). Because Flexbox lends itself well to multiple screen sizes (meaning the overall width of your container will change), this book uses percentages. But you can use any unit you want.

Later in the chapter, you will learn about an even better way to define the width of child containers, called `flex-basis`, so keep an eye out for that!

In the next task, the goal is to take the provided markup and make a two-column layout where the `<article>` element is 70 percent of the width of the `<main>` container, with the `<aside>` occupying the other 30 percent.

To create a two-column layout with Flexbox:

Here is the starting markup:

```
<main>
    <article>
        ...
    </article>
    <aside>
        ...
    </aside>
</main>
```

1. In your style sheet, target the element you want to use Flexbox on. In this case, type `main {`.

2. On a new line, type `display: flex;`.

3. On a new line, type `}` to close the style declaration.

4. Target the children of the element you're using Flexbox on. Type `main article {`.

5. On a new line, type `width: 68%;`.

   Since the `width` property doesn't take into account padding, you need to account for it so you don't break the main container with overflowing elements. Because of that, subtract 2 percent from the overall 70 percent width you want the `<article>` element to take up.

6. On a new line, type `padding: 2%;`.

7. On a new line, type `}`.

8. Now target the other child element. On a new line, type `main aside {`.

   Just as with `<article>`, to prevent the content from overflowing the container, subtract the padding from the width of the element.

9. On a new line, type `width: 28%;`.

10. On a new line, type `padding: 2%;`.

11. On a new line, type `}`.

This gives you a two-column layout that stacks properly (**FIGURE 16.8**).

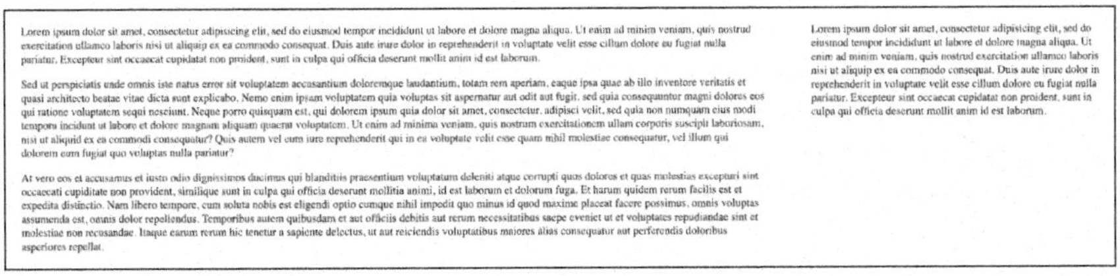

FIGURE 16.8
A two-column layout with `flex`

Wrapping elements

If you want child elements (also known as *flex items*) to naturally move to a new row so they maintain their defined widths instead of being forced onto one line, use the **flex-wrap** property. It has three values:

- **nowrap** is the default value. It forces all flex items onto one line. If no widths for flex items are defined, each item will take up a width equal to that of its parent. If widths are defined, **nowrap** may cause overflow.

- **wrap** breaks the flex items up into multiple lines.

- **wrap-reverse** behaves like **wrap** but reverses the order of the flex items.

Here's a simple example of the syntax:

```
main {
    display: flex;
    flex-wrap: wrap;
}
```

With this property, you will also need to apply a **width** (or **max-width**) to the child elements. That's because if they are block elements, they'll naturally take up the full width of the parent container.

To create a three-column layout with flex-wrap:

The markup is six <p> tags inside a **<main>** element:

```
<main>
    <p>...</p>
    <p>...</p>
    <p>...</p>
    <p>...</p>
    <p>...</p>
    <p>...</p>
</main>
```

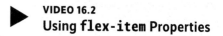

VIDEO 16.2
Using flex-item Properties

Flexbox comes with a set of properties to apply to items. In this video, you'll learn how to use them, instead of **width**, to create the two-column layout.

1. In your style sheet, type `main {`.

2. On a new line, type `display: flex;`.

3. On a new line, type `flex-wrap: wrap;`.

4. On a new line, type `}`.

5. On a new line, type `main p {`.

6. On a new line, type `width: 30%;`.

7. On a new line, type `padding: 1.5%;`.

   This is so that the total left/right padding is 3 percent, giving the total column width 33 percent. This divides the `<main>` element neatly into three equal columns.

8. Type `}`.

This gives you even columns split across two rows (**FIGURE 16.9**).

TIP When you create columns using the `float` property, you need to use the `clear` property to make sure elements line up properly under the floated area. Note that you don't need to use `clear` on any of the elements that use Flexbox. The Flexbox properties are designed to create columns and position multiple pieces of content.

You can also set a more dynamic width that will take other parameters (like margins and spacing) into account by using the `flex-basis` property, which allows you to set the basic size of the flex item. It accepts any unit that `width` accepts (**px**, **em**, **%**, etc.).

The `flex-basis` property also accepts a number of keywords, but most don't have browser support. To see a list of them and how they work, view this page in Firefox: developer.mozilla.org/en-US/docs/Web/CSS/flex-basis.

Lorem ipsum dolor sit amet, consectetur adipisicing elit, sed do eiusmod tempor incididunt ut labore et dolore magna aliqua. Ut enim ad minim veniam, quis nostrud exercitation ullamco laboris nisi ut aliquip ex ea commodo consequat. Duis aute irure dolor in reprehenderit in voluptate velit esse cillum dolore eu fugiat nulla pariatur. Excepteur sint occaecat cupidatat non proident, sunt in culpa qui officia deserunt mollit anim id est laborum.

Sed ut perspiciatis unde omnis iste natus error sit voluptatem accusantium doloremque laudantium, totam rem aperiam, eaque ipsa quae ab illo inventore veritatis et quasi architecto beatae vitae dicta sunt explicabo. Nemo enim ipsam voluptatem quia voluptas sit aspernatur aut odit aut fugit, sed quia consequuntur magni dolores eos qui ratione voluptatem sequi nesciunt. Neque porro quisquam est, qui dolorem ipsum quia dolor sit amet, consectetur, adipisci velit, sed quia non numquam eius modi tempora incidunt ut labore et dolore magnam aliquam quaerat voluptatem. Ut enim ad minima veniam, quis nostrum exercitationem ullam corporis suscipit laboriosam, nisi ut aliquid ex ea commodi consequat? Quis autem vel eum iure reprehenderit qui in ea voluptate velit esse quam nihil molestiae consequatur, vel illum qui dolorem eum fugiat quo voluptas nulla pariatur?

At vero eos et accusamus et iusto odio dignissimos ducimus qui blanditiis praesentium voluptatum deleniti atque corrupti quos dolores et quas molestias excepturi sint occaecati cupiditate non provident, similique sunt in culpa qui officia deserunt mollitia animi, id est laborum et dolorum fuga. Et harum quidem rerum facilis est et expedita distinctio. Nam libero tempore, cum soluta nobis est eligendi optio cumque nihil impedit quo minus id quod maxime placeat facere possimus, omnis voluptas assumenda est, omnis dolor repellendus. Temporibus autem quibusdam et aut officiis debitis aut rerum necessitatibus saepe eveniet ut et voluptates repudiandae sint et molestiae non recusandae. Itaque earum rerum hic tenetur a sapiente delectus, ut aut reiciendis voluptatibus maiores alias consequatur aut perferendis doloribus asperiores repellat.

Lorem ipsum dolor sit amet, consectetur adipisicing elit, sed do eiusmod tempor incididunt ut labore et dolore magna aliqua. Ut enim ad minim veniam, quis nostrud exercitation ullamco laboris nisi ut aliquip ex ea commodo consequat. Duis aute irure dolor in reprehenderit in voluptate velit esse cillum dolore eu fugiat nulla pariatur. Excepteur sint occaecat cupidatat non proident, sunt in culpa qui officia deserunt mollit anim id est laborum.

Sed ut perspiciatis unde omnis iste natus error sit voluptatem accusantium doloremque laudantium, totam rem aperiam, eaque ipsa quae ab illo inventore veritatis et quasi architecto beatae vitae dicta sunt explicabo. Nemo enim ipsam voluptatem quia voluptas sit aspernatur aut odit aut fugit, sed quia consequuntur magni dolores eos qui ratione voluptatem sequi nesciunt. Neque porro quisquam est, qui dolorem ipsum quia dolor sit amet, consectetur, adipisci velit, sed quia non numquam eius modi tempora incidunt ut labore et dolore magnam aliquam quaerat voluptatem. Ut enim ad minima veniam, quis nostrum exercitationem ullam corporis suscipit laboriosam, nisi ut aliquid ex ea commodi consequat? Quis autem vel eum iure reprehenderit qui in ea voluptate velit esse quam nihil molestiae consequatur, vel illum qui dolorem eum fugiat quo voluptas nulla pariatur?

At vero eos et accusamus et iusto odio dignissimos ducimus qui blanditiis praesentium voluptatum deleniti atque corrupti quos dolores et quas molestias excepturi sint occaecati cupiditate non provident, similique sunt in culpa qui officia deserunt mollitia animi, id est laborum et dolorum fuga. Et harum quidem rerum facilis est et expedita distinctio. Nam libero tempore, cum soluta nobis est eligendi optio cumque nihil impedit quo minus id quod maxime placeat facere possimus, omnis voluptas assumenda est, omnis dolor repellendus. Temporibus autem quibusdam et aut officiis debitis aut rerum necessitatibus saepe eveniet ut et voluptates repudiandae sint et molestiae non recusandae. Itaque earum rerum hic tenetur a sapiente delectus, ut aut reiciendis voluptatibus maiores alias consequatur aut perferendis doloribus asperiores repellat.

FIGURE 16.9 Using `flex-wrap` to make a three-column layout

Aligning elements

There are even more clever ways you can use Flexbox properties to align and space columns without the need to do mental math to figure out the amount of padding needed. One way is for horizontal alignment, and one is for vertical.

In the last example, you used the `padding` property to get evenly spaced columns. But there is a better way: the `justify-content` property. Before jumping into that, though, there's another property you should know about: `flex-direction`.

The `flex-direction` property tells the browser how to align the items. It has four values:

- `row` (the default) displays items left to right.
- `row-reverse` displays items right to left.
- `column` displays items vertically, top to bottom.
- `column-reverse` displays items vertically, bottom to top.

TIP If the browser is set to display text from right to left (as required by some languages, such as Hebrew and Arabic), HTML elements flow onto the page in the same direction. Using either `row` or `row-reverse` with `flex-direction` will reverse the flow. You can also set the direction with the `dir` attribute in HTML or the `direction` property in CSS.

To convert a row of items to a column:

1. In your style sheet, type `main {`.
2. Type `display: flex;`.
3. Type `flex-direction: column;`.
4. Type `}`.

This gives you a single, contained column of content (**FIGURE 16.10**). To better demonstrate how the property works, I applied a 45 percent width to the child elements.

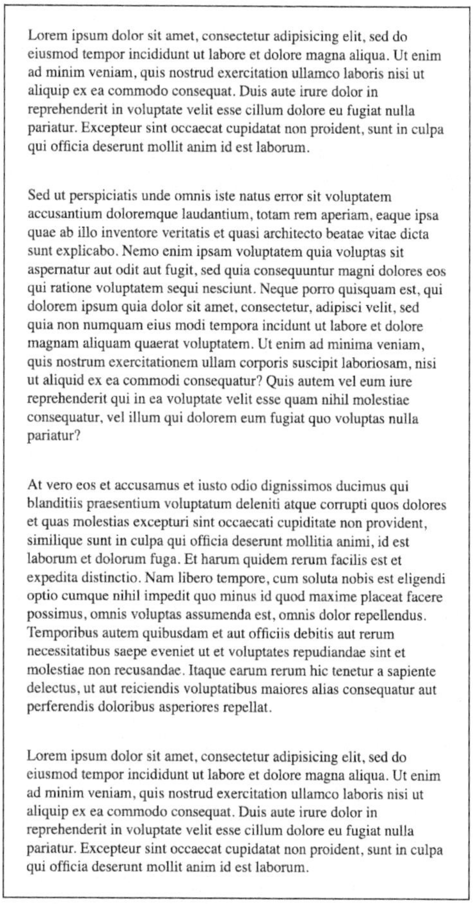

Lorem ipsum dolor sit amet, consectetur adipisicing elit, sed do eiusmod tempor incididunt ut labore et dolore magna aliqua. Ut enim ad minim veniam, quis nostrud exercitation ullamco laboris nisi ut aliquip ex ea commodo consequat. Duis aute irure dolor in reprehenderit in voluptate velit esse cillum dolore eu fugiat nulla pariatur. Excepteur sint occaecat cupidatat non proident, sunt in culpa qui officia deserunt mollit anim id est laborum.

Sed ut perspiciatis unde omnis iste natus error sit voluptatem accusantium doloremque laudantium, totam rem aperiam, eaque ipsa quae ab illo inventore veritatis et quasi architecto beatae vitae dicta sunt explicabo. Nemo enim ipsam voluptatem quia voluptas sit aspernatur aut odit aut fugit, sed quia consequuntur magni dolores eos qui ratione voluptatem sequi nesciunt. Neque porro quisquam est, qui dolorem ipsum quia dolor sit amet, consectetur, adipisci velit, sed quia non numquam eius modi tempora incidunt ut labore et dolore magnam aliquam quaerat voluptatem. Ut enim ad minima veniam, quis nostrum exercitationem ullam corporis suscipit laboriosam, nisi ut aliquid ex ea commodi consequatur? Quis autem vel eum iure reprehenderit qui in ea voluptate velit esse quam nihil molestiae consequatur, vel illum qui dolorem eum fugiat quo voluptas nulla pariatur?

At vero eos et accusamus et iusto odio dignissimos ducimus qui blanditiis praesentium voluptatum deleniti atque corrupti quos dolores et quas molestias excepturi sint occaecati cupiditate non provident, similique sunt in culpa qui officia deserunt mollitia animi, id est laborum et dolorum fuga. Et harum quidem rerum facilis est et expedita distinctio. Nam libero tempore, cum soluta nobis est eligendi optio cumque nihil impedit quo minus id quod maxime placeat facere possimus, omnis voluptas assumenda est, omnis dolor repellendus. Temporibus autem quibusdam et aut officiis debitis aut rerum necessitatibus saepe eveniet ut et voluptates repudiandae sint et molestiae non recusandae. Itaque earum rerum hic tenetur a sapiente delectus, ut aut reiciendis voluptatibus maiores alias consequatur aut perferendis doloribus asperiores repellat.

Lorem ipsum dolor sit amet, consectetur adipisicing elit, sed do eiusmod tempor incididunt ut labore et dolore magna aliqua. Ut enim ad minim veniam, quis nostrud exercitation ullamco laboris nisi ut aliquip ex ea commodo consequat. Duis aute irure dolor in reprehenderit in voluptate velit esse cillum dolore eu fugiat nulla pariatur. Excepteur sint occaecat cupidatat non proident, sunt in culpa qui officia deserunt mollit anim id est laborum.

FIGURE 16.10 `flex-direction` in action

► VIDEO 16.3
Using flex-basis, flex-flow, and justify-content

Flexbox allows you to easily do some clever things with your columns. In this video, you'll see three helpful properties in action.

TIP You can use **flex-flow** as shorthand for the **flex-direction** and **flex-wrap** properties. You would write the rule like this: **flex-flow:** *[flex-direction-value] [flex-wrap-value]*.

With the **justify-content** property, you are able to distribute the content evenly or to one side. The property has several values, some of which are listed below, and you can see them demonstrated in Video 16.3. The values distribute the content according to the flow established by **flex-direction**:

- **flex-start** (the default): Items are placed at the beginning of the container (similar to left alignment).

- **flex-end**: Items are placed at the end of the container (similar to right alignment).

- **center**: Items are centered within the parent.

- **space-between**: Items are evenly distributed within the parent, with no space between the items and the edge of the parent container.

- **space-around**: Items are evenly distributed within the parent, with equal space between them (but not evenly spaced between the edges).

- **space-evenly**: Items are distributed within the parent, with equal space between them and the edges.

To create evenly spaced columns without padding:

1. In your style sheet, type `main {`.

2. Type `display: flex;`.

3. Type `justify-content: space-evenly;`.

4. Type `flex-wrap: wrap;`.

5. Type `}`.

6. Type `main p {`.

7. Type `flex-basis: 30%;`.

   We're using **flex-basis** here instead of **width** because it's a little smarter. It can control width or height, based on **flex-direction**.

8. Type `}`.

This gives you the same results seen in Figure 16.9, without the need for the additional **padding** declaration.

`flex-grow`, `flex-shrink`, and `flex`

`flex-basis` is often used with **flex**, which is a shorthand property for **flex-grow**, **flex-shrink**, and **flex-basis**. These are applied to the flex items.

`flex-grow` is how much each item should grow relative to the remaining space in the parent container, if necessary, and is represented as a single unit. So **flex-grow: 2** says, "This item should take up twice as much of the remaining space as the other items if it needs to grow."

Conversely, `flex-shrink` is how much each item should shrink relative to the space in the parent container. So **flex-shrink: 2** says, "This item should take up half as much space as the other items if it needs to shrink."

These are combined into **flex**, which is the recommended property for setting **flex-item** sizes. Taking the example in the previous task, we might instead write:

```
main {
    flex: 1 1 30%;
}
```

where the values represent **flex-grow**, **flex-shrink**, and **flex-basis**, respectively.

However, you could write the rule by omitting **flex-shrink**:

```
main {
    flex: 1 30%;
}
```

Using **flex** allows the browser to intelligently determine the other values and is smart enough to know how to use the values provided.

Vertical alignment

You can use Flexbox to align elements vertically. While you can use **vertical-align** in specific instances, which you saw in Chapter 13, you may not always get the results you expect. The **align-items** property improves upon **vertical-align**.

For flex items, use the **align-items** property, which can have the following values:

- **stretch** (the default) fills the full height of the container with the content.

- **flex-start** starts content at the top of the container.

- **flex-end** starts the content at the bottom of the container.

- **center** centers the content vertically in the container.

- **baseline** aligns items on the "baseline" of the content—where the text sits.

The **align-items** property accepts many more values, which are listed and described at developer.mozilla.org/en-US/docs/Web/CSS/align-items#Syntax.

You can see these values in action in Video 16.4.

VIDEO 16.4
The align-items Property in Action

Much as with **justify-content**, it's better to see the **align-items** property in action. In this video, you'll see the effects of each value on real content.

To create a set of bottom-aligned columns:

1. In your style sheet, type **main {**.
2. Type **display: flex;**.
3. Type **align-items: flex-end;**.
4. **}**.

Your result will look like **FIGURE 16.11**. I applied additional styles to the children to highlight the changes.

These properties and examples will give you a great start to using Flexbox. Check out the sidebar "Resources Galore!" to learn more and go even deeper.

But now it's time to look at a way to do layouts that's even more flexible: CSS Grid.

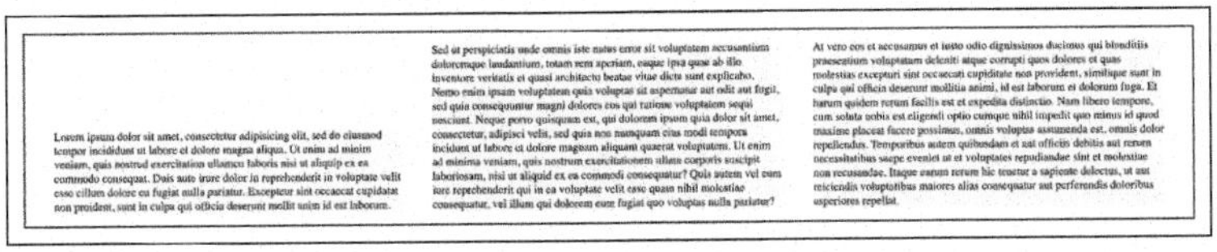

FIGURE 16.11 Bottom-aligned columns using Flexbox

Using CSS Grid Layout

CSS Grid Layout (or Grid, as it's more commonly known) also requires the use of the `display` property, but you'll need to use a second property: `grid-template-columns`. This tells the browser how many columns to create and how wide they should be. If you want three equal-width columns, the code looks like this:

```
main {
    display: grid;
    grid-template-columns: 30% 30% 30%;
}
```

That results in **FIGURE 16.12**.

You can also space them out a bit using `grid-gap`, which works similarly to `padding`, except the two values are for row and column spacing, respectively:

```
main {
    display: grid;
    grid-template-columns: 30% 30% 30%;
    grid-gap: 10px 20px;
}
```

If there's one value (`grid-gap: 15px`), it's applied to both rows and columns.

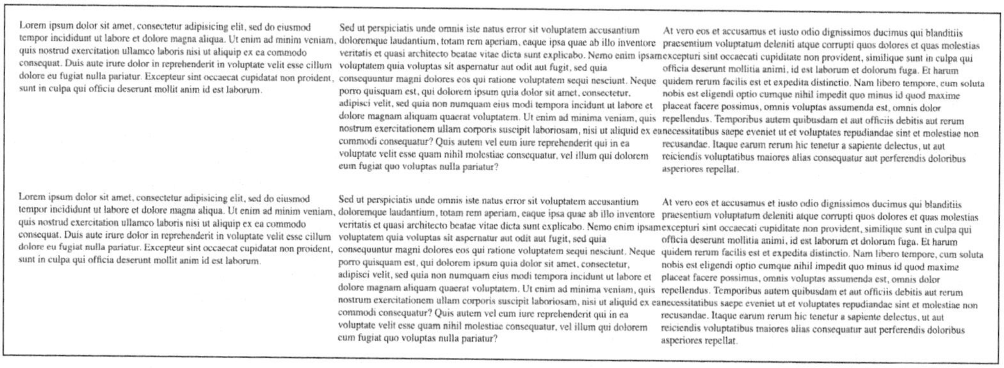

TIP You can use the `grid-template-rows` property to set up rows in your Grid layout, similar to the way you use `grid-template-columns` to create columns.

TIP An entire book could be written about Grid—and it has been: Rachel Andrew's *The New CSS Layout* (abookapart.com/products/the-new-css-layout).

TIP The same rules for children and descendants that apply for Flexbox apply for Grid.

FIGURE 16.12 Paragraphs with Grid applied

To create a two-column layout with Grid:

Here is the starting markup:

```
<main>
    <article>
        . . .
    </article>
    <aside>
        . . .
    </aside>
</main>
```

1. In your style sheet, type `main {`.

2. Type `display: grid;`.

3. Type `grid-template-columns: 68% 28%;`.

4. Type `grid-gap: 15px;`.

5. Type `}`.

This gives you a nice two-column layout (**FIGURE 16.13**).

Using the `fr` unit

You might have noticed in the last task that once again, some weird math was required to make sure everything fit properly in the container. But CSS Grid introduces a much, much better way to do it: the `fr` (fractional) unit. Here's an example:

```
grid-template-columns: 1fr 2fr 1fr;
```

The `fr` unit is a single integer measurement that basically reads like a recipe: "This column should be 1 part of the leftover (or available) space, this column 2 parts, and the last column should be 1 part of the leftover space."

The fantastic thing about the `fr` unit is that it takes into account all space already taken up, like **padding** and **grid-gap**. That means no mental math! Here's the new ruleset for **main**, with a two-column layout:

```
main {
    display: grid;
    grid-template-columns: 2fr 1fr;
    grid-gap: 15px;
    padding: 15px;
}
```

This gives you a clean, evenly spaced set of columns (**FIGURE 16.14**).

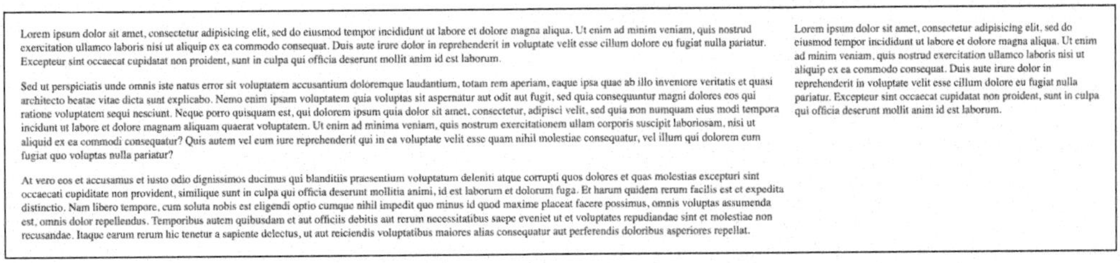

FIGURE 16.13 A two-column layout with Grid

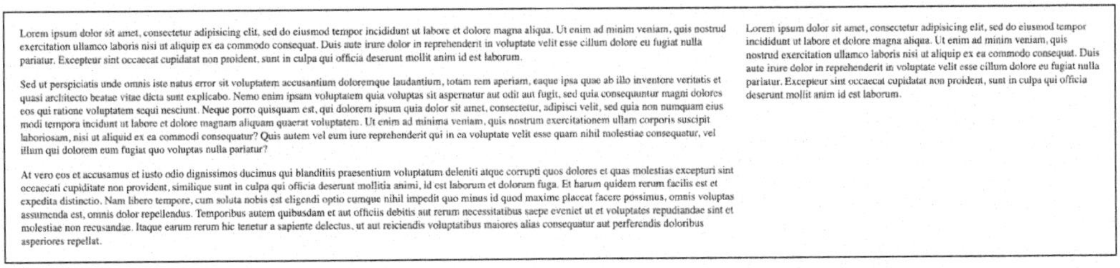

FIGURE 16.14 A two-column layout using `fr` units

Creating Grid templates

Another truly fantastic feature of Grid is the ability to define templates right in the CSS. You'll get a quick explanation here, but for a more in-depth look, check out Video 16.5.

Here's an example (in HTML markup and CSS statements) that you can work from. The HTML defines three principal elements in the class **wrapper** (**CODE 16.1**).

And now the CSS for these elements (**CODE 16.2**).

The first set of rules (for **header**, **main**, and **aside**) does something really important here: it tells the CSS how these elements will be referenced by name in the Grid template using a property called **grid-area**. This property allows you to reference the selector by a friendlier name in the property **grid-template-areas**.

In the rule for **.wrapper**, the differentiator from other code examples in this chapter is the use of **grid-template-areas**, which allows you to reference the names assigned by **grid-area** and define what columns and rows each **grid-area** should span. Note that **grid-template-areas** does not assume the **grid-area** names will match the HTML elements or selectors. Any non-numeric string can be used. For example, note that I assigned the name **sidebar** to the **aside** element.

Because this is a three-column grid (as we established with the **grid-template-columns** property), **grid-template-areas** shakes out like this:

- Each line is a row.
- Each string is a cell/column in the grid.

VIDEO 16.5
Grid Templates

In this video, you'll get an in-depth look at defining and using Grid templates.

CODE 16.1 The HTML

```html
<div class="wrapper">
    <header>
        ...
    </header>

    <main>
        ...
    </main>

    <aside>
        ...
    </aside>
</div>
```

CODE 16.2 The CSS

```css
header {
    grid-area: header;
}

main {
    grid-area: main;
}

aside {
    grid-area: sidebar;
}

.wrapper {
    display: grid;
    grid-template-columns: 1fr 1fr 1fr;
    grid-template-areas:
        "header header header"
        "main main sidebar";
    grid-gap: 20px;
    width: 900px;
    margin: 0 auto;
}
```

You can align elements in Grid very similarly to how you would do so in Flexbox. This video runs through those examples.

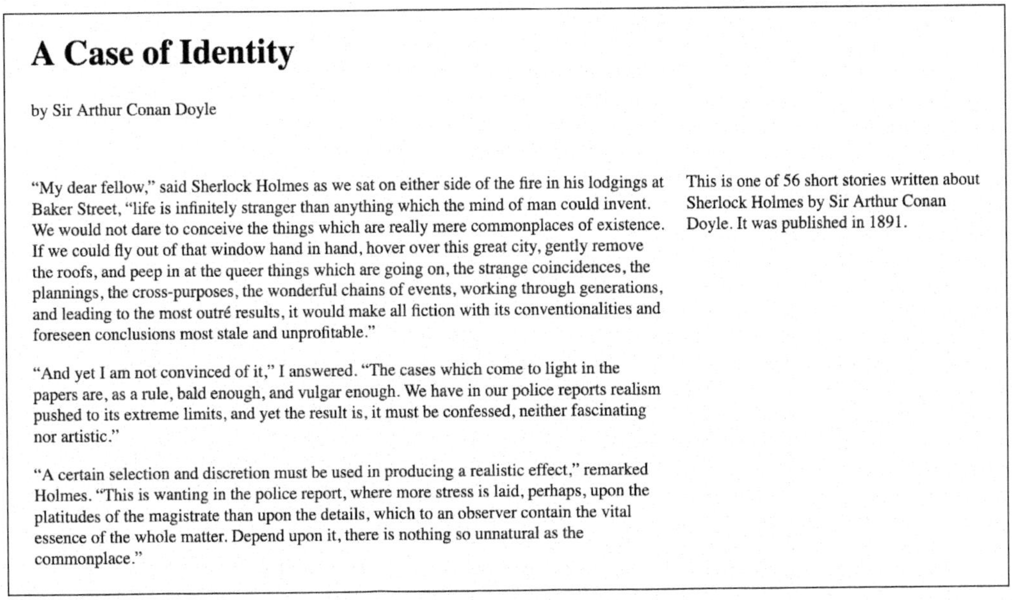

What this says is, "On the first row, the **header** grid area should take up all three columns. On the second row, **main** should take up the first two columns, with **sidebar** taking up the last." The result is something like **FIGURE 16.15**.

As you can imagine—and as you'll see in Video 16.5 and Chapter 17—this is a powerful way to define flexible layouts for the content.

> **TIP** If you want to leave a column or cell blank, use a period (.).

A Case of Identity

by Sir Arthur Conan Doyle

"My dear fellow," said Sherlock Holmes as we sat on either side of the fire in his lodgings at Baker Street, "life is infinitely stranger than anything which the mind of man could invent. We would not dare to conceive the things which are really mere commonplaces of existence. If we could fly out of that window hand in hand, hover over this great city, gently remove the roofs, and peep in at the queer things which are going on, the strange coincidences, the plannings, the cross-purposes, the wonderful chains of events, working through generations, and leading to the most outré results, it would make all fiction with its conventionalities and foreseen conclusions most stale and unprofitable."

"And yet I am not convinced of it," I answered. "The cases which come to light in the papers are, as a rule, bald enough, and vulgar enough. We have in our police reports realism pushed to its extreme limits, and yet the result is, it must be confessed, neither fascinating nor artistic."

"A certain selection and discretion must be used in producing a realistic effect," remarked Holmes. "This is wanting in the police report, where more stress is laid, perhaps, upon the platitudes of the magistrate than upon the details, which to an observer contain the vital essence of the whole matter. Depend upon it, there is nothing so unnatural as the commonplace."

This is one of 56 short stories written about Sherlock Holmes by Sir Arthur Conan Doyle. It was published in 1891.

FIGURE 16.15 Our previous two-column example, now using Grid templates

Browser Support

The next important consideration when using CSS is browser support. In Chapter 10, you learned about caniuse.com and the fact that some browsers are faster to implement new features than others. That's even more evident with CSS than with HTML. There is greater disparity among browsers as to which features are implemented and how they are implemented.

In **FIGURE 16.16** you can see that with the most recently available version of each major browser (excluding Internet Explorer 11, as development has shifted to Microsoft Edge), there's a mixed bag of support, from not supported and partial support to fully supported.

You might also notice the boxes with text in the upper-right corner of some cells. Those are called *vendor prefixes*.

Supported (some prefix)

	Edge 79		Firefox 72		Chrome 79		Safari 13	
CSS color-adjust	Yes	-webkit-	Yes		Yes	-webkit-	Yes	-webkit-
CSS line-clamp	Yes	-webkit-	Yes	-moz-	Yes	-webkit-	Yes	-webkit-
CSS :read-only and :read-write selectors	Yes		Yes	-moz-	Yes		Yes	
CSS text-orientation	Yes		Yes		Yes		Yes	-webkit-
CSS text-stroke and text-fill	Yes	-webkit-	Yes	-moz-	Yes	-webkit-	Yes	-webkit-
CSS user-select: none	Yes		Yes		Yes		Yes	-webkit-
Media Queries: resolution feature	Yes		Yes		Yes		Partial	-webkit-
CSS Backdrop Filter	Yes		No		Yes		Yes	-webkit-
CSS Cross-Fade Function	Yes	-webkit-	No		Yes	-webkit-	Yes	
CSS image-set	Yes	-webkit-	No		Yes	-webkit-	Yes	
CSS Reflections	Yes	-webkit-	No		Yes	-webkit-	Yes	-webkit-
CSS position:sticky	Partial		Yes		Partial		Yes	-webkit-
CSS Masks	Partial	-webkit-	Yes		Partial	-webkit-	Partial	-webkit-
:matches() CSS pseudo-class	Partial		Partial	-moz-	Partial		Yes	
CSS Appearance	Partial	-webkit-	Partial	-moz-	Partial	-webkit-	Partial	-webkit-
CSS scrollbar styling	Partial	-webkit-	Partial		Partial	-webkit-	Partial	-webkit-
:focus-visible CSS pseudo-class	No		Yes	-moz-	No		No	
CSS Canvas Drawings	No		No		No		Yes	-webkit-
CSS Initial Letter	No		No		No		Partial	-webkit-

FIGURE 16.16 The caniuse.com table showing browser support of recent CSS features

Using Prefixing Tools

There are loads of tools to help you automatically add the prefixes you need, so you don't need an encyclopedic knowledge of which prefixes to use and when:

- CSS-Tricks's writeup: css-tricks.com/how-to-deal-with-vendor-prefixes/
- Autoprefixer: autoprefixer.github.io/
- Should I Prefix: shouldiprefix.com/

You can also use a CSS preprocessor like Sass, which you'll learn about in Chapter 20.

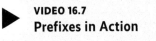

VIDEO 16.7
Prefixes in Action

In this video you'll see how prefixes affect different CSS properties, adding support for new and experimental features.

Vendor prefixes

Vendor (or browser) prefixes are vendor-specific CSS properties that can be used for experimental or beta features. Prefixes are used for a few reasons:

- They don't use any specific property from the CSS spec. Instead, they use a "working copy" of some property. For example, there's a property called `transition`, which might have a working, but not finalized, definition. Prefixes allow browsers to implement their version of `transition` based on the working spec.

- They allow web designers to use features of CSS that are implemented in some browsers without worrying they will break the website in browsers that don't support that feature.

- Once the CSS property is fully implemented, the prefixed property is ignored and its presence doesn't break the site. That means prefixes keep websites backward and forward compatible. Even so, you should clean up old prefixes when they're not needed.

> **TIP** At the time of this writing, vendor prefixes are still common practice, but as noted on MDN's web documentation, browsers are "working to stop using vendor prefixes for experimental features." One reason is to prevent the use of highly experimental features on a production website. You can read more about it at developer.mozilla.org/en-US/docs/Glossary/Vendor_Prefix.

The major browser prefixes are as follows:

- `-webkit-` is used for Chrome, Safari, newer versions of Opera, and all iOS browsers.
- `-moz-` is used for Firefox.
- `-o-` is for older versions of Opera.
- `-ms-` is for Internet Explorer and Microsoft Edge.

TIP Besides `-ms-`, Microsoft Edge supports a number of `-webkit-` prefixed features to improve compatibility.

When formatting your declarations, order them so that all the prefixes come before the non-prefixed property (due to the cascade!).

As an example, see the following code for a CSS transition. It creates a simple animation when any property for **a** changes (for example, if the background color changes on hover). You'll learn about CSS animations in Chapter 18.

```
a {
    background: #880000;
    -webkit-transition: all 1s linear;
    -moz-transition: all 1s linear;
    -ms-transition: all 1s linear;
    -o-transition: all 1s linear;
    transition: all 1s linear;
}
```

You'll learn more about testing later in the book, but as far as prefixes go, it's best to see what support new features have and use them accordingly.

For the purposes of simplicity, examples in this book exclude prefixes.

Wrapping Up

There's a lot to digest here, and you've only scratched the surface. However, this gives you a fantastic jump-off point for building incredible layouts in CSS.

The whole reason for this type of power is the topic covered in Chapter 17: responsive design. Being able to flexibly change how content is laid out without having to modify the markup allows you to create fantastic content no matter what screen your site is being viewed on.

Responsive Design and Media Queries

In today's world, websites can be viewed on computers, tablets, phones, watches, glasses, or even kitchen appliances. It's impossible to design for every single scenario, and that's where responsive web design (RWD) comes in. RWD ensures that your website looks good no matter what device it's viewed on.

This is achieved through media queries—we can write CSS that essentially asks the browser questions and then presents styles based on the answers.

Defining Media Queries

Unlike most of the CSS declarations you've seen so far, media queries aren't just sets of properties and values. They are containers for other rulesets. Those rulesets are then implemented based on the results of the media query. All media queries are formatted like this:

```
@media [media type] and ([media
 features]) {
    [Rulesets go here]
}
```

As you'll see later, there are lots of different types and features to check for. But for now, here's a common media query:

```
@media screen and (min-width: 600px) {
    main {
        display: flex;
    }
}
```

This says, "If the user is viewing this site on a screen whose viewport is at least 600px wide, display all `<main>` elements as `flex`."

Throughout the book you've seen references to screen size, window width, and browser size. While each term refers to how wide an area your website renders in, the most succinct term is *viewport*, which refers to the exact area of the screen that is rendering your website.

Other media types include `all`, `print` (for printing a webpage), and `speech` (for use with screen readers).

Using breakpoints

A common term in RWD is *breakpoint*, the point at which your layout changes to accommodate the viewport. It allows you to make your layouts more useable based on the size of the device your users are viewing the site on.

For example, if you have a navigation menu that is 601px wide, it won't look great on devices with a viewport of less than 601px. You can use a breakpoint to say, "Once the viewport is wider than this size, change the layout of the navigation menu."

So if you select a media query for `min-width: 600px`, your breakpoint is 600px.

Choosing breakpoints is an important decision because it ensures your layout

RWD Best Practices

There have been lots of discussions over the years as to the best practices for responsive web design. Should you use `em` or `px`? How should you organize your media queries? Should you start big and get smaller or vice versa?

Here is what I do in this book:

- Use `px` because there is less ambiguity about the actual width than with `em` and `rem`; `px` is more predictable (10px is always 10px), and that's especially useful for learning.
- Organize style sheets based on media query, with the base CSS before the media queries.
- Take a mobile first approach.

Mobile first is the web design strategy that posits that you design for the smallest screen first and move up from there. Its main benefit is that it forces you to assess your content and design elements. It helps you include only what you need, and then hopefully you realize that's all you need!

doesn't, well, break. Many breakpoints focus around specific devices—usually iOS devices—but as the field of screen sizes increases, this is not a good approach.

Instead, choose your breakpoints based on the point at which your content starts to look bad.

If you're starting mobile first, that means adding a breakpoint that takes effect when the page is on devices with larger screens. As the viewport expands past the breakpoint, it can switch to different layout settings, such as multicolumn layouts or layouts that are centered in the screen.

If you're starting by designing your pages for large screens (a large tablet or desktop), when the page is viewed on a smaller device you select your breakpoint by resizing the browser window (and therefore the viewport) down until the content becomes unreadable.

Ultimately, you'll probably have three major breakpoints (where there's a major shift in content) and three to four minor breakpoints (with smaller fixes for specific content). But that's a guide, and it's completely up to you. Do what works best for your design.

TIP **Since this book works with relatively basic layouts, it covers two or three total breakpoints.**

▶ **VIDEO 17.1**
Choosing Breakpoints

In this video, you'll see how to choose breakpoints by resizing the browser window until a site starts to look bad.

Responsive Layouts

So how do you make responsive layouts? Where do you start, and how do you structure your code? I recommend setting all the base styles *above* any media queries (as in, write them down in your style sheet first) and starting with the smallest layout. Media queries should modify your website as the viewport gets bigger. Here's a simple example to start.

To change the background color at 600px:

1. In your style sheet, type **body** to establish the default values for the page.
2. Type **{** to begin the rule.
3. Type **background:** followed by the hex code for the starting background color. For this example use #FF0000; .
4. Type **color:** followed by the hex code for the text color. In this case, use #FFFFFF; .
5. Type **}** to close the rule.
6. Type **@media** to begin the media query.
7. Type the name of the media type you want to target. Because you want to implement a different style rule when the user's browser window changes, use **screen**.
8. Type **and**.
9. Type the name and value (in parentheses) of the media feature that should trigger a change in the background color. This value is your breakpoint for the page, and you want the break to occur when the browser window is 600px or wider, so use **(min-width: 600px) {**.
10. Type the element you want this rule to affect. In this case, **body {**.

11. Type the attribute and value that you want to change at the breakpoint. In this example, use **background: #0000FF;**.

12. Type **}**.

13. Type **}** to close the media query.

Now resize the browser window. When it is below 600px wide, the background is red (**FIGURE 17.1**). When it's 600px or wider, the background is blue (**FIGURE 17.2**).

Note that the font color was set outside the media query. The goal is to avoid repetition in your code that might bloat your style sheet. Any styles set inside media queries will apply only when the media query is true. So if you have multiple media queries but don't want the color to remain the same, you'd have to set it in every media query.

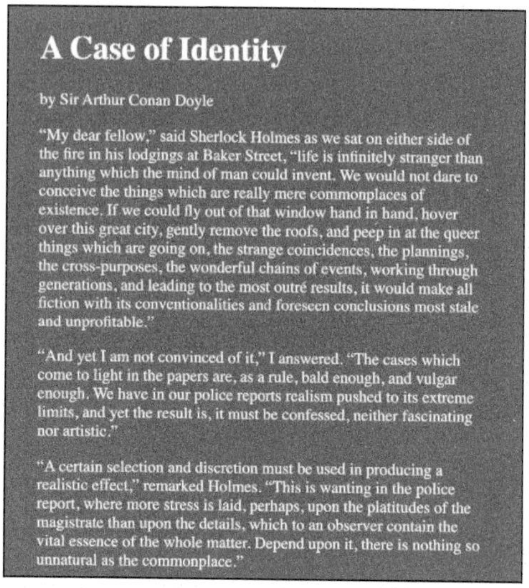

A Case of Identity

by Sir Arthur Conan Doyle

"My dear fellow," said Sherlock Holmes as we sat on either side of the fire in his lodgings at Baker Street, "life is infinitely stranger than anything which the mind of man could invent. We would not dare to conceive the things which are really mere commonplaces of existence. If we could fly out of that window hand in hand, hover over this great city, gently remove the roofs, and peep in at the queer things which are going on, the strange coincidences, the plannings, the cross-purposes, the wonderful chains of events, working through generations, and leading to the most outré results, it would make all fiction with its conventionalities and foreseen conclusions most stale and unprofitable."

"And yet I am not convinced of it," I answered. "The cases which come to light in the papers are, as a rule, bald enough, and vulgar enough. We have in our police reports realism pushed to its extreme limits, and yet the result is, it must be confessed, neither fascinating nor artistic."

"A certain selection and discretion must be used in producing a realistic effect," remarked Holmes. "This is wanting in the police report, where too much stress is laid, perhaps, upon the platitudes of the magistrate than upon the details, which to an observer contain the vital essence of the whole matter. Depend upon it, there is nothing so unnatural as the commonplace."

FIGURE 17.1 The page when the browser window is less than 600px wide

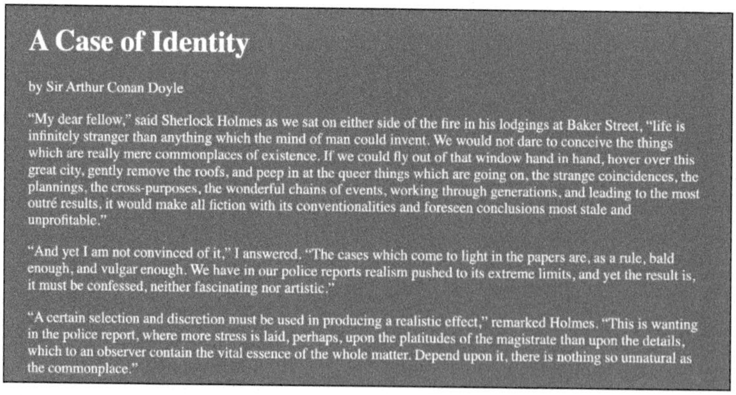

A Case of Identity

by Sir Arthur Conan Doyle

"My dear fellow," said Sherlock Holmes as we sat on either side of the fire in his lodgings at Baker Street, "life is infinitely stranger than anything which the mind of man could invent. We would not dare to conceive the things which are really mere commonplaces of existence. If we could fly out of that window hand in hand, hover over this great city, gently remove the roofs, and peep in at the queer things which are going on, the strange coincidences, the plannings, the cross-purposes, the wonderful chains of events, working through generations, and leading to the most outré results, it would make all fiction with its conventionalities and foreseen conclusions most stale and unprofitable."

"And yet I am not convinced of it," I answered. "The cases which come to light in the papers are, as a rule, bald enough, and vulgar enough. We have in our police reports realism pushed to its extreme limits, and yet the result is, it must be confessed, neither fascinating nor artistic."

"A certain selection and discretion must be used in producing a realistic effect," remarked Holmes. "This is wanting in the police report, where more stress is laid, perhaps, upon the platitudes of the magistrate than upon the details, which to an observer contain the vital essence of the whole matter. Depend upon it, there is nothing so unnatural as the commonplace."

FIGURE 17.2 The page when the browser window is 600px or wider

This is another benefit of the mobile first approach. You will likely start at default displays for smaller screens and then introduce changes as the page is displayed in larger viewports, allowing you to set as many default styles as possible before you start making changes.

For example, here is a simple CSS Grid layout that shows the pitfalls encountered when defining the bigger screen first (**CODE 17.1**). It tells **div**s to display their children in columns as long as the viewport is wider than 599px. At 599px or smaller, it display **div**s as a block.

CODE 17.1 Styles for a CSS Grid layout, designing for larger screens first

```
div {
    display: grid;
    grid-template-columns: 1fr 1fr 1fr;
    grid-gap: 15px;
    padding: 15px;
}
@media screen and (max-width: 599px) {
    div {
        display: block;
        padding: 0;
    }
}
```

CODE 17.2 Much more succinct Grid code, designing for smaller screens first

```
@media screen and (min-width: 600px) {
    div {
        display: grid;
        grid-template-columns: 1fr 1fr 1fr;
        grid-gap: 15px;
        padding: 15px;
    }
}
```

In the media query, you're actually *resetting* the **div** back to its default display mode.

You can avoid the dangers of designing for the large screen first by treating the larger screen as the special case, and allowing the smaller screen to use the browser's default settings.

And now, we'll define media queries used in designing for small screens first (**CODE 17.2**). You don't have to reset **div** to its original state because it maintains that state (**display: block**) until you change it for bigger viewports.

This is a seemingly trivial example, but in the mobile first layout, it wasn't necessary to define any special styles, because the browser defaults were adequate. The desktop-first layout required some resetting of styles. You can imagine that using multiple breakpoints, or more varied styles and layouts, will compound the cases in which you find yourself redefining styles.

TIP In a desktop-first layout, notice that **max-width** is 599px versus a 600px **min-width**. You might run into issues like that—where you have an "off by one pixel" declaration—if you want to get your designs pixel-perfect. If you want the design to change at 600px, **min-width** makes that a little clearer, since 600px is in the actual definition.

As you create your layouts, think about how to reduce the number of styles you override and how to make your style sheets easier to manage.

Making a Full-width Layout Responsive

So what goes into making a fully respon-sive layout? Here, you'll build it in sections. **CODE 17.3** shows the HTML markup you'll work with. **CODE 17.4** shows the initial CSS styles, in a `style.css` file. Both are available at github.com/jcasabona/html-css-vqs/Ch17/.

CODE 17.3 The HTML markup for the rest of this chapter

```
<div class="wrapper">
    <header>
        <h1>A Case of Identity</h1>
        <p class="byline">by Sir Arthur Conan Doyle</p>
    </header>
    <main>
        <p> "My dear fellow," said Sherlock Holmes as we sat on either side of the fire in his
         lodgings at Baker Street, "life is infinitely stranger than anything which the
         mind of man could invent. We would not dare to conceive the things which are really
         mere commonplaces of existence. If we could fly out of that window hand in hand,
         hover over this great city, gently remove the roofs, and peep in at the queer things
         which are going on, the strange coincidences, the plannings, the cross-purposes,
         the wonderful chains of events, working through generations, and leading to the most
         outré results, it would make all fiction with its conventionalities and foreseen
         conclusions most stale and unprofitable."</p>
    </main>
    <aside>
        This is one of 56 short stories written about Sherlock Holmes by Sir Arthur Conan
         Doyle. It was published in 1891.
    </aside>
    <footer>
        <p>The <i>Sherlock Holmes</i> series is in the public domain.</p>
    </footer>
</div>
```

```css
@import url('https://fonts.googleapis.com/css?family=Playfair+Display:400,400i,500,500i,600,
    600i,700,700i,800,800i,900,900i&display=swap');
body {
    font-family: 'Playfair Display', serif;
    background-color:#fcf6e7;
    margin: 0;
    padding: 0;
}
header,
footer {
    background: #282009;
    color: #FFFFFF;
    padding: 30px;
    text-align: center;
}
h1 {
    font-weight: 900;
}
main,
aside {
    margin: 30px;
}
aside {
    background: #272727;
    color: #FFFFFF;
    padding: 30px;
}
.byline {
    font-family: Futura, sans-serif;
    font-style: italic;
}
p {
    font-size: 18px;
    margin: 30px 0;
}
```

FIGURE 17.3 shows the smallest screen and **FIGURE 17.4** the largest screen.

TIP To keep the source code clean, we define only the essential styles.

Starting small: mobile first styles

Most of the styles in Code 17.4 are for general look and feel and are not related to layout. On the smallest screens, everything will be a single column, so the browser's default styles for the elements will work. The changes you see for margin, padding, fonts, and colors were just to add some personality to the page and make the layout changes more obvious (like giving the aside a different background color from the body).

So now it's time to answer the question of when to start changing the layout—at what point can you begin to space the content out a bit more?

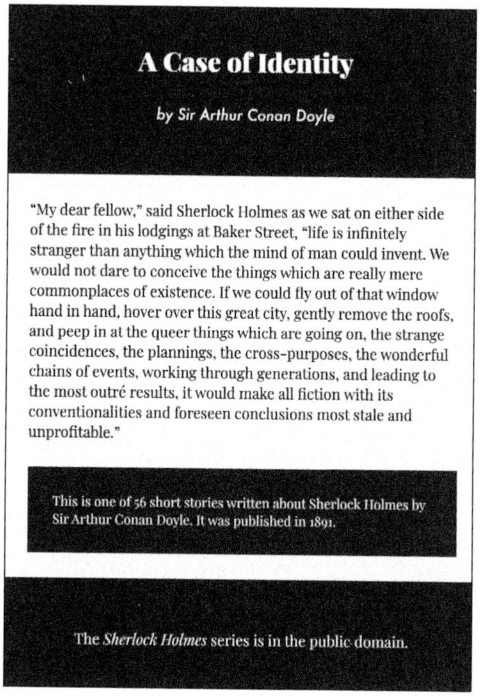

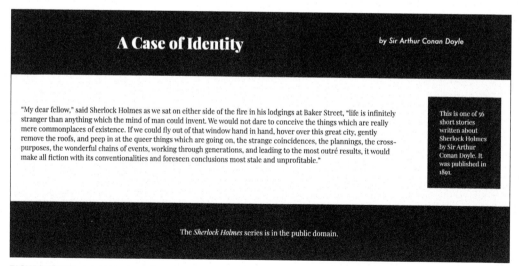

FIGURE 17.3 The mobile layout

FIGURE 17.4 The desktop layout

As you try to figure this out, the best thing to do is resize your browser. Since this layout lends itself very well to a one-column format, not a whole lot needs to be done in terms of adjusting it. Complicated layouts require more complicated media queries.

However, there are a few things that can be done to take advantage of more screen real estate.

The mid-sized screen layout

One way you can take advantage of more screen space when your page is being viewed on bigger devices is to spread out the header text a bit. One way to do this is to set up a grid on the <header> element and use columns to space the child elements.

 TIP The examples in this chapter use the styles shown in **CODE 17.4**, which you should add to your **style.css** file, as the starting point. Continue to add the new styles presented in each task to the end of the same file.

▶ **VIDEO 17.2**
Making a Full Three-Column Layout Responsive

Though this book preaches mobile first, you may be in a situation where you have a full site design and need to make it mobile friendly. This video shows you how to do just that. Then you'll see what it looks like as the browser resizes.

To create a two-column layout at a breakpoint:

1. Start by defining your media query, based on the breakpoint at which you've chosen to change your layout. Type `@media screen and (min-width: 768px) {`.

   Add this code to the end of your style sheet (assuming you're using the code from Code 17.4).

2. Target the element you'd like to change at your determined breakpoint. Type `header {`.

3. Add the styles for this element at the specific breakpoint, one per line. Type `display: grid;`.

4. Type `grid-template-columns: 2fr 1fr;`.

5. Type `grid-gap: 15px;`.

6. Type `justify-items: center;`.

7. Close the ruleset for your element by typing `}`.

8. Close the media query by typing `}`.

Once you extend your browser window to a width of at least 768px, your header will move the byline out from under the heading and to its right (**FIGURE 17.5**).

This is a good first step, but the real fun starts at the next breakpoint: 1000px.

A Case of Identity

by Sir Arthur Conan Doyle

FIGURE 17.5 The header once the viewport is widened beyond 768px

The large-screen layout

On a large screen, you can really take advantage of the screen real estate. Using a multicolumn layout for large screens is a great way to show more information to the user, now that they have the room for it. A `wrapper` `div` comes in handy here. This `div` "wraps" the elements—`header`, `main`, `aside`, and `footer`—so that they are all siblings. That means you can apply `display: grid` to the `.wrapper` selector and easily control how each child element (or grid item) is displayed.

Since the large screen layout builds upon all the styles added to `style.css` before it, add the following styles to the end of `style.css`.

To set up a grid layout at a specific breakpoint:

1. You want this layout to go into effect at the largest breakpoint you determined works best for your layout. Type `@media screen and (min-width: 1000px) {`.

2. You will also need to create the grid-areas. Based on Code 17.3, type `header { grid-area: header; }`.

   Because of the cascade, this will essentially be added on to previous rulesets targeting header.

3. On a new line, type `main { grid-area: main; }`.

4. On a new line, type `aside { grid-area: sidebar; }`.

5. On a new line, type `footer { grid-area: footer; }`.

Be sure to leave off the } that would close the media query. We're not done with it yet!

With those defined, it's time to convert the wrapper div into a grid with a template layout.

To convert `wrapper` to a grid layout:

1. It's time to target your entire layout at this breakpoint. Type `.wrapper {`.

2. A grid lends itself well to controlling each element of the layout. On a new line, type `display: grid;`.

3. On a new line, type `grid-gap: 15px;`.

4. Determine how many columns you want in your layout. For this example, choose five to make it clear we won't have a `main` section and `aside` that are the same widths. On a new line, type `grid-template-columns: 1fr 1fr 1fr 1fr 1fr;`.

5. Type `grid-template-areas:`.

6. Type `"header header header header header"`.

   Remember from the mid-sized layout task, that `header` is also using `grid`. This controls the width of the `header` element, which we want to extend across the entire page.

7. Type `"main main main main sidebar"`.

8. Type `"footer footer footer footer footer";`.

9. Close the `.wrapper` ruleset by typing `}`.

10. Close the media query. On a new line, type `}`.

Now the sidebar shows up to the right of the main content, just like in Figure 17.4.

Now for the fun part: resize the browser window and watch your layout change!

There are a few more stylistic changes you can make, like increasing the heading font size and tightening up some styles, but you've just taken your first layout and made it responsive.

The rest of this chapter explores other functions of CSS media queries.

A common pattern for responsive design is replacing the menu items with a single label or icon that, when clicked or tapped, reveals the menu. In this video, you'll learn how to do that.

FIGURE 17.6 Trying to print a webpage

Not Just for Screen Widths

The only media type you've seen in action so far is `screen`, and the only feature you've seen is related to `width`. While these are the most common implementations for media queries, they aren't the only ones. For starters, there's another common media type to look at: `print`.

Creating a print style sheet

Because computers print websites more or less exactly as they appear in the browser window, such printouts often aren't very helpful to those who want readable text (**FIGURE 17.6**).

Luckily, you can add a media query to apply print styles to the page. Here's how to do it, starting with the markup from the previous section.

To add printer styles to a website:

1. At the bottom of your style sheet, type `@media print {` to target printers.

2. Type the elements you want to include in the printout. For this example, you want the whole page, so include `body, header, aside, footer {`.

3. On a new line, type `background: #FFFFFF;`.

   This step and the next set the background color and text to white and black, respectively, so the text is more easily readable when printed.

4. On a new line, type `color: #000000;`.

5. On a new line, type `}`.

6. On a new line, type `.wrapper {`.

   This is the crux of the print styles.

7. On a new line, type `display: block;`.

   Simply setting the display to `block` makes the browser ignore all grid-related properties (like `grid-template-columns`) and moves the content into one column.

8. On a new line, type `width: 75%;`.

   This is a stylistic decision on my part, but it gives the reader plenty of margin on either side of the content.

9. On a new line, type `margin: 0 auto;`.

10. On a new line, type `}` to close the `.wrapper` ruleset.

11. On a new line, type `}` to close the media query.

This creates a single column of black text that looks great when printed (**FIGURE 17.7**).

Aside from media types (`all`, `print`, `screen`, `speech`), you can also target specific media features.

On Hiding Elements

One all-too-common practice in responsive design is just hiding elements that don't "fit" on smaller screens. While the mobile first approach should help solve this, it's still something to be mindful of. If you need to hide an element for small screens, you should question whether you need it at all.

One exception to this rule is print styles. If your goal is to make sure the main content is readable when printed, it might be a good idea to hide certain elements (like comments or images).

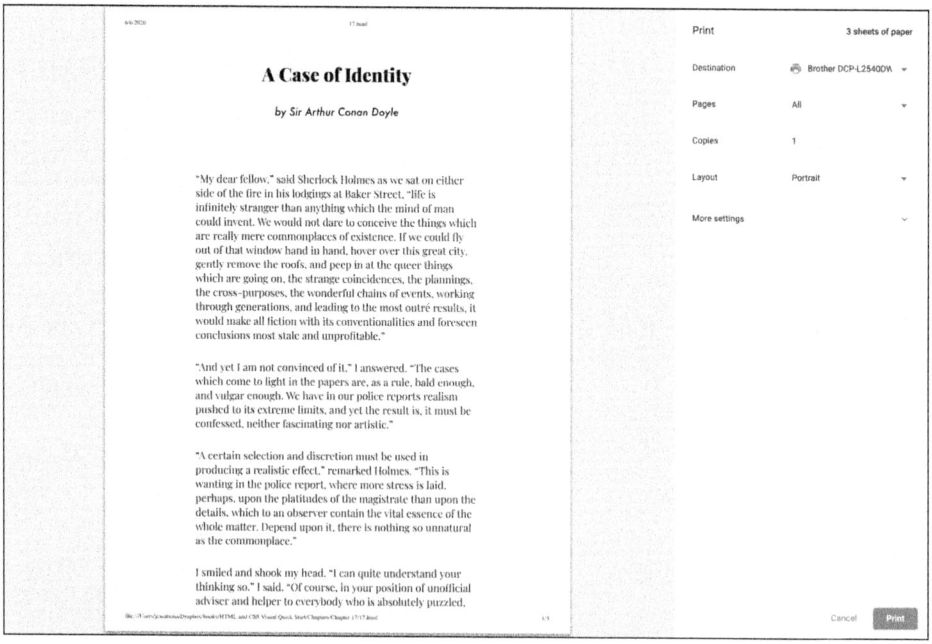

FIGURE 17.7 The printed page

Targeting specific media features

TIP You can get a list of media features at developer.mozilla.org/en-US/docs/Web/CSS/@media. But keep in mind that specific devices might have their own implementation.

You might want to target a specific feature on touch devices, check if a device is in portrait or landscape, or much more. This is what the extended media features are for. A great example is checking to see whether a user has enabled dark mode.

To apply dark mode styles:

1. At the bottom of your style sheet, type `@media screen`.

2. To specify one or more media features, type **and** followed by the name of the media feature in parentheses. To check for dark mode, type `(prefers-color-scheme: dark) {`.

3. Type the selectors you want the style to apply to; in this case, `body, header, aside, footer {`.

4. To make sure the text harmonizes with the overall inky environment, reverse the usual black-on-white colors. Type `background: #272727;` to make the page a dark gray.

5. Type `color: #FFFFFF;` to make the text white.

6. Because it's light text on a dark background, a bit more spacing will make the text easier to read. Type `line-height: 2em;`.

7. Type `}`.

8. Type one more `}`.

Now, when you visit the site on a device using dark mode, it will look like **FIGURE 17.8**.

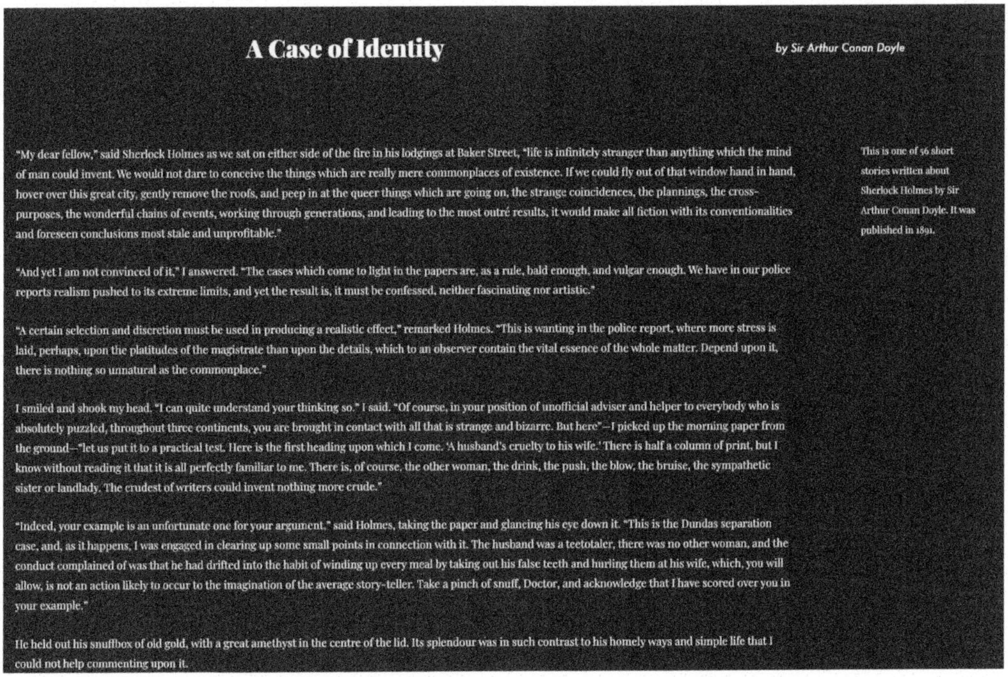

FIGURE 17.8 Dark mode styles applied to a webpage

Experiment with more of these media features, as you can do checks for the following:

- Pointer (cursor) support (with `any-pointer`)

- Hover support (with `any-hover`)

- Retina displays (with `resolution`, `min-resolution`)

- Inverted colors (with `prefers-color-scheme`)

And much more. The possibilities for customizing a website's experience are growing quickly!

▶ **VIDEO 17.4**
Advanced Media Queries

The examples in this book only scratch the surface of what you can do with media queries. In this video, you learn how to write more advanced media queries by combining checks and using logical operators.

Wrapping Up

Media queries are essential to creating great user experiences no matter what device your site is being used on. From adjusting layout based on width to swapping out colors in dark mode, your styles are completely customizable based on the user's preferences and their browser's capabilities.

And now that you're familiar with everything from the basics to layouts in CSS, it's time to get a little more advanced and look at CSS animations.

CSS Transformations and Animations

It used to be that if you wanted to add a little extra flourish to your webpages, you'd need to use JavaScript or, if you go far back enough, Flash. The added flourish could be a simple transition or a little animation, but now CSS has the ability to apply transformations to properties as well as to create frame-by-frame animations.

While you won't be making the next *Toy Story* in your browser, you will be able to easily create interactions that improve a user's experience with your website. This chapter gives you a small taste of what's possible!

CSS Transitions

CSS transitions are some of the simplest but most delightful effects you can apply to your elements. Normally, when you change the value of a CSS property, the change happens instantaneously. A CSS transition allows you to change those values over time, which adds nuance and visual cues to your user interface. They generally occur due to some user interaction, like a hover.

The main property here is **transition**, and it's a shorthand property for **transition-property**, **transition-duration**, **transition-timing-function**, and **transition-delay**. In **transition**, they are replaced by these four values:

- **property**: The CSS property that you want to animate. It can be any CSS property that supports transitions—which is most but not all of them. See a full list at developer.mozilla.org/en-US/docs/Web/CSS/CSS_animated_properties.

- **duration**: The amount of time, in seconds, the transition should take.

- **timing-function**: The mathematical description of the rate at which the property changes, which can itself change over time. Common examples are **ease** (the default), **linear**, **ease-in**, **ease-out**, and **ease-in-out**. You can even make your own timing function with **cubic-bezier**.

- **delay**: The amount of time, in seconds, before the transition starts.

When you write the **transition** property, it accepts the four values in this order:

transition: *[property] [duration]*
  [timing-function] [delay]

Further, each option can have a value of 0 or 1, except **property**, which should have a value of **none**, **all**, or a specific CSS property. Listing just a property will assume default values for **duration** (0s), **timing-function** (ease), and **delay** (0s). And if you supply two numbers (in seconds), the **timing-function** defaults to **ease**.

TIP Transitions can be applied in other ways, such as through adding a class in JavaScript.

▶ **VIDEO 18.1**
Demo of Transition Functions

It's easiest to show how these transitions work in a video. So here, you'll see each as a 1.5-second transition applied to the **width** property.

CODE 18.1 The background color of this button will change when the user hovers their pointer over it.

```
<!--Here's the HTML for the button. -->
<a class="button" href="#">Click Here</a>

/*Here follows the CSS that defines the
↪ appearance of the button.*/
a.button {
    background: #880000;
    border-radius: 40px;
    color: #ffffff;
    display: block;
    font-size: 1.5rem;
    max-width: 150px;
    padding: 15px;
    text-align: center;
    text-decoration: none;
}
/*And let's add a hover state to the
↪ button.*/
a.button:hover {
    background: #008800;
}
```

FIGURE 18.1 button produced by Code 18.1 in its initial state.

One common application of transitions is to change background colors. **CODE 18.1** shows a button defined in CSS (**FIGURE 18.1**).

In this example, when the user hovers their pointer over the button, only one thing changes: the **background** property changes from dark red to dark green. But it's a sudden, simple change. Adding a transition can make that change smoother.

To add a **background** transition to an element with CSS:

1. Using the sample CSS as a starting point, after **text-decoration** in the **a.button** ruleset, type **transition:**.

2. Next to **transition:**, type **background 1s ease-in;**.

   This says, "Add a 1-second ease-in transition to the **background** property."

That's it! Mouse over your button to watch a much smoother transition from dark red to dark green. As an added bonus, the browser reverses the timing function when you un-hover, so you get a nice transition both on hover and when you move off the element.

TIP For a transition to work, the property you wish to target must be defined in both states, and those properties must have different values.

TIP The transition in this example is purposefully a little longer than usual so you can see the effect in action. A more common duration is half a second.

As mentioned earlier, you can also use a delay value to introduce a pause before the transition. You do this by adding a fourth value to the **transition** property—a number in seconds. Here's an image with a transition effect on hover (**FIGURE 18.2**):

```
img {
    padding: 20px;
    width: 250px;
    transition: width 2s ease 0.5s
}
img:hover {
    width: 350px;
}
```

The last point we'll make about transitions in this chapter is that you can use the keyword **all** to target all the properties in the style declaration.

To enlarge an input field on focus:

1. In your style sheet, type **input {**.

2. Type **font-size: 1.5rem;**.

3. Type **padding: 5px;**.

4. Type **transition:** **all** **1s ease-out;**.

    This transition applies the timing function **ease-out** (start fast and get slower) to all properties with different values upon state change, over the course of 1 second.

5. **}**.

6. Type **input:focus {**.

7. Type **font-size: 2rem;**.

8. Type **padding: 10px;**.

9. Type **}**.

Your input field will now enlarge when the user clicks it, taps it, or activates it by pressing the Tab key.

FIGURE 18.2 An image before and after the transition to the hover state is invoked

VIDEO 18.2
Increasing the Size of an Input Field

In this video, you create an input field that increases in size when the cursor is focused on it.

CSS Transformations

Another way to add simple effects to your webpages is with CSS transformations. While commonly triggered by actions by the user—like hovering, clicking, or focusing on a form element—that's not necessarily the case, as you'll see later in this chapter.

TIP This chapter talks a lot about 2D and 3D planes. As a refresher, the x axis is the horizontal axis, going left to right. The y axis is the vertical axis, going down to up. The z axis is the depth axis, going front to back (where back is away from the viewer).

VIDEO 18.3
Transformation Examples

In this video, you'll see the visual effect created by each transformation.

The **transform** property lets you transform an HTML element by rotating it, scaling it, skewing it, or repositioning it in the horizontal and/or vertical directions. It's even possible to combine several transformations to achieve interesting visual effects:

- **scale(x,y)** changes the size of the element. It affects **font-size**, **height**, **width**, and **padding**. Use **scaleX()** and **scaleY()** to scale only a single axis. Units are a multiplier (**0.5** to shrink by half, **2** to double the size, etc.).

- **skew(x,y)** tilts an entire container based on the values. Use **skewX()** and **skewY()** to skew only a single axis. Units are degrees.

- **translate()** moves a container from side to side, up and down, or both. Generally combined with the **animate** property. Units are standard measurement units you've seen throughout the book (**px**, **em**, etc.), as well as other advanced units that can represent numbers to the browser.

- **rotate()** rotates the element clockwise from its current position. Units are degrees.

TIP There are two more functions—**matrix()** and **perspective()**—but they are a little more complicated to implement. To learn more, read this article: css-tricks.com/almanac/properties/t/transform/.

TIP It's easy to get carried away implementing transformations because they can do cool things to your elements, but unless you're creating advanced animations, use them sparingly so they stand out.

Writing transformations

The syntax for writing a transformation is a little simpler than for transitions, but transformations can be used for more advanced animations, as you'll see later. Here's a basic declaration that incorporates a transformation:

```
div.diamond {
    background: #FF0000;
    width: 200px;
    height: 200px;
    margin: 50px;
    transform: rotate(45deg);
}
```

The above code results in a rotated 200 by 200 square, which looks like a diamond (**FIGURE 18.3**). Note that this is a static transformation, which can serve as a design element. Other transformations, like **scale()**, are better served when combined with a user event or an animation.

TIP You'll notice that the **transform** property takes elements out of their original flow. That's something to keep in mind as you move forward.

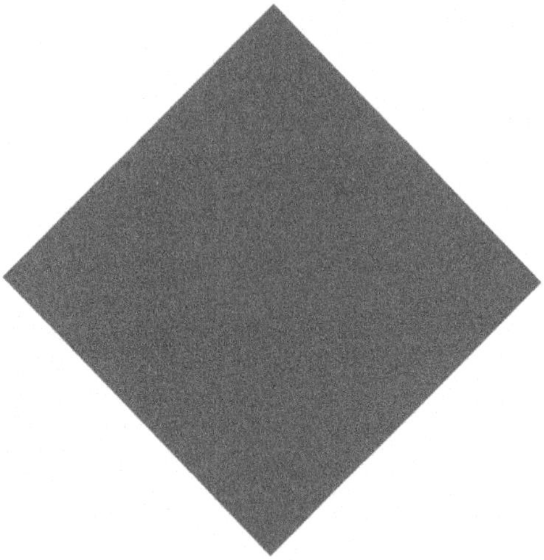

FIGURE 18.3 A rotate transformation applied to a square

FIGURE 18.4 A square with a `skewX()` transformation applied on hover

▶ **VIDEO 18.4**
Creating an Image Gallery with Mouseover Effects

In this video, you'll learn how to combine transformations and make an attention-grabbing effect when a user hovers over an image.

To skew a **div** slightly on hover:

1. In your style sheet, type `div {`.

2. Type `background: #FF0000;`.

3. Type `width: 200px;`.

4. Type `height: 200px;`.

5. Type `transition: transform 1s linear;`.

   This is so the element skews smoothly with a well-timed animation, instead of making the element jump to the skewed state.

6. Type `}`.

7. Type `div:hover {`.

8. Type `transform: skewX(-20deg);`.

   When you use degrees as the unit, you can also use negative values.

9. Type `}`.

Now when the user's mouse hovers over the square, it skews to the right (**FIGURE 18.4**).

3D Transformations

The following functions have 3D versions:

- `scale3d(x,y,z)`
- `rotate3d(x,y,z)`
- `translate3d(x,y,z)`
- `matrix3d()`

They each apply their transformations to the z axis as well, and this is where the `perspective()` function comes in handy—it sets the perspective for all child elements to make sure 3D animations are all based on the same viewpoint.

While this book doesn't get into the nitty-gritty of 3D transformations, they are good to know about if you want to take CSS animations to the next level or do some academically cool stuff.

CSS Animations

The final and most robust way to add flair to your webpages is CSS animations. These are done using two properties: **animation** and **@keyframes**.

@keyframes is a way for you to time-stamp the steps of your animations. This essentially puts your animations on a time-line that you can change. So you can say, "At start (0% of the timeline), the container should do this. At 50%, it should change to this, and at end (100%) it should be this." You reference the timeline (or keyframes) by assigning a name to them. See **CODE 18.2** for a simple example (**FIGURE 18.5**).

> **TIP** If two steps have the same value, use comma-separation as a form of shorthand: **@keyframes switch { 0%, 100% { background: red; } }**.

This code applies an animation that switches the background color from red to blue on a loop. **animation** is a short-hand property that lets you set the value of multiple properties. Here's what's used in Code 18.2:

- **animation-name**: This matches the **@keyframes** name.

- **animation-duration**: How long the animation should take in seconds.

- **animation-iteration-count**: How many times the animation should run. The keyword **infinite** is a placeholder for no limit.

CODE 18.2 A **div** with an animation applied to it. The **animation** property references the name (**switch**) that is given to the **@keyframes** controlling the animation.

```
div {
    width: 200px;
    height: 200px;
    background: red;
    animation: switch 4s infinite;
}
@keyframes switch {
    0% {
        background: red;
    }
    50% {
        background: blue;
    }
    100% {
        background: red;
    }
}
```

FIGURE 18.5
The two states of the **switch** animation

There are other animation properties that can be represented in the animation shorthand property. Here's the full list in the order they're expected:

- `animation-name`
- `animation-duration`
- `animation-timing-function`
- `animation-delay`
- `animation-iteration-count`
- `animation-direction`
- `animation-fill-mode`
- `animation-play-state`

Since this is an introduction to animations, this book doesn't cover everything. If you'd like to learn more, check out this MDN article: developer.mozilla.org/en-US/docs/Web/CSS/animation.

VIDEO 18.5
Rainbow Animation

In this video, you expand on the `switch` animation and use keyframe stops to change the `div` to every color in the rainbow.

TIP There are several other animation properties you can add as well, including delays and timing functions. Check out all the properties here: css-tricks.com/almanac/properties/a/animation/#article-header-id-0.

Combining animations

You can add more than one animation at once. To demonstrate, you'll convert the `switch` square to a circle. `border-radius` is used for this task because the value you provide for the property lets you set how much you want to "round off" the corners, as a percentage. Setting it to 50 percent rounds them so much that the square looks like a circle.

To convert a square to a circle:

1. In the 0% keyframe, below `background: red;`, type `border-radius: 0%;`.

2. In the 50% keyframe, below `background: blue;`, type `border-radius: 50%;`.

3. In the 100% keyframe, below `background: red;`, type `border-radius: 0%;`.

This creates a red square that transforms into a blue circle (**FIGURE 18.6**).

FIGURE 18.6
Red square transforming to blue circle

Animations using the transform property

Using **transform** in animations is a great way to save performance and do neat things like actually moving objects. This is where the **translate()** function from earlier comes into play. Using the CSS code below as a starting point, you'll make the ball that is generated by the following style declaration bounce up and down (**FIGURE 18.7**). In your HTML, add the following:

```
<p class="ball"></p>
```

And in your CSS, add the following:

```
p.ball {
    width: 50px;
    height: 50px;
    border-radius: 50%;
    background: #000000;
}
```

FIGURE 18.7 The ball that will bounce in the next task.

To bounce the ball:

1. In **p.ball**, after **background: #000000;**, type **animation: bounce 1s infinite alternate;**.

   bounce is the name we're giving to the animation we're about to define.

   The **infinite** value means "Loop this animation and never stop it."

   The **alternate** value means "Execute the animation, and then play the animation in reverse."

2. Type **animation-timing-function: linear;**.

   This timing function, **linear**, says that the item should animate at an even, consistent speed the whole time.

3. Type **}** to close the **p.ball** declaration.

4. Type **@keyframes bounce {**.

   This is where we define our animation. Notice that the name, bounce, is also referenced in the animation property in step 1.

5. Type **0% {**.

On Performance

Adding too many animations to your pages can cause performance issues in the browser. That's because they place heavy demands on the CPU (central processing unit), and they can potentially crash the browser.

There are a few animations you can use safely because the browser itself implements them, which means the GPU (graphics processing unit) can assist. They are the standard transform properties built into CSS with the addition of opacity:

- opacity
- translate
- rotate
- scale

To learn more, check out this fantastic article: www.html5rocks.com/en/tutorials/speed/high-performance-animations/.

```css
p.ball {
    width: 50px;
    height: 50px;
    border-radius: 50%;
    background: #000000;
    animation: bounce 1s infinite
     ▸ alternate;
    animation-timing-function: linear;
}

@keyframes bounce {
    0% {
        transform: translate(0px,0px);
    }
    100% {
        transform: translate(0px, 400px);
    }
}
```

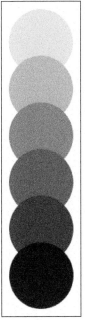

FIGURE 18.8 The ball starts at the top of the parent, bounces to the bottom, and then repeats.

6. Type **transform: translate(0px, 0px);**.

We define no translation at 0 percent (or the first step of the animation) so that the ball returns to its starting state.

7. Type **}**.

8. Type **100% {**.

This sets a keyframe at the very end of the animation (at 100 percent of the timeline).

9. Type **transform: translate(0px, 400px);**.

Since the **translate** property moves the element along the *x* and *y* axes, this says, "Move the ball 400px along the *y* axis." Since the starting point is 0px, the ball will move down 400px.

10. Type **}**.

11. Type **}**.

For a complete listing of the final CSS see **CODE 18.3**. To see the results (and expand upon them), check out Video 18.6 (**FIGURE 18.8**).

VIDEO 18.6
Follow the Bouncing Ball

In this video, you expand on the **bounce** animation and make the ball bounce from one corner of the container to the other and then back.

Wrapping Up

What a chapter! Now you know how to add effects and animations to your elements. This will help you create more dynamic pages, and it allows for smoother, less jarring state changes to let the user know what's happening on your page.

Of course, you've only scratched the surface. There's a ton to know about CSS animations, and lots of fantastic examples out there. To go deep with CSS animations, check out this article on CSS-Tricks: css-tricks.com/almanac/properties/a/animation/.

And if you want to see what you can do, the "picked pens" on CodePen never disappoint: codepen.io/.

You may have noticed a lot of repetition of CSS properties (like **font**, **color**, and **background**) in this chapter and elsewhere. The next chapter shows you how to remove some of that repetition with CSS variables.

19

CSS Variables

As you start to build more complex websites, your style sheets will also grow in complexity. Luckily, there are ways to manage complex CSS and get it under control.

In Chapter 20, you will be introduced to *CSS preprocessors*, which are essentially programming languages that are mostly CSS with added functionality. But if you're not yet ready to dive into something like that, CSS natively supports variables, which will go a long way toward taming your CSS.

TIP The official specification name for variables is *custom properties*: developer.mozilla. org/en-US/docs/Web/CSS/--*.

What Are Variables?

So far, as you've written CSS you've needed to manually type styles each time you want to use them. For example, let's say you have an accent color on your website of **#EB1DFE** ( ). You can apply that to buttons, borders, links, and so on. But for each instance, you'll need to type **#EB1DFE**.

But what if you decide to change it to a different accent color? You'll need to find all the references and manually change them. More so, if you want to change only some of them, a file-wide Find/Replace won't work. But there's a better way. You can use *custom properties*, which are often referred to as *variables*.

Variables act like placeholders; they are a way to store information in order to reference it later, and they are a part of every programming language. With variables, there are two components: the name and the value. When you define (or set) a variable, you assign it a value. Then you can use the variable name instead of the value.

In CSS, to reference a variable, you use the function **var()** and place the variable between parentheses. A *function* in this instance is a way to execute a piece of code that tells the browser, "Grab the value of the variable and use that."

> **TIP** By convention, the names of variables use *camel case*. That means each word in the name except the first is capitalized, and there are no spaces between the words: **thisIsCamelCase**.

The beauty of variables is you only need to change the accent color value in one place, and it will update everywhere.

To make a CSS variable assignment:

1. In your style sheet, at the top, type **:root {**.

   This defines the scope of the variable (more on that later).

2. Now it's time to make the assignment. Type **--accentColor: #EB1DFE;**.

   Every variable needs to start with a double hyphen (**--**). The name should describe what it's representing.

   The value can be any valid CSS value. In this case, it's a hex representation of a color.

3. Type **}**.

4. On the next line, type **a {** to assign the style to links.

5. Type **color: var(--accentColor);**.

6. Type **}**.

This makes all your links a nice pink (**FIGURE 19.1**).

To see the full syntax, check out **CODE 19.1**.

FIGURE 19.1 A link using the color assigned by a CSS variable

CODE 19.1 The code that creates and uses the variable **--accentColor**

```
:root {
    --accentColor: #EB1DFE;
}

a {
    color: var(--accentColor);
}
```

VIDEO 19.1

Changing Multiple Elements by Changing a Single Variable

Using CodePen, I show you how a single variable change updates multiple elements on a page.

It may seem trivial here, but imagine you've used the color dozens of times through multiple style sheets. It can be a daunting task to remember where the instances are and then update all of them, especially if a simple find and replace won't work—what if you want to keep some of the values but not all of them?

Since variables are native CSS, they work just like any other property or ruleset:

- They cascade, which means they can easily be overwritten.

- They can be manipulated by JavaScript (which is outside the scope of the book).

- They don't require any additional tools to work.

> **TIP** You can also include a fallback value in the `var()` function. This means that if you try to use a variable that has no value assigned to it, a default value will be used. For example, if you write `color: var(--primaryColor, #FF0000);`, the color #FF0000 will be used if the `--primaryColor` variable is not valid.

Variable scope

When you talk about variables, you can't ignore a discussion about *scope*. The scope of a variable determines the context in which it's "visible," or can be referenced. In the accent color task, you used the keyword :root, which means, "The scope of this variable is the entire document." But you could have just as easily used **div** or **p**, making the scope only those elements. You can also change the scope by defining the same variable in a different ruleset (**FIGURE 19.2**).

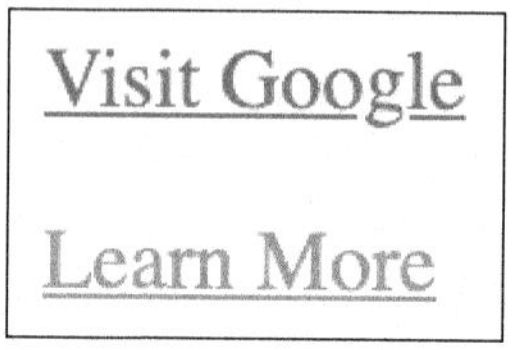

To change the scope of a CSS variable:

Here is your HTML:

```
<main>
<a href="https://google.com">
 Visit Google</a>
</main>
<aside>
    <a href="https://casabona.org">
     Learn More</a>
</aside>
```

1. In your style sheet, type :root {.

2. Type --accentColor: #EB1DFE;.

3. Type }.

4. On a new line, type the name of the element whose property you want to change. In this case, use **aside** {.

5. Type the name of the variable for the property you want to change. For this example, use --accentColor: #008800;.

6. Type }.

7. On a new line, type **a** {.

Visit Google

Learn More

FIGURE 19.2
Changing the scope of a variable changes the styles.

When you change the scope of a variable, you can more succinctly update your rule-sets. Here's a demo on CodePen.

8. Type `color: var(--accentColor);`.

   This single declaration is all that is needed. If the `<a>` tag is the descendant of an `<aside>` element, its `--accentColor` value will be #008800. Otherwise, it will be #EB1DFE.

9. Type `}`.

You can think of variables as phone numbers, where the area code is the scope. Two people in the US can have the same phone number if they aren't in the same area code (just ask anyone whose number is 867-5309, from the Tommy Tutone song "Jenny").

If you don't dial the area code, your local area code is assumed. If you dial the area code, you're changing the scope of the phone number. Variables are the same way.

Spanning Multiple Files

It hasn't been discussed much in this book, but you're not limited to one CSS file per website. You can have multiple CSS files and use them to organize different aspects of your styles.

While there is much debate over what loads faster (one giant CSS file or several smaller CSS files), there is some benefit to using multiple CSS files, especially as it pertains to variables. You can keep all of your variables in a single file—say, `variables.css`—and load it before any other CSS file. You would list this as the first `<link>` reference in your HTML. The browser loads CSS files (and all files) in the order in which it encounters them.

Then you can cleanly define variables and their scopes and leave the actual rulesets to a separate CSS file (often named `main.css` or `style.css`).

Simplifying Styles with Variables

The ability to change the scope of CSS variables means you can write more succinct CSS. In the scope task, you saw that there were two variable definitions but only one ruleset for the `<a>` tag. This doesn't just apply to element rulesets. You can change variables through media queries too.

This gives you the chance to define nearly all of your styles early in your CSS, without the need to create large sections of code dedicated to media queries. If you change only the variable values, and not entire styles, your media queries will be much shorter, and there's less work for the browser to do, making your website more efficient.

To create a grid using variables and media queries:

Here's the HTML code you're working with:

```
<div>
    <p>This is grid item 1</p>
    <p>This is grid item 2</p>
    <p>This is grid item 3</p>
</div>
```

1. At the top of your style sheet, type `:root {`.

   This line will define the default values for our CSS variables. We start mobile first, so the grid template will be a single column.

2. On a new line, type `--gridTemplate: 1fr;`.

   Remember here that we are only defining the variable, and not the style. That comes later.

3. On a new line, type `--gridGap: 0;`.

4. On a new line, type `}`.

5. On a new line, type `@media screen and (min-width: 600px) {`.

   This is the only reference to a media query, and its sole purpose is to change the values of the variables, not to assign actual styles. At the 600px breakpoint, the variables will change.

6. On a new line, type `:root {`.

   Since the scope of the variables in step 1 is `:root`, we need to reference that same scope in the media query.

7. On a new line, type `--gridTemplate: 1fr 1fr 1fr;`.

   At 600px, we want the grid layout to change from one column to three columns, so we're changing the value of the variable.

8. On a new line, type `--gridGap: 10px;`.

   The same goes for the gap between columns. Changing the variable here will change the styles at the 600px breakpoint.

9. On a new line, type `}` to close the `:root` variable declarations.

10. On a new line, type `}` to close the media query.

11. On a new line, type `div {`.

    This is the only `div` ruleset we'll need, thanks to CSS variables.

12. On a new line, type `display: grid;`.

13. On a new line, type `grid-gap: var(--gridGap);`.

    The variable `--gridGap` will change based on the media query declaration above, making this `div` responsive without explicitly putting it into its own media query ruleset.

Taking the grid task a step further, this video shows you how to make a complex layout using CSS variables.

This is grid item 1

This is grid item 2

This is grid item 3

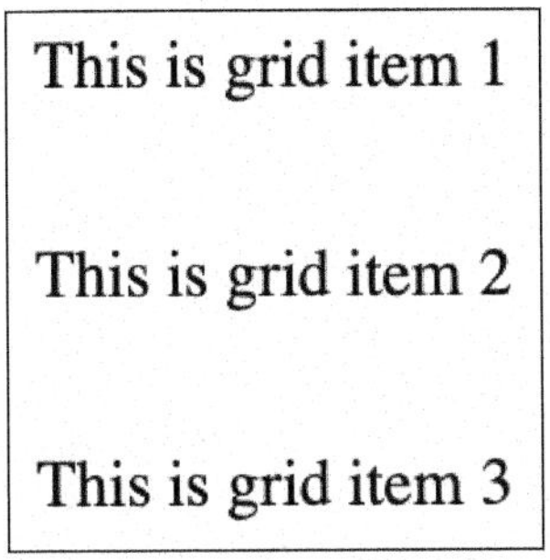

FIGURE 19.3 The CSS variables produce a single column of grid items when the viewport is less than 600px wide.

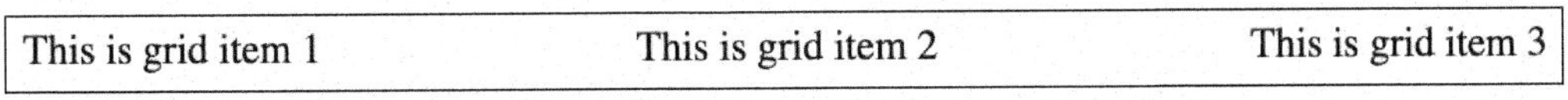

This is grid item 1   This is grid item 2   This is grid item 3

FIGURE 19.4 Once the viewport is 600px or wider, the values of the CSS variables change, creating a three-column grid.

14. On a new line, type `grid-template-columns:` → `var(--gridTemplate);`.

Same goes for `--gridTemplate`. This value will change based on the breakpoint.

15. On a new line, type `}` to close the **div**.

The resulting code stacks paragraph elements inside the div in a single column when the viewport is narrow (**FIGURE 19.3**). If the viewport is widened beyond 600px, the paragraphs are distributed into three columns (**FIGURE 19.4**). See **CODE 19.2** for the complete code listing.

For comparison's sake, **CODE 19.3** shows the code you'd have to write if you didn't use CSS variables.

CODE 19.2 This concise code uses variables to create a responsive grid layout.

```
:root {
    --gridTemplate: 1fr;
    --gridGap: 0;
}
@media screen and (min-width: 600px) {
    :root {
        --gridTemplate: 1fr 1fr 1fr;
        --gridGap: 10px
    }
}
div {
    display: grid;
    grid-template-columns:
    → var(--gridTemplate);
    grid-gap: var(--gridGap);
}
```

CODE 19.3 The code to create a very simple grid without CSS variables. This quickly gets much more complicated with bigger grids or more breakpoints!

```
div {
    display: grid;
    grid-gap: 0;
    grid-template-columns: 1fr;
}

@media screen and (min-width: 600px) {
    div {
        grid-gap: 10px;
        grid-template-columns: 1fr 1fr 1fr;
    }
}
```

Calculations with Variables

Aside from the **var()** function, CSS also provides the **calc()** function, which allows you to perform basic arithmetic operations in CSS. You can do the following:

- Addition with the plus sign (+)
- Subtraction with the minus sign (-)
- Multiplication with the asterisk (*)
- Division with the forward slash (/)

This allows you to include calculations either in new variables or on the fly—that is, in the property definition. One big benefit is that you can mathematically define padding and properly scale font sizes, making your styles more consistent.

In other words, we can size various properties proportionally derived from a couple of base values.

To proportionally change a variable with `calc()`:

This HTML is straightforward:

```
<h1>This is a heading</h1>
<p>This is body text!</p>
```

1. At the top of your style sheet, type `:root {`.

2. On a new line, type `--fontSize: 1.25rem;`.

3. On a new line, type `--fontSizeHeading: calc(`.

    This opens up the **calc()** function for us.

4. Type `var(--fontSize) * 3`.

    This is the operation. Remember that we need to use the **var()** function to get the value of `--fontSize`. Then we multiply it by 3. We'll use this calculated value for **h1**, and we want it to be three times as large as the body's font size.

Manipulating Variables with JavaScript

Though JavaScript is generally outside the scope of this book, it's worth talking about it in the context of variables.

One of the most powerful aspects of CSS variables is their ability to be manipulated by JavaScript. This allows you to make changes to variables, and therefore to your layout and styles, in real time and on the fly.

Perhaps you want to change the background color based on how long a user has been on your site. You can change the CSS variable that controls the background, based on a JavaScript counter.

As you begin to master HTML and CSS, learning JavaScript is the next logical step, and this is one more reason to check it out.

CODE 19.4 The CSS that uses `calc()` to create a heading size proportional to the body font size

```
:root {
    --fontSize: 1.25em;
    --fontSizeHeading: calc(var(
      --fontSize) * 3 );
}

body {
    font-size: var(--fontSize);
}

h1 {
    font-size: var(--fontSizeHeading);
}
```

5. Close the function with `);`.

6. On a new line, type `}`.

7. On a new line, type **body** `{`.

8. On a new line, type
   `font-size: var(--fontSize);`.

9. On a new line, type `}`.

10. On a new line, type **h1** `{`.

11. Type
    `font-size: var(--fontSizeHeading);`.

    You could also use
    `font-size: calc(var(--fontSize) * 3);`
    and forgo defining a second variable.

12. On a new line, type `}`.

You can see the full CSS in **CODE 19.4**. The result is that the body copy is slightly bigger than the browser default, and the <h1> tag is three times as big as the body copy (**FIGURE 19.5**).

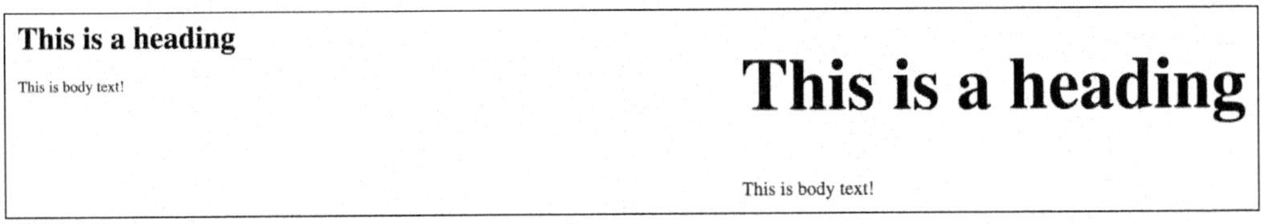

This is a heading

This is body text!

This is a heading

This is body text!

FIGURE 19.5 On the left are the default sizes for Chrome. On the right, the new sizes, including the heading size resulting from the `calc()` function.

Wrapping Up

CSS variables can change the way you write CSS, especially as it becomes more complex. Between overriding it easily and making calculations, you can do some pretty powerful stuff.

And there's something else that can take your CSS to the next level: preprocessors.

CSS Preprocessors

CSS includes functions that make writing rulesets easier, but there are even more powerful tools that can streamline and optimize your CSS code.

These tools are called *CSS preprocessors*, and they operate at a level above CSS. That is, they take what you write and convert it to CSS. Preprocessors add features that otherwise wouldn't exist in CSS, the ability to reuse rulesets easily without copying and pasting, and loops (a way to automatically write code based on a set of criteria). Let's take a closer look.

How CSS Preprocessors Work

A CSS preprocessor is essentially a programming language that produces valid CSS. You write in the unique syntax of the preprocessor (which you'll learn about in this chapter), and the preprocessor takes what you write and converts it into CSS.

Doing this allows the preprocessors to add new features to CSS without changing how the browser works. Think of it this way: if you want more storage space in your laptop, you're probably not going to crack it open to replace the hard drive—you'll buy an external hard drive. It sits on the outside of your computer, but it still offers more space for you.

CSS preprocessors act similarly. They add more features you can use to write CSS without cracking open the browser to add the support. And the beauty of most preprocessors is that they look enough like CSS that if you already know CSS you can quickly get started using one.

Why use a preprocessor over native CSS?

With CSS variables, CSS Grid, Flexbox, and the continued evolution of CSS, the gap between native CSS and preprocessors is closing (**FIGURE 20.1**).

Still, preprocessors offer a number of benefits over native CSS:

- Easier nesting and cascading. Instead of writing out the entire selector (like `div.wrapper main section p.alert`), you can nest a selector inside another one to create a visual hierarchy similar to HTML. You'll learn more about this later.

- Repeatable/reusable rulesets. You saw this a bit with variables, but preprocessors allow you to programmatically generate CSS rulesets. For example, instead of manually writing the calculations for scaled headings, as you did in Chapter 19, you can write a few lines of code saying, "Starting with **h1**, decrease the size of each heading by 20 percent."

- Built-in functions. Easily generate color schemes, perform advanced math operations, and more with built-in functions.

- Organization. Create multiple preprocessor files and compile them into a single CSS file.

- Auto-prefixing. Automatically prefix your CSS properties without having to add them manually every time.

Your mileage will vary based on the preprocessor you choose. On that note, while there are a few different preprocessors to choose from, this book uses Sass/SCSS.

```
$bgColor: #EB1DFE;

body {
    background: $bgColor;

    h1 {
        background: #FFFFFF;
        padding: 15px;
    }
}
```

```
body {
    background: #EB1DFE;
}
body h1 {
    background: #FFFFFF;
    padding: 15px;
}
```

FIGURE 20.1 What Sass syntax looks like, and the CSS it outputs

TIP This chapter is a primer on preprocessors; it is a little less hands-on than previous chapters because entire books have been written about specific preprocessors. But as you continue your web design education, it's highly likely you'll come across one.

Popular CSS Preprocessors

There are many CSS preprocessors to choose from, but there are two very popular preprocessors: Sass (sass-lang.com) and Less (lesscss.org).

They differ in nuances of features and syntax, but if you're starting from zero, either one should be fine for you.

Statistically (at the time of this writing), Sass is a lot more popular, which means you'll likely find more tutorials, examples, and support.

If neither appeals to you, there's also Stylus (stylus-lang.com), which has been praised for its simple and clean syntax.

Getting Started with Sass

When deciding whether it's worthwhile to use Sass or any other CSS preprocessor, keep in mind that you will need to add a compiler to your workflow. Throughout this book, you've been able to write HTML and CSS in your text editor, save it, and immediately open the file in your browser. With Sass there's an extra step involved: the Sass file needs to be compiled.

Before you get started, you should know there are *technically* two versions of Sass you can write: Sass and SCSS. The main difference is the syntax. Sass looks more like a programming language, and SCSS looks more like CSS. This book uses SCSS. All files written with SCSS use the file name extension `.scss`.

For the purposes of this book, there are two ways you can get started with Sass:

- You can use CodePen. This does not require installing anything additional on your computer. You can practice writing it, see the results, and then determine later if you'd like to continue with it. As an added bonus, you can copy the compiled CSS and paste it right into your own `.css` files.

- You can install an app that compiles Sass. This allows you to write Sass files and create CSS files, which you can then use on your websites.

Here's how to do both.

To write Sass using CodePen:

1. Go to codepen.io.

2. Do one of the following to create a Pen (a scratchpad for code snippets):

    If you already have an account and are logged in to it, click Pen in the left sidebar under the Create heading (**FIGURE 20.2**).

    If you do not have an account or you are logged out, click the Start Coding button.

3. In the new Pen, find the CSS box, and click the Open CSS Settings button; it has a cog icon ( ).

4. In the dialog box that opens, click the CSS Preprocessor menu (**FIGURE 20.3**).

5. Choose SCSS from the CSS Preprocessor menu.

6. Click Close. Now the CSS box should be labeled CSS (SCSS).

    You're able to type Sass syntax into it now.

7. Let's start small. You'll learn about variables later in the chapter, but for now, know that the syntax is a dollar sign (**$**) and the variable name. Create a variable for background color by typing **$bgColor: #EB1DFE;**.

    This creates a variable assignment where **$bgColor** has the value **#EB1DFE**.

8. On a new line, type **body {**.

9. On a new line, type **background: $bgColor;**.

    The background of the pen should immediately turn a dark pink.

FIGURE 20.2 Two ways of creating a new Pen: first, for users logged into an account; second, for users who aren't logged in.

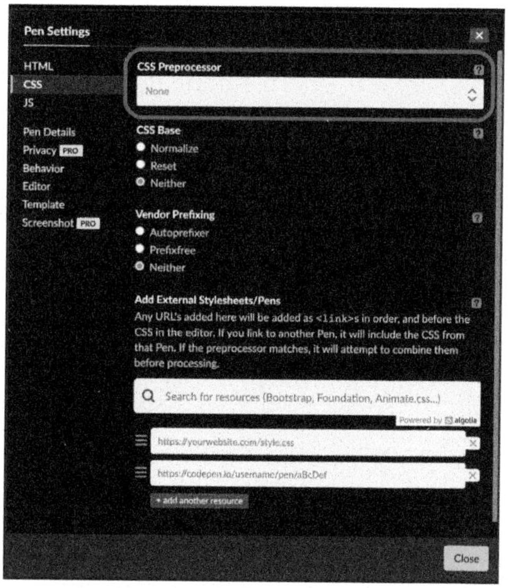

FIGURE 20.3 The CSS Settings dialog box on CodePen

10. On a new line, type }.

11. To view the compiled CSS, click the arrow button on the right (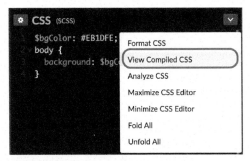).

12. Choose View Compiled CSS (**FIGURE 20.4**).

Your SCSS code is replaced with compiled CSS, and "Compiled" appears in the title bar of the CSS box.

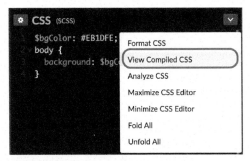

FIGURE 20.4 The menu that allows you to display compiled CSS in the pen

To write Sass using an app on your computer:

1. Go to scout-app.io.

2. Under Sass for Web Designers, download the version of Sass for your computer's operating system (**FIGURE 20.5**).

For macOS, click the OSX button; for a PC, click Windows.

3. Install the application.

When the installation is complete, you'll add a project to Scout.

FIGURE 20.5 The Scout-App website, showing the download buttons

4. On your desktop, create a new website folder. I've called mine **website**. Then create two new subfolders named **scss** and **css**.

5. Launch Scout-App, and click the folder icon under Import Projects (**FIGURE 20.6**).

A file navigation folder opens.

6. Select the website folder you created in step 4.

7. On the Add Project screen (**FIGURE 20.7**), click in the Input Folder field and navigate to the scss folder you just created.

Scout-App is now watching the input folder for any changes.

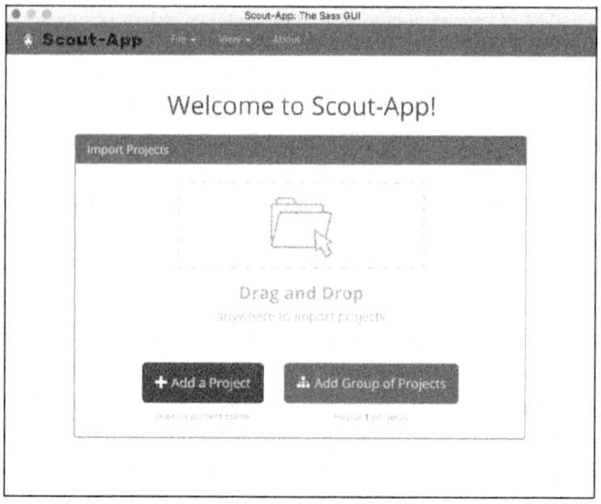

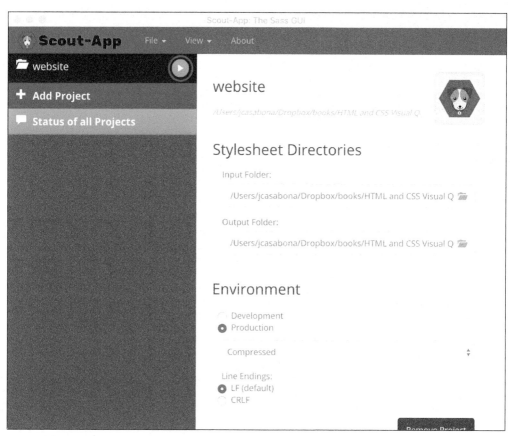

FIGURE 20.6 You can load an existing website into Scout-App by dragging its folder into the Import Projects area or by clicking the folder icon.

FIGURE 20.7 The Scout-App Project screen is where you manage your projects.

8. Click in the Output Folder field, and select the css folder you just created.

   Scout-App will automatically save any changes from the input folder into this output folder.

9. Test this out. In a text editing program, create a new file (it doesn't need any content) and save it as **style.scss** in the scss folder.

10. Check the css folder. You should now have a new file named `style.css`.

   If you don't, you may need to press the play button next to the project name.

TIP One great feature of Sass is that it can compile a *minified* version of your CSS—meaning without spaces or line breaks. This reduces the file size and lets browsers download it faster. You will learn more about the advantages of this in Chapter 23.

▶ **VIDEO 20.1**
Configuring Sass on Your Computer

If you want to write Sass and generate CSS from it, you'll need a Sass compiler. Here's how to install one on your machine.

Writing Sass

At the beginning of this chapter I mentioned that there are full books and courses created just for Sass. But there are a few features worth highlighting:

- Nesting selectors
- Variables that don't rely on browser support
- Math operators
- Extending rulesets

Nesting CSS selectors in Sass

One of the cooler features of Sass is its ability to reformat selectors in nested form, which saves you from having to write out increasingly long selectors for specificity. The benefit, besides a better visual representation of the family tree than in normal CSS, is that you can include declarations alongside the dependents you want. For example, this Sass code:

```
.wrapper {
    background: #000000;
    color: #FFFFFF;
    main {
        aside {
            border: 1px solid #FFFFFF;
        }
    }
}
```

... compiles to this in CSS:

```
.wrapper {
    background: #000000;
    color: #FFFFFF;
}
.wrapper main aside {
    border: 1px solid #FFFFFF;
}
```

Notice that the CSS targets **aside** elements that are children of **main** and grandchildren of **.wrapper**. By writing the ruleset as nested selectors, it reads, "**aside** is inside **main**, and both of them are inside **.wrapper**." This ensures specificity and makes your CSS easier to read. And as your CSS grows, you won't have to worry about specificity as much—as long as you have the proper nesting.

An important character for nesting is the ampersand (**&**). It serves as a placeholder for the parent selector. So **.wrapper main** would become **& main**. This is helpful, as it allows you to use the parent (or outer) selector in more advanced ways, like for pseudo-selectors. Here's how to use the parent selector.

To target :first-child while nesting in Sass:

1. In your **style.scss** file, type **p {**.

2. Type **color: #880000;**.

3. On a new line, indent and type **&:first-child {**.

4. Type color: #008800;.

5. Type **font-size: 1.5rem;**.

6. Type **}**.

7. Type **}**.

The resulting Sass will look like this:

```
p {
    color: #880000;

    &:first-child {
        color: #008800;
        font-size: 1.5rem;
    }
}
```

It will be compiled to this CSS:

```
p {
    color: #880000;
}
p:first-child {
    color: #008800;
    font-size: 1.5rem;
}
```

If you're using Scout-App, your output might look a little different. Make sure that in your project settings, Production is selected and Expanded is chosen from the Output Style menu (**FIGURE 20.8**).

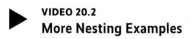

FIGURE 20.8 The settings in Scout-App that will give you fully expanded CSS output

▶ **VIDEO 20.2**
More Nesting Examples

I demonstrate more examples of nesting that use the **&** feature, as well as some media queries.

Variables and mathematical operators

In Chapter 19, you learned about CSS custom properties (variables) and functions. While variables in Sass became popular before the advent of custom properties in CSS, the preference for web developers today is to use CSS's built-in variables.

Still, Sass variables are worth covering, as you'll likely see them if you continue to develop with Sass.

Variables and math in Sass work very similarly to native CSS variables. The main difference is the syntax. To define a variable in Sass, instead of using two hyphens (--), you use a dollar sign ($):

```
$bgColor: #EB1DFE;
```

Then you just type the variable name, as opposed to using the `var()` function, like in CSS:

```
body {
    background: $bgColor;
}
```

Most of the same benefits (like the ability to change multiple values at the same time by reassigning a variable) apply to Sass variables, with a few exceptions:

- They cannot be changed in real time.
- They cannot be manipulated by JavaScript.
- They don't cascade.

To define and use a variable in Sass:

1. At the top of your `style.scss` file, before any other declarations, type `$fontSize: 1.25rem;`.
2. On a new line, type `body {`.
3. Type `font-size: $fontSize;`.
4. Type `}`.
5. Save the file.

6. Open the `style.css` file and examine the compiled CSS. It should look like this:

```
body {font-size: 1.25rem;}
```

While this is a single declaration using a variable, you can imagine using the `$fontSize` variable in several places. If that ever needs to change, all you'd need to do is reassign `$fontSize` and then recompile the Sass.

The arithmetic operations in Sass are the same as in CSS (+, -, *, /) and there is one more: *modulo* or "remainder," and that's represented by a percent sign (%).

The modulo operator divides two numbers, but instead of returning a result, it returns the remainder. For example, `15 % 2` returns the value `1`.

Using the same Sass from the previous task, you can use a multiplier on the font size.

To increase font size with multiplication:

1. In your `style.scss` file, on a new line after the closing } on the body ruleset, type `h1 {`.
2. Type `font-size: $fontSize * 3;`.
3. Type `}`.

The compiled CSS will look like this:

```
h1 {font-size: 3.75rem; }
```

Notice that you don't have to specify the unit on the multiplier—it will use the unit provided in the variable. If you use different units in arithmetic operators (like `rem` * `px`), you will get an error.

> **TIP** Math in Sass doesn't stop with arithmetic operators. There are also built-in math functions for rounding, min, and max. Learn more here at sass-lang.com/documentation/modules/math.

Repeatable rulesets with @extend

In CSS, variables make it easier to reuse repeatable properties, as you saw in Chapter 19. But what if you could do it with entire rulesets? With the **extend** rule in Sass, you can! The **extend** rule allows one selector to use (or inherit) the ruleset from another selector. It's written @extend *[selector]*.

To use @extend for alerts:

1. In your **style.scss**, file, create the class you want to extend. For this task, it will be a class that's used for alert boxes. Type .alert {.

2. Type background: #880000;.

3. Type color: #FFFFFF;.

4. Type padding: 10px;.

5. Type text-align: center;.

6. Type }.

7. Now it's time to create the class that extends .alert. This class will change the alert slightly, showing a different background color to denote a "friendly," less urgent message. Type .alert-good {.

8. Type @extend .alert;.

   This tells Sass that .alert-good should use all of the rules defined in .alert.

9. Type background: #000088;.

   This overrides the original rules to show the change in .alert-good. In this instance, it's only the background color.

10. Type }.

11. Save the file and examine the compiled CSS file (**CODE 20.1**).

With **extend** rules, you don't need to copy and paste or otherwise rewrite rulesets! Sass also neatly compiles classes that use **extend** rules to prevent code bloat. Notice how it combines the selectors into a comma-separated list instead of repeating the rulesets for each selector (**FIGURE 20.9**).

CODE 20.1 The resulting CSS after using extend for the .alert and .alert-good classes

```
.alert, .alert-good {
    background: #880000;
    color: #ffffff;
    padding: 10px;
    text-align: center;
}
.alert-good {
    background: #000088;
}
```

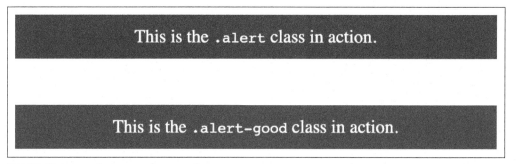

FIGURE 20.9 The .alert and .alert-good classes in use

You can also use multiple extends in a ruleset, which allows you to include multiple definitions without having to write them (**FIGURE 20.10**). The class will simply inherit the styles from both selectors. So if you have a class called `.big`:

```
.big {
    font-size: 3rem;
}
```

You can do something like this, using the Sass from the previous task:

```
.alert-good {
    @extend .alert;
    @extend .big
    background: #000088;
}
```

The resulting CSS can be seen in **CODE 20.2**.

Finally, you can also write placeholder classes that exist only to be extended. There are no references to placeholder classes in the compiled CSS. This is strictly for you to use in Sass. Placeholders are great if you have a style you want to use across multiple rulesets, but you don't want those rulesets associated with a usable class, which would muck up your CSS.

You define a placeholder class with the percent sign (%). The % is an indicator in Sass that you're using a placeholder class and that it should not be compiled as a usable class in CSS.

To write a placeholder class:

1. In your **style.scss** file, type % followed by the name of the placeholder class you want to define. In this case, use `notify {`.
2. Type `margin: 0 auto;`.
3. Type `padding: 10px;`.
4. Type `text-align: center;`.
5. Type `}`.
6. Type `.alert {`.
7. Type `@extend %notify;`.
8. Type `background: #880000;`.
9. Type `color: #FFFFFF;`.
10. Type `}`.
11. Type `.error {`.
12. Type `@extend %notify;`.
13. Type `background: #FEB728; (`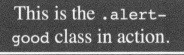`).`

FIGURE 20.10 The `.alert-good` class is extending both `.alert` and `.big`.

CODE 20.2 The results of `.alert-good` extending two other classes. Notice that `.alert-good` is referenced in both the `.alert` and `.big` declarations.

```
.alert, .alert-good {
    background: #880000;
    color: #ffffff;
    padding: 10px;
    text-align: center;
}

.big, .alert-good {
    font-size: 3rem;
}

.alert-good {
    background: #000088;
}
```

14. Type }.

15. Save the `.scss` file and examine the compiled CSS (**CODE 20.3**).

With placeholder classes, applying that class name to an element (**notify** in this case) will do nothing.

Notice there's no reference to **%notify**, and that all the properties from **%notify** are grouped together, leaving only the custom properties in their own rulesets (**FIGURE 20.11**).

> **TIP** There's one more aspect of Sass that's important: **mixin**. It is similar to **extend**, but there are some important differences to understand. I chose to include **extend** here because it's more in line with what you've already learned. If you want to learn about **mixin**, you can do so at sass-lang.com/documentation/at-rules/mixin.

Wrapping Up

This was only a brief introduction to CSS preprocessors, and you've only scratched the surface with Sass. But it's important to know about as you continue to build websites, and you're very likely to come across it.

With that, the CSS section of this book is complete. From here, you'll learn important concepts and tools to help you build better websites. But there's one important step to take first: we need to get your website online!

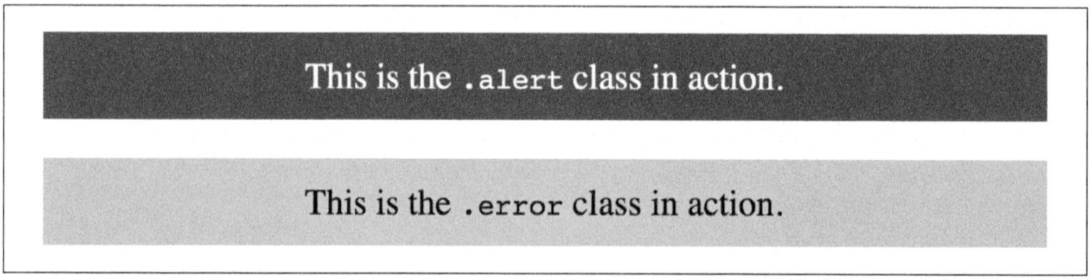

CODE 20.3 These classes were generated from a placeholder class in Sass.

```
.alert, .error {
    margin: 0 auto;
    padding: 10px;
    text-align: center;
}
.alert {
    background: #880000;
    color: #ffffff;
}
.error {
    background: #feb728;
}
```

This is the .alert class in action.

This is the .error class in action.

FIGURE 20.11 The .alert and .error classes generated from the %notify placeholder class

Getting Your Website Online

You have the HTML down. You have the CSS down. Your files are nice and organized. How do you show it to people?

Getting your website online requires two components you saw all the way back in Chapter 2: a domain and a server. Once you have those, there's a clear process you'll walk through to get your website online. Then you can send it to everyone you know!

Choosing Hosting and a Domain

The time has come for you to make some decisions. You need to purchase both a domain and web hosting for your website. When you purchase a plan from a hosting company, the company provides you with the technologies and services that you need for your website to be seen on the internet.

At the most basic level, your hosting provides you with a publicly accessible space on a server that stores and manages connections to your website. People will connect to your website via the domain.

There are lots of different hosting companies. Many specialize in specific types of websites, but any hosting you get will be able to serve up HTML and CSS. So how do you choose?

Evaluating hosting

When choosing the right hosting for your needs, there are a few ways to evaluate them. While there isn't a "one-size-fits-all" hosting company, drawing up a list of your needs will help you narrow down the requirements a bit. So what do you look for?

- Can you talk to a person? If you're going to be setting up and supporting your own website, you should make sure the hosting company you go with provides good technical support! Great documentation and videos are fine, but chat and phone support are incredibly important as well.

- Will there be automatic backups? This isn't a deal breaker as far as choosing the plan, but it's important to know whether you will need to make your own backups or if they handle that for you.

- Will they help make your site secure? This can come in many forms, including site monitoring, free SSL (see the "Secure Domains" sidebar), protection from cyber attacks, and repairing your website if it's hacked.

TIP Many people use the term *SSL* when speaking of website security in general, even though SSL technically refers only to the Secure Sockets Layer cryptographic protocol. That technology itself has been deprecated in favor of the newer Transport Layer Security (TLS) protocol.

Pricing can also be a factor. You generally get what you pay for, and at this stage of the game, you probably don't need anything too crazy, especially if you're still honing your skills. There are two hosts I'd recommend:

- Web Hosting for Students: If you need something really cheap to $25/year (**FIGURE 21.1**): webhosting forstudents.com/.

- SiteGround: Once you're ready to publish your site to the world (also known as "going live"), you'll need to move on from a basic service like Web Hosting for Students. SiteGround is versatile and works well for lots of types of sites (**FIGURE 21.2**). If you use the link from this book, you'll get a special offer for your first year: casabona.org/go/siteground/.

FIGURE 21.1 Web Hosting for Students

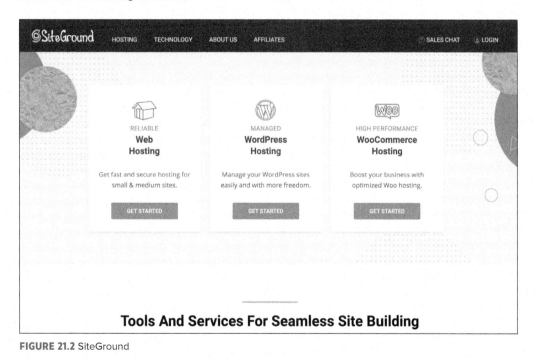

FIGURE 21.2 SiteGround

Choosing a domain

Usually, you can purchase domains from the same place you get your hosting, but it's not always recommended in case one day you decide you want to change hosts.

Certain companies offer one free domain with an account, but if you'd like to purchase a domain separately, which I recommended, hover.com is a great service. They offer a number of different top-level domains (TLDs) from .com and .org to .io, .me, and .xyz.

Tips on choosing a domain name:

- Make it unique and easy to remember. You want your domain to stand out, but not so much that it's difficult to remember when someone tries to visit.

- Make it easy to type and speak. A domain with a tricky name will send people to the wrong place or dissuade them from visiting at all. On that same token, try to avoid numbers and hyphens. They are very hard to speak (is the number typed out or is it the digit?), and hyphens are often forgotten about.

- Try to acquire a name in the .com domain first. About 70 percent of domains use the TLD .com, even as the number of TLDs grows. That means that most people will have an easier time remembering a .com domain and will likely try that first.

- Make it as short as possible. This goes back to making it easy to remember, speak, and type—joesbakery.com is easier to remember (and spell) than joesdowningtownbakery.com.

- Avoid copyrighted names. Make sure you're not using a copyrighted term in your domain. The last thing you want to do is change it because you've infringed someone's copyright. An example is *wordpress*. According to the WordPress Foundation, who holds the copyright for WordPress, you cannot use *wordpress* in a domain name.

- Be aware of word combinations. This sounds silly and somewhat juvenile, but you don't want to accidentally create a vulgar domain.

Secure Domains

You might notice that some domains use the http:// prefix and others use https://. The difference is that https:// indicates that the site accepts connections using the Hypertext Transfer Protocol Secure, which in turn employs Transport Layer Security, or TLS. In general conversation, TLS is often lumped in together with its predecessor, SSL. A domain using HTTPS will be offered a TLS certificate.

This means any data sent to and from your website will be transmitted securely; you will want this if you're processing payments, taking user information, or logging in with a username and password.

There are also search engine optimization (SEO) benefits. Google uses https as a "ranking signal"—something it uses to evaluate how high to rank your website in search results. In Chrome, it warns users when https is not in use.

This is configured by the server, and SiteGround offers free TLS/SSL certificates through Let's Encrypt.

- Snag the matching social media if you can. Matching domain names with social media accounts takes away the guesswork for users.

Keep in mind that *this is not a checklist*. If you have the perfect domain but it uses a number, use the number. Since you can point two domains to the same website, grab it spelled out and with a digit. If a .com isn't available, buy the .org instead.

The goal is to do the best you can, and most of all make it relevant to your website's topic.

One Note on Email

"Do I get an email address?" is a common question when purchasing a domain and hosting. Email is a separate service and therefore not always included.

You will usually find email offered as an add-on to hosting, but there are alternative solutions available. Hover.com offers email forwarding, for example.

You can also sign up for something like Google Apps for Business, though this requires extra setup.

To register your domain:

1. Visit hover.com.
2. Use the search box to type in your domain idea (**FIGURE 21.3**).

   You can include or exclude a TLD. Hover will still show you a full list of available domains.
3. Press Enter or click the search icon.
4. You'll be taken to a screen of available domains. Click the plus sign next to the one you want.
5. Click the Shopping Cart button in the top right (**FIGURE 21.4**).
6. Go through the checkout process and create your account!

▶ **VIDEO 21.1**
Registering a Domain

Here's the entire process, start to finish, of registering a domain with hover.com.

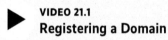

hover

DOMAIN PRICING   EMAIL   BLOG   WEBMAIL   ABOUT US   HELP

FIND A DOMAIN   TRANSFER   RENEW   SIGN UP   SIGN IN

Every great idea deserves a great domain name.

Find a domain for yours.

FIGURE 21.3
The search box on hover.com

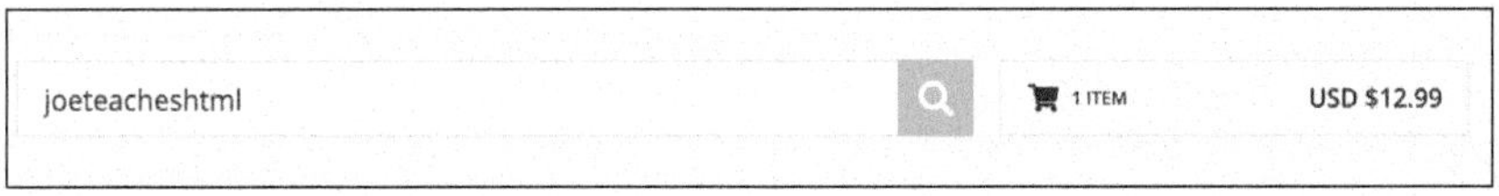

joeteacheshtml   🛒 1 ITEM   USD $12.99

FIGURE 21.4
The Shopping Cart button on hover.com

Connecting your domain

Once you've purchased your domain, if you haven't done it through your hosting company, you'll need to point it to your host. This will vary based on both your host and your domain registrar.

Your host should provide instructions for changing what's called the *DNS,* Domain Name System. You can think of it as a big lookup table (or address book), associating servers with domains.

TIP Once you purchase your domain and point it to a server, it may take 24 to 48 hours to work. This is a process known as *propagation.*

In Video 21.2, you'll see how to do it with Hover and SiteGround.

▶ **VIDEO 21.2**
Pointing Your Domain to SiteGround

Here's how you'll point your domain, registered through Hover, to SiteGround hosting.

Pre-Launch Check

Before taking your site online, you'll want to run through a quick checklist:

1. Is your website folder organized the way you'd like it to be? You will upload it just that way, so double-check.

2. Are all of your links, embeds, and references properly formatted? Make sure that if you're linking to something in a child folder, it's in the right place, and that all images and other media display properly.

3. Are there any references to files that start with `file:` or `C:`? These are absolute links to the files on your computer, and they will not work for anyone other than you once they are uploaded, so make sure to change them to relative links.

It's best to click through each page and make sure everything looks and works as you expect. Once you do that, you're ready to upload your files to your server.

Making Your Site Live

With your hosting and domain purchased, it's time to get your site online—sometimes referred to as *deploying* your site. To do that, you'll need to use something called *File Transfer Protocol*, or FTP.

FTP is how you send files from your computer to the server. To do this, you'll need an FTP program. A free (and widely used) one is FileZilla (**FIGURE 21.5**). You can download it at filezilla-project.org.

Finding FTP Information

Finding the FTP information for your server will vary from host to host. For SiteGround, it's best to use their documentation, just in case it changes after the time of this writing: www.siteground.com/tutorials/ftp/accounts/.

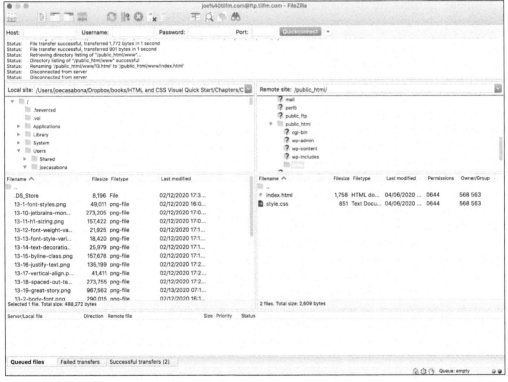

FIGURE 21.5 FileZilla, a popular FTP program

Once you download that, you'll see you need some information:

- Host

  This might also be listed as host address, IP address, domain, or server address.

- Username

- Password

- Port

  A port is a communication gateway in a computer (or other device) defined in software. Usually, individual ports allow for a specific network service to pass through. You can think of it as a docking bay or as a locker that you have the key to.

This information can be found through your hosting account. Look for a section of the documentation that includes "FTP" in the title.

Once you find that information, you'll fill it into the appropriate fields in FileZilla. Then you'll connect to your server. Once you connect, you'll see two panels: on the left-hand side will be your computer; on the right, your server.

To send files to your server with FileZilla:

1. Using the information from your hosting provider, fill in the host, username, password, and port.

2. Click Quickconnect.

3. Once the right panel populates, you'll want to locate the `public_html` or `www` folder. This is where all web-accessible files will live.

   You might already be in that folder. You can use the Remote Site bar above the right panel to see where you are (**FIGURE 21.6**).

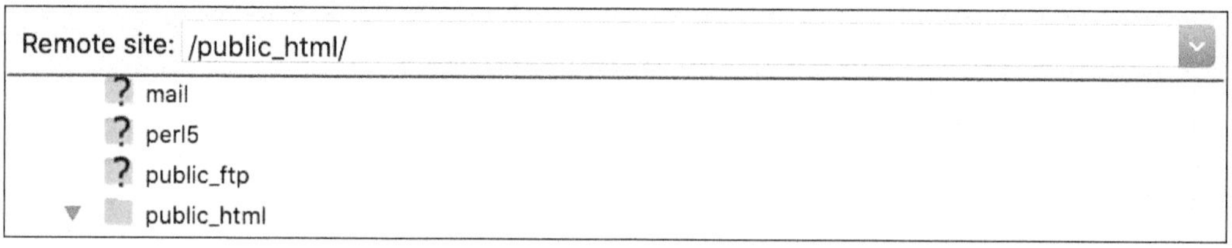

Remote site: /public_html/	
? mail	
? perl5	
? public_ftp	
▼ public_html	

FIGURE 21.6 The Remote Site box in FileZilla will show you where you're uploading files to on your server.

▶ **VIDEO 21.3**
Uploading Your Files

You'll get a quick tour of FileZilla, find your FTP information (if you use SiteGround), and then upload your files.

4. In the panel on the left, make sure you're displaying the contents of your website folder.
5. Drag each file and folder in your website folder from the left panel to the right panel (**FIGURE 21.7**).

   Remember not to just drag the website folder over. This will result in your website files being located in a child folder.
6. Once the files upload, visit your domain with a browser. The files on your website should render properly and display as you designed them!

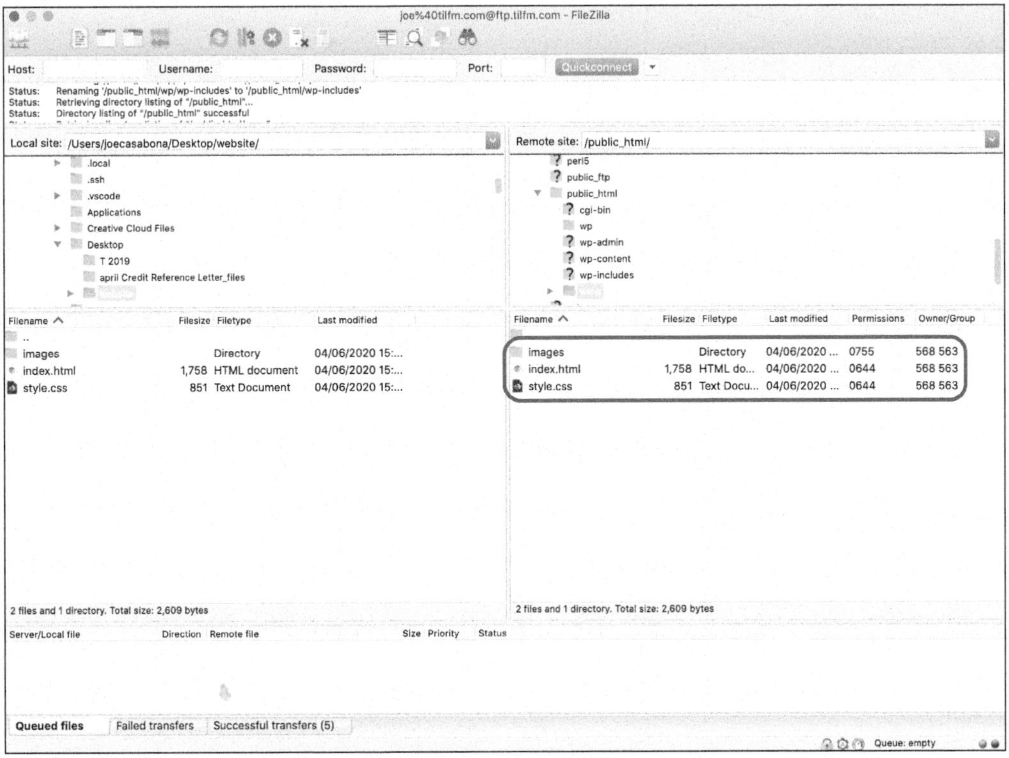

FIGURE 21.7 The state of FileZilla once you upload your site

Testing Your Site

Now that your website is uploaded to the server, it's time to give it a test. Use your browser to visit your site at the domain you purchased, click through all of the links, and make sure your images and other media are showing up properly.

Check each file

If you can, check the site on a computer other than your own to double-check that you didn't leave any absolute links to files on your computer in the HTML documents. Those will still work for *you* (because they're located on your computer), but they won't work for anyone else.

The same goes for all links. You'll want to make sure internal links are still going to your site, and that external links are reaching the intended destination.

Test in common browsers

You'll learn more about testing in the next chapter, but for the purposes of making sure your freshly uploaded site is working properly, you'll want to check in at least a few browsers, like Safari, Edge, Chrome, and Firefox.

As you've seen, browsers handle things differently, and checking your site in multiple browsers will increase the changes that you'll find something that's broken before your users do.

Wrapping Up

Congratulations! You did it! You've uploaded your site to a server and it's now live. But your job is not done.

With all of the basics down, it's time to dive into some advanced but important topics. And the first is testing your site for a multitude of issues, from broken HTML and CSS to device support.

404 Errors

Something you haven't seen yet, for your own site at least, is a 404 error. This is a common error for websites that means "file not found."

If someone tries to visit a file on your website that doesn't exist, the server will send a 404 error, alerting the user that what they're trying to access isn't there.

404 errors can happen because of a typo in a file, because of a file that was never uploaded to the server, or when a link to an external site lacks the `https://` prefix, among other reasons.

Testing Your Website

Now that you know how to build and launch a website, it's time to look at some other areas of web design that you should become familiar with. The first is testing.

Up until now you've been writing some code and checking it in whatever browser you use. Perhaps you've been resizing the browser to see how it looks at different sizes. But there's a bit more you can and should do.

In This Chapter

Why Test Your Website?

You might be wondering why you have to test your website beyond just checking it in your browser to make sure it doesn't look broken. Because websites need to run properly everywhere that a web browser can run (which is basically everywhere), we need to test everywhere. That means testing in major browsers, on different platforms, and at different device screen sizes.

There are also a lot of unknowns in web development. You don't know what users are going to do. You don't know if they have an ad-blocker that's somehow affecting your website. You don't know the speed of their internet connection.

Finally, since HTML is very forgiving—you can write HTML in several different ways and the code will still work for you—you could run into situations where devices other than your own interpret your markup differently. This is especially true if your HTML is not *valid*—that is, written properly to specification, as defined by the DOCTYPE.

When you test your website, you should follow a three-pronged plan:

- Validate your HTML and CSS.
- Test in browsers.
- Test on devices.

As you do those things, you can troubleshoot the problems you encounter using some very helpful tools.

Validating Markup

You want to validate your markup first because it will find any glaring errors in your HTML—absent closing tags, improper usage, or *syntax errors*.

Syntax errors are found in code that's incorrectly typed (**FIGURE 22.1**). Perhaps the closing bracket (>) is missing from a tag or you left a quotation mark out of your HTML. These lapses can cause big errors on your page that could go unnoticed if your browser of choice doesn't flag them.

Luckily, there's a single validator that will check your HTML and CSS and even look for broken links.

The W3C markup validator

The World Wide Web Consortium (W3C) is the international organization that creates the standards and specifications for HTML and CSS.

They also happen to have a markup validator that you can use to make sure your HTML and CSS code meets their standards (**FIGURE 22.2**).

There are three ways to send your markup to the validator:

- Provide the URI (or the domain) of the file.
- Upload the file.
- Copy and paste the markup into a textbox (called *direct input*).

Since the CSS for your site is in a separate file, file upload and direct input will be a little tricky (though not impossible). In general, you should choose the URI option.

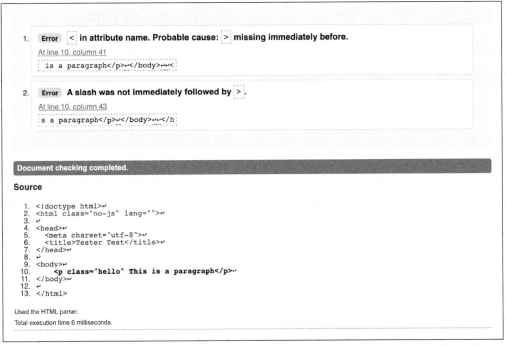

FIGURE 22.1 Invalid code alerts generated by a syntax error in HTML. These are two of the many issues the error causes.

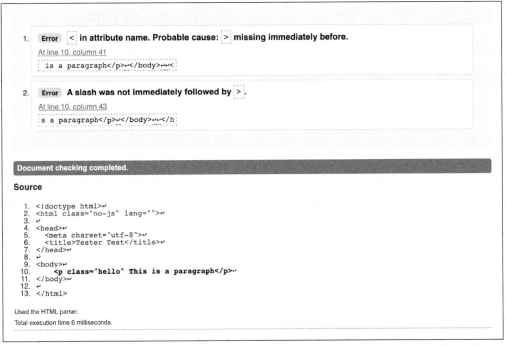

FIGURE 22.2 The W3C Markup Validation Service home page (validator.w3.org/)

To validate your markup:

1. Visit validator.w3.org.

2. Click the Validate by URI tab.

3. Type your website's domain into the Address field.

4. Click the Check button.

5. Review your results and fix the errors. These can break your site in certain browsers.

   You may also see warnings that indicate improper or unnecessary use. You can (and should) fix these, but they do not risk breaking your website.

Though validating your code will likely save you a lot of time by helping you eliminate errors on your website, that doesn't mean it will solve all of your issues. For that, you'll need to do your own testing, starting with different browsers.

▶ **VIDEO 22.1**
Using the W3C Markup Validator to Find and Fix Errors

Now that you know how to use the validator, it's time to see how to use the information it provides to make fixes.

Browser Testing

The low-hanging fruit for testing is browser testing. That's when you view your website in the major browsers to make sure everything looks good. Remember that browsers may not implement new HTML features at the same time, and each browser interprets CSS differently. So you'll want to check your website in the following desktop browsers. You can get three of the four depending on your operating system:

- Chrome (download for macOS/Windows)
- Firefox (download for macOS/Windows)
- Safari (macOS only; comes on macOS)
- Edge (comes on Windows; download for macOS)

For each browser, check each page of your website to make sure things don't look completely broken. That means broken or misaligned layouts, unreadable text, or other things that look completely off.

Websites do not need to look the same in every browser, though! So if there are some minor differences due to padding, that's okay. The CSS reset method mentioned in Chapter 12 should take care of most of those issues, but don't sweat the minor differences too much (**FIGURE 22.3**).

FIGURE 22.3 Comparing a website in Chrome and Safari. The site looks exactly the same in both browsers—huzzah!

Browser and device testing tools

You won't always have access to every browser or to a wealth of devices to test your websites on. Luckily, there are several tools that will help you with your testing when you need it.

The longtime favorite for many pros is BrowserStack (browserstack.com), which will provide real-time testing on actual devices, giving you a more robust and accurate testing environment (**FIGURE 22.4**).

They offer a free tier if you're starting out, but it can get expensive pretty quickly, especially if you need to test for more than 30 minutes. Another option is LambdaTest (lambdatest.com). There is a free tier here that will let you perform a limited amount of real-time browser testing. It should be enough for the types of sites created in this book.

Device Testing

In the world of mobile browsers and the *Internet of Things* (a system that connects almost any kind of object to the internet), it's important to make sure your websites work on mobile devices and on networks with different internet speeds.

While BrowserStack is a great option for doing browser testing to test on browsers and devices you don't natively have access to, it's important for you to test on devices you're physically using as well (even if it's not all of them). You'll want to make sure that your site:

- Resizes correctly on a real screen
- Loads quickly
- Is using supported features or appropriate fallbacks

FIGURE 22.4 Testing a website with BrowserStack

It's important to use real devices for this because although you can check actual devices through your computer on BrowserStack or by emulating devices (using a computer-generated version of the device), there's nothing like the real thing.

What you should test

There is a seemingly infinite number of combinations of devices, operating systems, and connection speeds, and it's impossible to test all of them. So what do you do?

For devices, you should check a resource like Device Atlas, which will tell you the most popular mobile devices by country (deviceatlas.com/device-data/explorer/).

On the actual devices, you should test the built-in browser. You should look up what the most popular browsers are to make sure you're covering the bases. Statcounter has good data for this: gs.statcounter.com/ (**FIGURE 22.5**).

You'll want to test the most popular browsers and devices at least, to make sure everything is working.

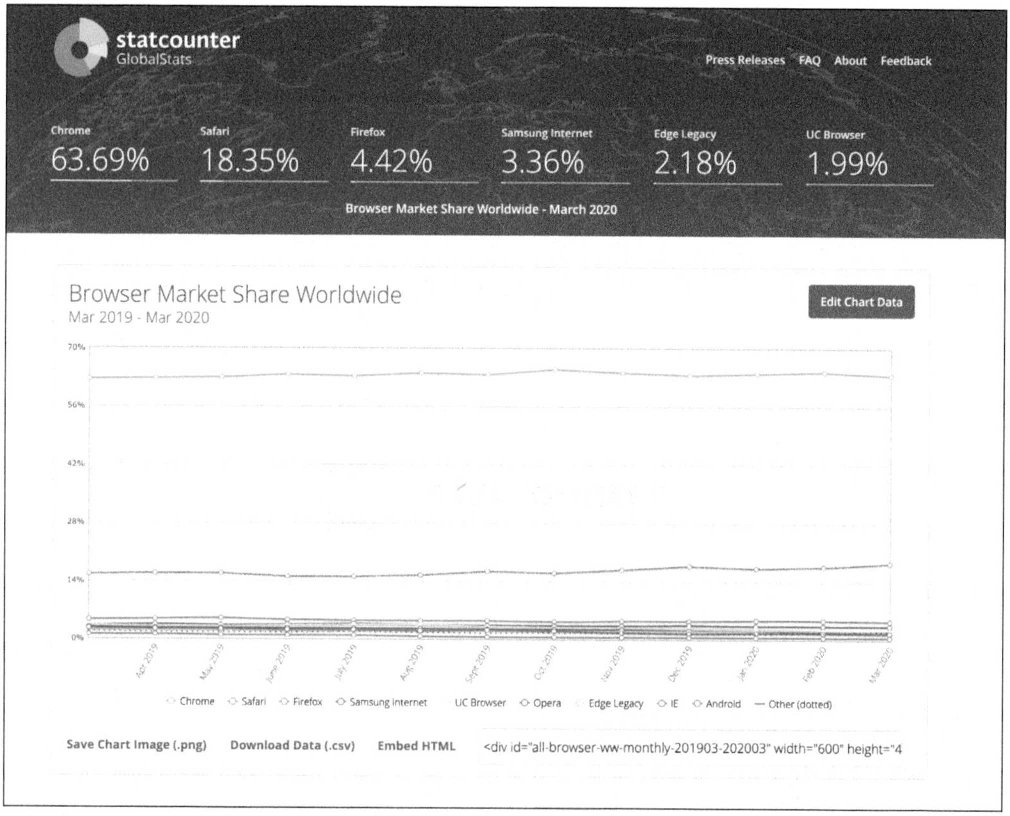

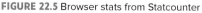

statcounter
GlobalStats
Press Releases
FAQ
About
Feedback
Chrome
63.69%
Safari
18.35%
Firefox
4.42%
Samsung Internet
3.36%
Edge Legacy
2.18%
UC Browser
1.99%
Browser Market Share Worldwide - March 2020
Browser Market Share Worldwide
Mar 2019 - Mar 2020
Edit Chart Data
70%
56%
42%
28%
14%
0%
Chrome
Safari
Firefox
Samsung Internet
UC Browser
Opera
Edge Legacy
IE
Android
Other (dotted)
Save Chart Image (.png)
Download Data (.csv)
Embed HTML
<div id="all-browser-ww-monthly-201903-202003" width="600" height="4

FIGURE 22.5 Browser stats from Statcounter

Internet connection speeds are a little easier to simulate. There are a few testing tools you'll learn about later in this chapter, and in Chapter 23 when you learn about improving performance. But for now, here's a short list of connections you should check:

- High-speed internet (if your site loads slowly here, you'll need to make some adjustments).

- Current cellular internet connections—5G at the time of this writing.

- Two previous generations of cellular networks (4G and 3G at the time of this writing).

- Extremely slow internet.

  For this you might try a crowded coffee shop or library.

The goal here is to make sure your site doesn't load too slowly. It creates a poor user experience.

Finding test devices

Whereas checking browsers and simulating slow internet connections can be done in software, testing on actual devices requires access to hardware.

You're probably not buying a ton of hardware to test your websites, but you can send the site to a few friends who have different devices and different-sized devices.

You can also leverage social media here. Send out a message asking people to visit your site and send a screenshot or report what's going on. You can even ask them to use yourbrowser.is (yourbrowser.is /generate) to generate a report about their device so you don't need to guess (or have them guess) (**FIGURE 22.6**).

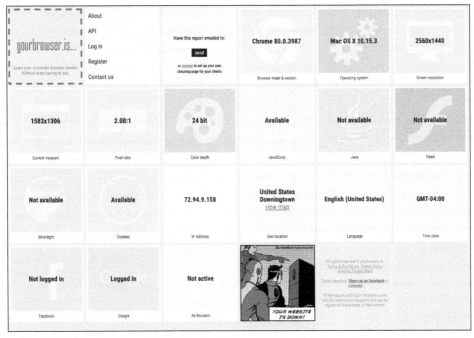

FIGURE 22.6 My browser information, as reported by yourbrowser.is

As a last-ditch effort, you could always go to a cellphone carrier's store and test devices there! I've done it when in a pinch (though just be aware that they might not like it).

If you're really stuck, an emulator is better than nothing. By using Xcode on macOS (**FIGURE 22.7**) and Android Studio on macOS or PC, you can emulate devices to test on.

To emulate an iPhone with Xcode for macOS:

1. In your Applications folder, double-click the Xcode icon.

   If it's not pre-installed, you can download it from the App Store. You may need to update it. If you do, run those updates.

   If the Welcome To Xcode window opens, click the X in the upper-left corner to dismiss it.

2. After Xcode opens, in the main menu bar, choose Xcode > Open Developer Tool > Simulator.

   Simulator might take a few minutes to open, depending on the speed of your machine.

3. Once Simulator loads the iOS or iPadOS device, click the Safari icon.

4. In the address bar, type the URL of your website.

5. If you want to test other devices, you can choose Hardware > Device, then choose the operating system and device you want to test.

Even if you already have an iPhone, this is an easy way to test your site on other iPhone versions or on various iPad models.

FIGURE 22.7 The iPhone 11 Pro Max, displayed in XCode's Simulator

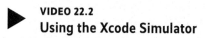

VIDEO 22.2
Using the Xcode Simulator

Once you access the Simulator in Xcode, there are several features worth exploring. Here's a quick tour of them.

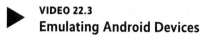

VIDEO 22.3
Emulating Android Devices

If you already have an iPhone but want to test your site on Android devices, you can do so with Android Studio. Here's how.

Troubleshooting with Chrome Developer Tools

One staple of web development troubleshooting has been to use the development tools built into web browsers. All of the major browsers offer these, but we'll use the developer tools provided in Chrome, officially named Chrome DevTools. This is a set of tools you can use to check markup, CSS, webpage load speed, and downloads. You can also test responsive web designs as well as perform a whole host of other tasks that will make your job as a web designer easier.

To access Chrome DevTools:

1. In Chrome, click the menu button in the upper-right corner of the window (⋮) to open a menu.

2. Choose More Tools > Developer Tools from the menu.

A new screen will pop up on the right, showing the source code of your website (**FIGURE 22.8**).

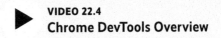

VIDEO 22.4
Chrome DevTools Overview

In order to quickly familiarize you with Chrome DevTools, you'll get an overview of what each tab does and how to navigate the panel.

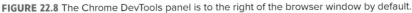

FIGURE 22.8 The Chrome DevTools panel is to the right of the browser window by default.

A common use case for Chrome DevTools (and for the developer tools in any browser) is to change part of the CSS on the site to get a preview of how it looks before committing those changes to code.

For example, if your intended three-column layout is displaying as two columns, you can adjust the CSS in developer tools, note the required changes, and then make them to the actual source file.

This is a bit faster than making the changes in code, saving, uploading, and testing.

You can also test color schemes, fonts, and other styles much more quickly.

To modify CSS with Chrome DevTools:

1. Visit your website.

2. Open Chrome DevTools.

3. Select one of the elements from your markup by clicking it in DevTools (**FIGURE 22.9**).

4. In the Styles tab (which displays the CSS for the page), at the bottom of the Elements panel below the HTML listing, click next to the opening curly brace for that element's ruleset (**FIGURE 22.10**). This will create a new line in the ruleset.

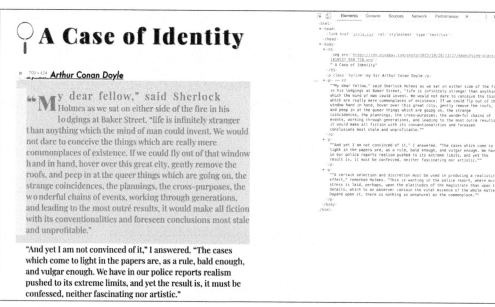

FIGURE 22.9 Selecting an HTML element in Chrome DevTools

FIGURE 22.10 Modifying CSS in Chrome DevTools

5. Place your cursor on that new line, and type `color:`.

6. Press Return/Enter to move to the next field.

7. Type #FF0000;.

Now, all of the next in that element should turn red.

Mobile device testing with Chrome DevTools

Another common use case for Chrome DevTools is to test different screen widths and even connection speeds. While this isn't a substitute for actual device testing, this will help you find media query and performance issues.

To test in different screen sizes:

1. Visit your website.

2. Open DevTools.

3. Click the Toggle Device Toolbar button (⬚).

4. Notice that your website's width has now changed (**FIGURE 22.11**), and there's a new toolbar with an item labeled Responsive. Click that label and choose one of the other devices from the list.

5. Now click the menu again and choose Responsive. In this mode, you can manually change the width. Change it to one of your breakpoints.

FIGURE 22.11 The Responsive device test section of Chrome DevTools

6. In that same toolbar, there's a menu labeled Online. That lets you control the load time of the website. Choose Low-End Mobile and refresh the page. You should notice it takes much longer for your website to load.

You can see exactly how long by consulting the Network tab of the Elements panel. See more in **VIDEO 22.5**.

▶ **VIDEO 22.5**
Responsive Testing in Chrome

Chrome offers a robust set of tools for testing your website on a variety of mobile devices and networks. Here's a walkthrough of those features and the information you can get from them.

Wrapping Up

Testing is an important part of web design because it ensures your website works for as many people as possible. By checking for valid markup and viewing your website in as many browsers and on as many devices as feasible, you're helping your website visitors.

Another way you can help your visitors is by making sure your website loads quickly. Let's look at how to do that in the next chapter.

Improving Website Performance

Depending on the study cited, from 40 to 80 percent of users will abandon a website if it takes more than four seconds to load. According to one study, Amazon loses $1.6 billion per year for every second of load time (medium.com/@vikigreen).

While *your* losses won't be quite that great (at least when you're starting out), you should always look to improve the performance of your website because a slow website will cost you users. Aside from that, better performance will improve your site's user experience (UX), increase user engagement with your content, and even help boost your site's page rank in Google.

What Do We Mean by Performance?

Before getting too far into the weeds, you need to know what web professionals mean by *performance*. Getting to the heart of it, performance is measured by two criteria:

- Load time: How long it takes for a website to be delivered to the user from the time they request it.

- Interface efficiency: How long it takes for something to happen once a user interreacts with your website—clicking a link, filling out a form, and so on.

TIP Load time is sometimes also measured as "perceived" load time. This essentially means that if you show the user *something*, even if it isn't the entire website, they'll feel like the website is loading faster.

TIP Interface efficiency is also referred to as "responsiveness." So as not to confuse this with the practice of designing websites for all screen sizes, I use the term *efficiency*.

The goals in making your site perform as well as possible in terms of page load speed and how quickly it reacts to user interactions (referred to as being more *performant*) are a fast load time (under three seconds for any network speed) and to provide the user with feedback as soon as they do something on your website. This can be as simple as hover states on links.

Now that you know what performance means and why your website should be performant, let's take a look at the how.

Know How Your Website Performs

Before you start optimizing for performance, you need to know how well your website performs in the first place. Often this has to do with the amount of data you're sending from the server to the user's browser. The more data, the slower a website loads.

Common performance factors

You'll learn about some tools to help you pinpoint specific performance issues, but there are a few common culprits:

- Images: Huge image files represent a lot of data that needs to be transmitted. And often, they don't need to be as big as they are.

- Other media: You might consider images first because they are more in your control. With other media, like audio and video files, you're probably uploading them to a service like SoundCloud or YouTube, and those services work hard on improving performance. Even so, embedding too many videos or pieces of audio on a page can still slow down your website.

- Bloated HTML and CSS: Using too much markup or too many styles can lead to bigger HTML and CSS files, which leads to slower load times. Later in this chapter I'll talk about ways to diagnose those problems and find solutions to them. On top of that, as you include more files (like JavaScript libraries), downloading each one requires a separate request to the server. More requests also lead to longer load times.

- Hosting: It's easy to blame hosting for performance issues, but the truth is a bad host will result in a slower site. If you're using a hosting company that overworks its servers or underinvests in resources for those servers, you can have a single line of text in a file load slowly. While you're learning, it's okay to skimp in this area because it's the biggest cost to you, but once you're ready to do this professionally, a good host is a must.

TIP I recommend SiteGround to *most* people when they need web hosting.

Performance Testing Tools

While media, bloated code, and hosting are all areas you can keep an eye on when developing your website, it's worth using third-party tools to help you pinpoint performance issues on your website.

There are several web-based tests that will load your website and then give you a list of areas to fix. Popular ones include PageSpeed Insights from Google (**FIGURE 23.1**), GTmetrix (**FIGURE 23.2**), and Pingdom (**FIGURE 23.3**).

They each use slightly different methods for measuring performance, but they'll all help by pointing out what you can improve.

TIP Some might argue that the best tool to pay attention to is Google's PageSpeed Insights because it will give your site a rank based on performance. However, the Google search algorithm may also affect your PageSpeed rank, so getting multiple opinions is a good idea.

FIGURE 23.1 Google's PageSpeed Insights for Casabona.org (developers.google.com/speed/pagespeed/insights/)

FIGURE 23.2 GTmetrix ratings for Casabona.org (gtmetrix.com/)

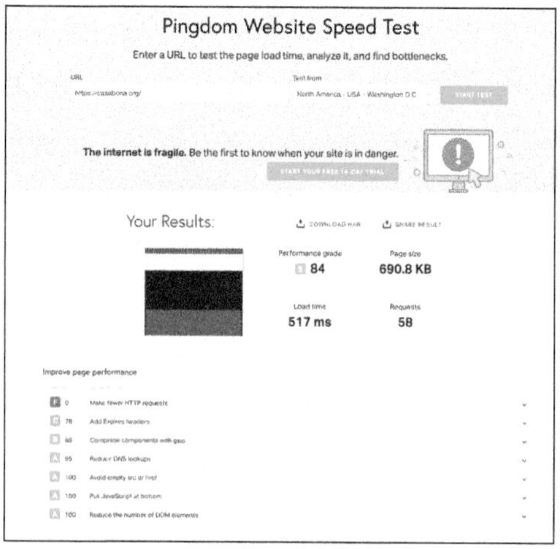

FIGURE 23.3 Pingdom's rating for Casabona.org (tools.pingdom.com/)

▶ **VIDEO 23.1**
Doing a Live GTmetrix Test

GTmetrix is an in-depth performance testing tool that pulls scores from multiple sources and gives you suggestions based on each. This video takes you on a quick tour of the interface, and gives you advice on what to do with the information the service provides.

To use PageSpeed Insights:

1. In your browser, visit developers.google.com/speed/pagespeed/insights/.

2. In the text box labeled Enter A Web Page URL, type your website's address (**FIGURE 23.4**).

3. Click the Analyze button.

   Once the tool completes analysis, you're given two scores: one for mobile and one for desktop.

4. Click Desktop, on the left toward the top of the page (**FIGURE 23.5**).

   PageSpeed Insights gives you data based on how well your website has performed for other people. It then gives you detailed descriptions of each metric.

5. Click the three-line icon next to Lab Data to view those descriptions (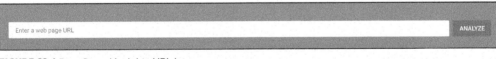).

6. Under both Opportunities and Diagnostics, you see scores and recommendations. Click the down arrow (∨) to view the recommended fixes you can make.

FIGURE 23.4 PageSpeed Insights URL box

FIGURE 23.5 The Mobile and Desktop buttons that reveal, and let you switch between, the scores on PageSpeed Insights

The Chrome DevTools Network tab

Chrome DevTools, which you learned about in Chapter 22, has more than just tools for reviewing HTML, CSS, and responsive design.

You learned how to test in Chrome on low-speed internet connections, but the Network tab will give you a more detailed breakdown of your website's performance (**FIGURE 23.6**).

To view results in the Network tab in Chrome DevTools:

1. Visit your website in Chrome.

2. Open Chrome DevTools by clicking the menu button and choosing More Tools > Developer Tools.

3. Click the Network tab.

4. On macOS, press Command-R to reload the page and see the network activity results. On Windows, press Ctrl-R.

Your website reloads, and the Network tab is populated with data organized into two sections: a timeline and a list of all the files (HTML, CSS, images, etc.) that your website loads, with load times.

Using the information from the Network tab, you can look at slow-loading files and determine how you can optimize your site.

Speaking of which, let's look at a few techniques for optimizing your website, starting with some low-hanging fruit: making your HTML and CSS files smaller.

▶ **VIDEO 23.2**
A Closer Look at the Network Tab

Knowing how the Network tab works can help you fast-track performance testing based on internet speeds and other factors. Let's take a closer look at this fantastic tool.

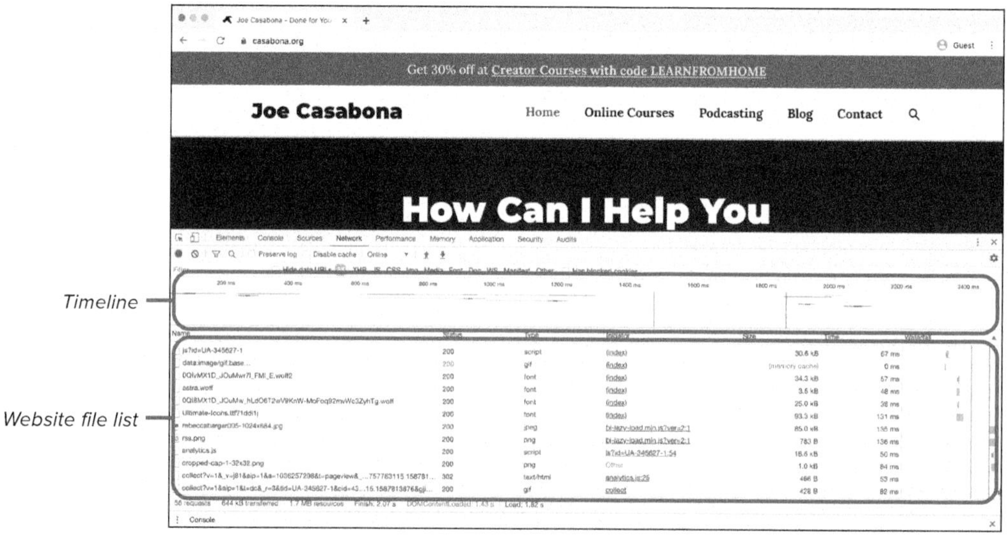

FIGURE 23.6 The Network tab in Chrome DevTools with results loaded from Casabona.org

Minify HTML and CSS Files

Minifying HTML and CSS files is the act of removing unnecessary characters in order to make the files as small as possible.

When you write HTML, every character counts towards the total file size, even spaces and line breaks—the computer still needs to represent them as data. Generally, one character = one byte (though some characters use more). So "Hello World" has a size of 11 bytes. Since you generally see sizes in kilobytes (KB), megabytes (MB), or gigabytes (GB), **TABLE 23.1** shows how many bytes are in each unit of measurement. You may see people use a simple power of 10 conversion (1000 bytes in a KB; 1,000,000 bytes in a MB, etc). However, when converting values to computer storage, you should use the exact values provided in the table.

In both HTML and CSS, spaces and line breaks are unnecessary; they are only there because it's easier for us to read the files with proper spacing included. The same goes for comments. While they give cues to developers as to what's going on in the code, they do not affect how the browser renders a site, so they aren't needed. Removing spaces, line breaks, and comments can lead to considerable space savings (**FIGURE 23.7**).

TABLE 23.1 Byte Conversion Chart

Unit	Size in Bytes
Kilobyte (KB)	1024
Megabyte (MB)	1,048,576
Gigabyte (GB)	1,073,741,824

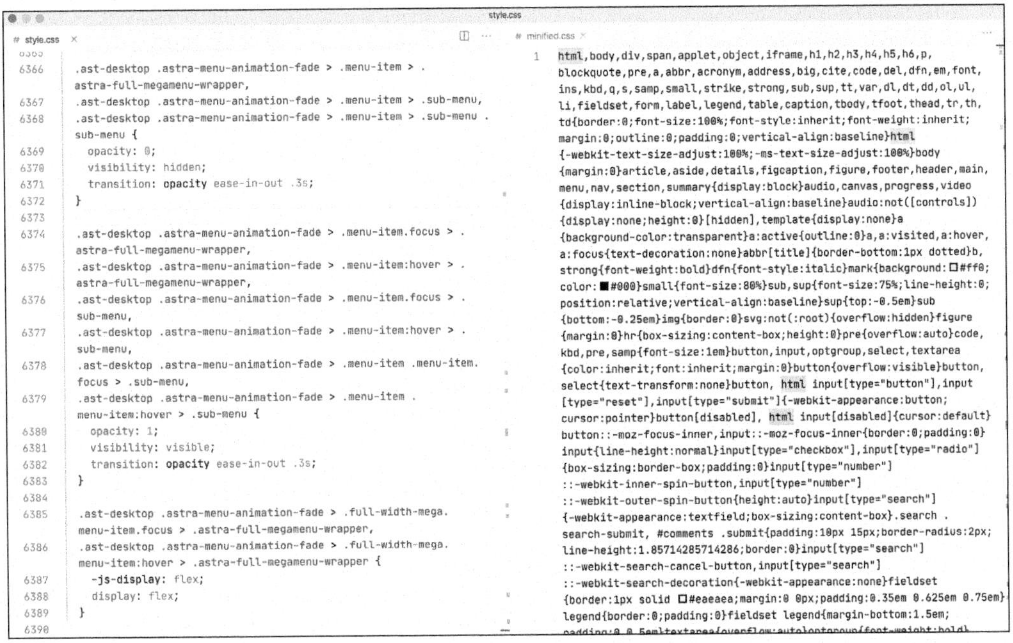

FIGURE 23.7 On the left you see the CSS from Casabona.org, which is nearly 6400 lines of code and 129KB in size. On the right, you see the minified version, one (very long) line and 97KB. That's 40 percent smaller!

There are lots of online tools for minifying both HTML and CSS. Some give you options for degrees of minification (just remove line breaks, remove all spaces, etc.). Make sure that whatever minification is done, it doesn't end up breaking your code. I've gotten consistent (and good) results from Minify Code (**FIGURE 23.8**).

To minify HTML using Minify Code:

1. Visit minifycode.com.

2. Click the HTML Minifier button.

    If your browser window is a smaller size, you may see a blue icon in the top right. Click it to reveal the navigation menu.

3. Open the `index.html` file for your website in a text editor.

4. Copy all the text from your `index.html` file.

5. Paste the text into the textbox on the Minify Code page.

6. Click the Minify HTML button.

    Your HTML is replaced with the minified version.

7. Copy that code.

8. Create a new folder called **minified**.

9. In that folder, create a new file called index.html.

10. Paste the minified HTML into the new index file and save the file.

11. Upload the new, minified version of `index.html` to your web server.

Your mileage will vary depending on how much markup you have in your file. The bigger savings are often seen with minifying CSS. That process looks exactly the same as the previous task, but you'll use the CSS minifier on minifycode.com instead of the HTML minifier.

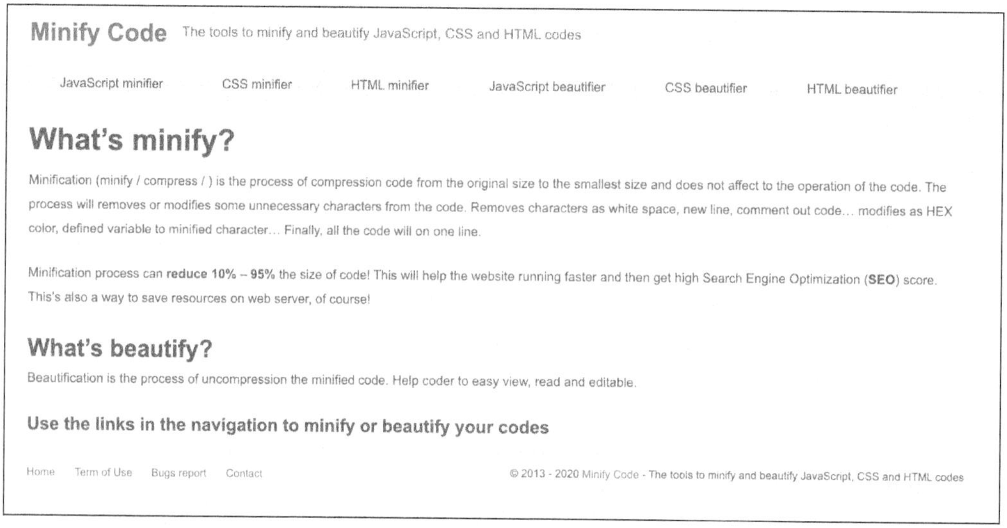

Minify Code The tools to minify and beautify JavaScript, CSS and HTML codes

JavaScript minifier   CSS minifier   HTML minifier   JavaScript beautifier   CSS beautifier   HTML beautifier

What's minify?

Minification (minify / compress /) is the process of compression code from the original size to the smallest size and does not affect to the operation of the code. The process will removes or modifies some unnecessary characters from the code. Removes characters as white space, new line, comment out code... modifies as HEX color, defined variable to minified character... Finally, all the code will on one line.

Minification process can **reduce 10% – 95%** the size of code! This will help the website running faster and then get high Search Engine Optimization (**SEO**) score. This's also a way to save resources on web server, of course!

What's beautify?

Beautification is the process of uncompression the minified code. Help coder to easy view, read and editable.

Use the links in the navigation to minify or beautify your codes

Home   Term of Use   Bugs report   Contact   © 2013 - 2020 Minify Code - The tools to minify and beautify JavaScript, CSS and HTML codes

FIGURE 23.8 Minifycode.com allows you to minify HTML, CSS, and JavaScript.

Optimize Your Images

Another quick win for improving performance is optimizing your images. There are three ways you can do this.

First, when you can, use SVG for simple graphics, since they are inherently smaller than pixel-based images like JPEGs.

Second, if you are using pixel-based images, make sure your images are the appropriate size for the space they're in. For example, if you have an image sized to 500x250, you shouldn't be shrinking a 2000x1000 image by 75 percent; use a 500x250 image sized at 100 percent. You can do this easily in HTML using the techniques you learned in Chapter 7.

Another image format that has gained popularity is WebP. Developed by Google, the format makes images about 26 percent smaller than their PNG counterparts. It uses the .webp extension, and it's supported by all major browsers except Safari at the time of this writing. You can learn more about how to use WebP at css-tricks .com/using-webp-images/.

Finally, you can *compress* your images. Compression is a way of shrinking a file size at the code level without altering what the file represents. In fact, minifying is a form of compression. We get a much smaller file size, but your website still looks the same. Another example is shorthand in text messaging or chat. Instead of "laugh out loud," most people write "LOL." It's much shorter but means the same thing.

Why compress images?

Images often contain extra information that bloats the file size, like metadata about the image. This can be where the photo was taken, what camera was used, date and time, and more.

None of this matters to people visiting your website, especially when it's loading slowly. So you can use compression and optimizing tools to remove that metadata and reduce image file sizes without losing quality (**FIGURE 23.9**).

There are several free image-optimizing tools for macOS and Windows, as well as web-based services. For macOS, I recommend ImageOptim (imageoptim.com/). It's been around for a long time, it works well, and it can integrate with other services through its API (for a price).

For Windows, RIOT (riot-optimizer.com/) is a free tool that works well.

ImageOptim also has a web interface with limited functionality (**FIGURE 23.10**).

FIGURE 23.9
On the left is the original image, and the compressed version is on the right. Notice that there's no difference in quality.

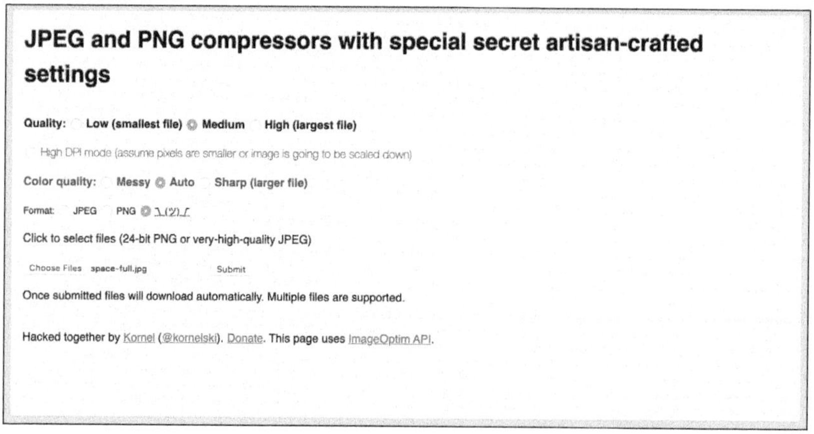

FIGURE 23.10
The interface for imageoptim.com/ online has several options for optimizing your images.

To use ImageOptim to compress an image:

1. Go to imageoptim.com/online.

2. Keep all the settings at their default values for now.

   You can always experiment with these settings!

3. Click Choose Files and select one of the images from your website folder.

   This website supports selecting multiple images if you want to process more than one at a time.

4. Once you've selected your image, click Submit.

5. After ImageOptim finishes compressing the image, you'll be prompted to download the new version. Save it to the minified folder you created in a separate task.

6. Upload the image to your website, replacing the old one.

Again, your mileage will vary depending on the image you use. But for the image used in Figure 23.9, the original was 4.3MB and the reduced version was 3.9MB.

Between using something like Image-Optim and sizing your images properly, your website should load a lot faster. But there's something else you can do that will make a huge difference, which I cover in the next section.

Getting Creative with Images

Aside from sizing and compressing, you can get creative with the way you process and display images.

For example, the less complex the image, the less space it takes up. Consider using black and white or duotone images instead of full color—that can go a long way toward reducing file size.

Advanced Hosting Techniques

There are two terms you'll likely hear as you learn more about webpage loading speed and performance.

The first is *cache*. Caching copies some of your website files to be stored on the visitor's computer for faster access. Much like the local storage you learned about earlier, a cache is where a browser stores certain files that are unlikely to change often (like images and your CSS). This reduces the number of requests your browser has to make to the server, because the files are already technically on the user's computer.

The second is *content delivery network (CDN)*. This is a set of servers your website files are distributed to. When a user makes a request to your website, the server closest to the user serves up the needed files.

You can think of cache and a CDN this way: imagine that your favorite ice cream place is 20 minutes away from your home. The "request" for ice cream would take 20 minutes.

With cache, it would be as if you bought a gallon of the ice cream to keep in your freezer.

With a CDN, it would be as if the ice cream shop worked out a deal with your grocery store, which is only 10 minutes away, to sell the ice cream there.

Load Your Critical CSS First

Another term you'll probably see, especially if you review your PageSpeed Insights results, is the term *render-blocking resources*. These are any files that need to be downloaded before the page can be displayed at all. The fewer render-blocking resources, the faster your page is perceived to load.

Imagine you're going on a trip but you didn't pre-pack a bag. Each time you get into your car, you realize you forgot something, so you run back inside to get it. It takes you much longer to get on the road. Each forgotten item is like a render-blocking resource. If you had packed a bag earlier, you would have been able to leave faster.

This is also known as time to *first paint*. The first paint is the very first render of your website. When users see a blank screen, they know the website is taking time to load. Your goal is to eliminate this blank screen as soon as possible, even if it's not the full site (**FIGURE 23.11**).

FIGURE 23.11 Filament Group's site employs several performance boosters, including critical CSS. You can see its first paint, where you can start reading the content, versus the last paint, which includes all the images, bells, and whistles.

Part of the reason I left this until last in the chapter is that it's more complicated than the other techniques we've covered. It's not just shrinking a file or some other basic task.

The lazy loading technique from Chapter 10 is one way to remove certain render-blocking resources and get your website loaded faster. However, everything you include in the <head> element of your website is also, by default, render-blocking.

For the purposes of this book, render-blocking resources means your CSS file. If it's absolutely massive, it will take your website longer to load. So you can employ the following technique:

Move the most important CSS—that is, the CSS required to style the first part of the website—to an internal style sheet (see Chapter 11). Load the rest of the CSS later in the document, like right before the </body> tag.

TIP There are lots of tools to help load only the critical CSS, and many are automatic. Unfortunately, they rely on tools we haven't learned about in this book. If you're curious, Smashing Magazine offers a good overview: www.smashingmagazine.com/2015/08/understanding-critical-css/.

Determine your critical CSS

If you're not using automated tools, your first job is to determine which CSS is critical and which is not. Many times, the determining factor is *the fold* (**FIGURE 23.12**). This is any content that shows up in the user's browser before they scroll.

> **TIP** The term *the fold* comes from the newspaper industry! Newspapers were always stacked folded. So of course only the part of the front page above the fold was visible, and thus it got by far the most attention.

When working with many different devices, determining the fold is impossible, but for the purposes of this book, let's work with your desktop browser window. Take a look at your website and see what renders in the browser before you do any scrolling. This is the stuff that you should target for your critical CSS.

You can also use a tool like the Critical Path CSS Generator by Sitelocity (**FIGURE 23.13**).

> **TIP** In critical CSS, you can also leave out certain special effects, like text shadows or box shadows. The goal is a fast first paint. You can add bells and whistles later.

Above the fold

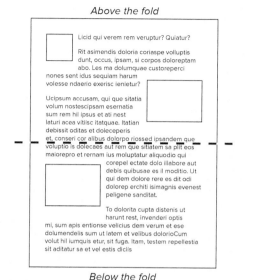

Below the fold

FIGURE 23.12 The fold is what loads in the browser without scrolling. Critical CSS should style for above the fold.

FIGURE 23.13 Sitelocity's Critical Path CSS Generator will help you determine what your website's critical CSS is (sitelocity.com/critical-path-css-generator).

CODE 23.1 shows a simple HTML example with a single comment denoting where I've determined the fold to be.

In this instance, you'll want to include some **body** styles and the **header** and `.primary-content` styles in your critical CSS. Everything else can be put in the `style.css` file. For simplicity's sake, **CODE 23.2** includes the critical CSS.

To add critical CSS inline:

1. Open your HTML file (or create a new one using Code 23.1).

2. On the line after the opening **<head>** tag, type **<style>**.

3. Add your critical CSS. If you're using the demo code, use Code 23.2 for this part.

4. On the next line, type **</style>**.

CODE 23.1 Critical CSS markup example

```
<html>
    <head>...</head>
    <body>
        <header>...</header>
        <main>
            <section class="primary-
            → content"> ...</section>
<!--Here is "the fold"-->
            <section class="secondary">...
            → </section>
        </main>
        <footer>...</footer>
    </body>
</html>
```

CODE 23.2 The critical CSS

```
body {
    max-width: 700px;
    padding: 30px;
    margin: 0 auto;
    font-family: 'Playfair Display', serif;
    background-color:#fcf6e7;
}

h1 {
    color: #282009;
    font-size: 4em;
    font-weight: 900;
    letter-spacing: 0.08em;
}

.byline {
    font-family: Futura, sans-serif;
    font-style: italic;
    font-weight: bold;
    text-decoration: underline;
}

header img {
    width: 50px;
    height: auto;
    vertical-align: middle;
}

.primary-content {
    background: #FFFFFF;
    padding: 30px;
}

p {
    font-size: 24px;
}
```

5. On a new line right before `</body>`, add a reference to your CSS file by typing `<link href="style.css" rel="stylesheet" type="text/css" />`.

6. Save your files and upload them to your server.

7. Visit the newly created HTML file. You should notice that some of the styles load initially, and then the rest of the styles finish loading once the browser gets to the `style.css` reference at the end of the document.

Wrapping Up

In this chapter you've learned some important principles and techniques for speeding up your website. A fast website is important because it keeps users from abandoning it, and we want as many people to use our site as possible.

In that same vein, another way to ensure anyone who wanted to view your website can is to make it accessible. Let's take a look at how in Chapter 24.

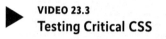

VIDEO 23.3
Testing Critical CSS

Once you add the critical CSS to your website, it's important to test your files to make sure that the first paint looks usable and that the rest of the styles fully load later. Let's create new HTML and CSS pages to see how quickly a page loads before and after adding the critical CSS.

Conditionally Load Style Sheets

Aside from loading your critical CSS and then all the rest of your CSS in a single file, you can separate it out further by loading it conditionally based on media queries.

For example, let's say you have three separate style sheets:

- One for general (noncritical) styles
- One for big device styles
- One for print styles

You can load them using media queries right in the HTML tag:

```
<link href="style.css" rel="stylesheet" type="text/css" />
<link href="large-screen-styles.css" rel="stylesheet" type="text/css"
 media="screen and (min-width: 1301px)"/>
<link href="print-styles.css" rel="stylesheet" type="text/css" media="print" />
```

This ensures that the last two style sheets are only loaded when they are needed.

Web Accessibility

Throughout this book, you've learned how to make websites. You've learned how to support devices of all shapes and sizes. And you've learned how to make your website load as quickly as it can on internet connections fast and slow. But there's one more way you can make sure your website works for whoever wants to view it: make it *accessible*.

Web accessibility means designing your website in such a way that people with disabilities can use it. This can be making sure your images have `alt` tags for screen readers, choosing color schemes that are readable for those who are color-blind, or even adding keyboard shortcuts to help those who can't use a mouse to navigate.

In This Chapter

Including as Many People as Possible

An important point to make at the outset is one that's often stated by accessibility advocates: web accessibility doesn't just help the disabled—it makes your website more usable for everyone.

Usability is a big reason this book has focused on semantics, using the right tags, and making your website work across multiple devices, screen sizes, and connection speed. You want to reach as many people as possible with your website. Another step in that process is realizing that you're not designing your website just for yourself.

TIP **This chapter scratches the surface of accessibility and describes a few things you can do. If you want to learn more, there's a fantastic book called *Accessibility for Everyone*, by Laura Kalbag: abookapart.com /products/accessibility-for-everyone.**

A Note on the Legal Side of Things

There are also certain legal ramifications in certain countries for not making your website accessible. In the United States, the retailer Target and the pizza delivery company Domino's both faced legal action for not having websites that were accessible enough.

While that shouldn't be the main reason you make your website accessible, it is important to keep in mind that having a website that isn't accessible is viewed as discriminatory.

Designing for a diverse set of users

When thinking about web accessibility, it's important to remember that not everyone uses a computer with a keyboard and mouse.

About 12 percent of the United States population has some disability. That could range from color blindness to motor impairments, and everything in between. Here's a short list of disabilities to think about, and how they can affect how people use your website:

- Partial eyesight loss can make small text hard to read and images hard to see clearly. Users may rely on a screen reader for help.
- Color blindness makes it hard to see or distinguish certain colors (**FIGURE 24.1**). If you're using a color scheme that doesn't have enough contrast, text may be completely invisible to some users (**FIGURE 24.2**).

- Full or partial hearing loss means users will not be able to listen to videos or audio on your website. The best fix for this is to include transcripts and captions or subtitles for videos.
- Motor impairments may cause users to have difficulty using traditional pointing devices like a mouse. A screen reader can help with input, and making your website navigable by keyboard will help as well.
- Cognitive impairments like dyslexia or memory deficits can affect how people use your website. Using good, clear fonts and keeping your website clear of distractions isn't just good UX, it can make it more accessible.

Making your website accessible, combined with tools available in browsers and other software, can make it so anyone can use your website without trouble.

> **TIP** Two good tools for figuring out workable color schemes are paletton.com/ and coolors.co/.

FIGURE 24.1 The same image as viewed by people with varying degrees of color blindness, from none to completely monochrome.

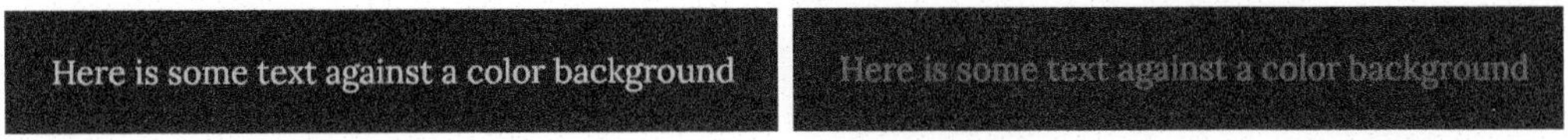

FIGURE 24.2 Green text on a black background is readable for those without color blindness. But for those who are green-blind, the text looks dark purple and becomes unreadable.

What You've Done so Far

Luckily, a lot of what you've done so far goes a long way toward making your website accessible. Using the appropriate HTML elements for sections of your website clues screen readers into what kind of content you're building.

Using heading tags (and the right heading tags) breaks up long blocks of text and makes them easier to consume and understand.

With forms, using different fields for different types of input helps users better understand the type of data they're inserting. Similarly, labels provide meaning to those fields.

Using the `alt` attribute on images allows images to be described when they can't be downloaded or viewed.

TIP For `alt` attributes, the more descriptive, the better. For Figure 24.1, an alt tag of "girl in yard" is better than nothing. But it's not as good as "A girl toddler wearing a backwards hat and holding a pink bucket in a fenced-in yard."

The testing you've learned about also helps with accessibility. By improving performance and testing on different browsers and devices, you're ensuring your website can work anywhere and everywhere.

You can see how well you've done by turning off the styles on your website and viewing just the HTML (**FIGURE 24.3**). This is what both search engines and screen readers will see. In Chrome, you can do this using the Web Developer extension you downloaded in Chapter 6.

To turn off CSS in Chrome:

1. Visit your website in Chrome.
2. Click the Web Developer cog icon (⚙).
3. Click the CSS Tab.
4. Click Disable All Styles.

With no styles, does your website make sense? Does the information flow the way you expect it to? Is the information that should be at the top actually at the top?

Great! Your website is well on its way to being accessible. But there is more you can do. In the rest of this chapter, you'll learn important tests and techniques that will help you make sure your website is accessible.

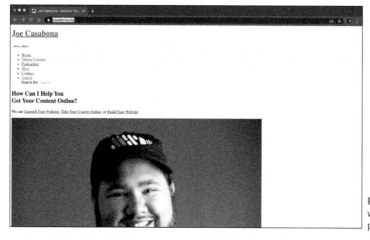

FIGURE 24.3 Casabona.org with all styles disabled. It's not pretty, but it's usable!

Additional Tags and Attributes

Accessibility is something you should plan for from the beginning of your project. Before you start using evaluation tools, do as much as you can during development to make your website accessible.

Using well-structured HTML is the best thing you can do to support accessibility, so make sure to use the skills you've learned throughout the book to make a website accessible at its core.

However, sometimes in the course of building your site you do need to use HTML elements that don't necessarily have any meaning, like **div** or **span**. You might also create an area of your site that does not have an HTML tag that would give it meaning. Luckily, that's where *ARIA* tags come in.

ARIA is the shorthand way of writing WAI-ARIA, or Web Accessibility Initiative–Accessible Rich Internet Applications. Most people just refer to it as ARIA.

ARIA is a way of providing to the browser more information about an element when the proper meaning isn't built into HTML. You can do that by using two different types of attributes:

- **role** defines a type of user interface component based on its function (examples include **button**, **alert**, and **search**). This does not change how the element is displayed; it just gives the element more meaning (**FIGURE 24.4**).

- States and properties provide further information about a particular element. For example, in a date selector, the value of the month may be a number (**10**, for example). The property **aria-valuetext** can have the value **October** so that screen readers can give the user more meaning for that particular element.

To add **role** to a **div**:

1. In an HTML file, right after the opening **<body>** tag, type **<div class="sale-alert"**.

2. Type **role="alert">**.

   Using the ARIA **role** attribute, we're telling browsers and screen readers that this **div** is an **alert** and should be treated as such.

3. Type **Now though Sunday, get 25% off!**.

4. Type **</div>**.

Now your browser knows that this particular **div** is an **alert** on your site. This is particularly useful for screen readers, which can now tell users more than just "This is a container on a page."

> **TIP** Get a full list of roles, states, and properties at developer.mozilla.org/en-US/docs/Web/Accessibility/ARIA/ARIA_Techniques.

Now though Sunday, get 25% off!

FIGURE 24.4 An **alert** with basic styles applied. It also contains the more meaningful **role="alert"** attribute.

States and properties

States and properties can be used to provide further descriptions of elements or to connect elements in a meaningful way. One way is by connecting a password hint to the password field with **aria-describedby** (**CODE 24.1** and **FIGURE 24.5**).

However, these can sometimes be a little tricky to apply for beginning users of HTML and CSS, since many are manipulated by JavaScript.

For example, you might design a menu that is shown and hidden by JavaScript based on a click event (like in Video 24.1). You can add **aria-expanded="true"** to the event when the menu is open, and **aria-expanded="false"** when it's closed.

▶ **VIDEO 24.1**
Changing ARIA States and Properties

ARIA states and properties are often updated in real time through JavaScript. This video shows an example of different sections of an accordion list expanding, causing the ARIA state to change.

CODE 24.1 A password field with the **aria-describedby** attribute applied

```
<label for="password">Enter a Password:</label>
<input type="password" id="password" name="password" aria-describedby="hint" />
<div id="hint">Must be at least 10 characters, and include a Capital letter, number, and
 special character.</div>
```

Enter a Password:
Must be at least 10 characters, and include a Capital letter, number, and special character.

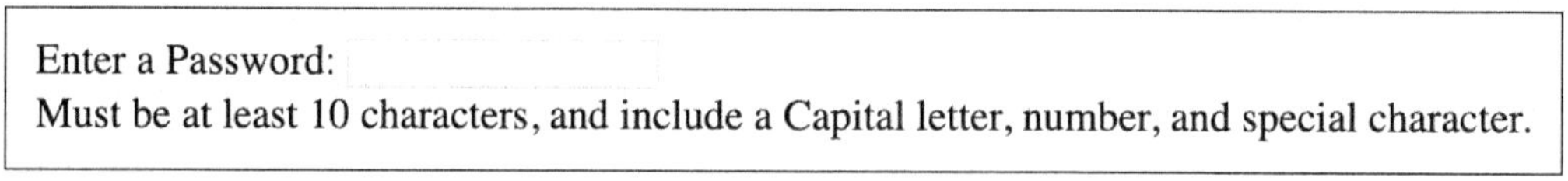

FIGURE 24.5 A password field with a hint box. Thanks to the use of the **aria-describedby** attribute, the browser knows the two elements are related.

TIP A *property* of an element is relatively static (for example, `aria-labelledby` identifies the label of an element), but a *state* is a dynamic property (for example, whether a checkbox is selected or unselected). In practice, though, it's not important to be aware of the distinction, and most people use *attribute* to refer to both of them.

TIP One interesting example of how ARIA properties are used is the `aria-live` property. It allows you to define *live regions*, or regions that get updated in real time. Setting its value to `polite` will announce a live change when the user isn't actively scrolling or typing. Setting the value to `assertive` will interrupt what the user is doing to make the announcement. You might use `polite` for something like Twitter, when there are new tweets. Use the `assertive` value for something truly important, like an error or warning.

Accessibility Tests and Validation

Once you've got your website created, there are a few ways to test and validate your work to ensure it is accessible.

The *Web Content Accessibility Guidelines (WCAG)* are maintained by the Web Accessibility Initiative (www.w3.org/WAI/standards-guidelines/wcag/). They are part of the World Wide Web Consortium (W3C), which develops and maintains web standards. You can test your website against WCAG to learn how to make your website more accessible.

The guidelines are currently in their second version (WCAG 2.1), and there are three levels of accessibility, ranging from Level A to Level AAA:

- Level A is the lowest level of conformance. This is a great place to start to make sure your website is minimally compliant.

- Level AA is the next level up, where your website meets more criteria in the guidelines. This is the goal most organizations aim for because it's reasonably achievable without much added cost.

- Level AAA is the highest level and very difficult (and costly) to achieve. For the most part, only accessibility-focused organizations aim for this rating.

Testing tools

There are three testing tools you'll learn how to use to evaluate your website:

- Our old friend Google Chrome Dev-Tools (**FIGURE 24.6**).

- WAVE by WebAIM gives detailed test results and feedback. It is highly recommended by web accessibility experts (**FIGURE 24.7**).

- A Chrome extension named Colorblindly tests for color blindness (**FIGURE 24.8**).

FIGURE 24.6 The accessibility audit built into Chrome

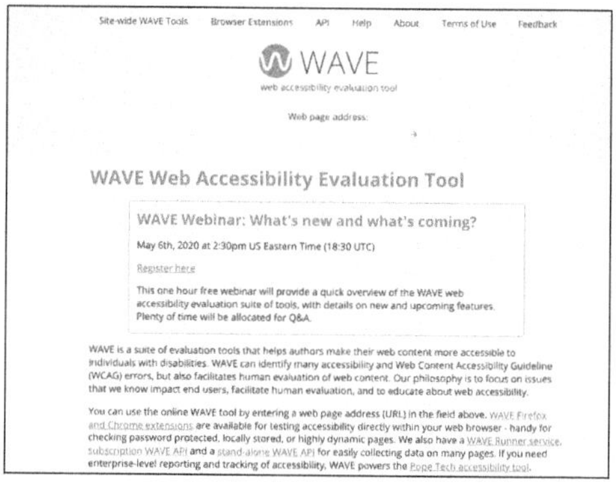

FIGURE 24.7 WAVE by WebAIM (wave.webaim.org/) is a tool for accessibility testing.

FIGURE 24.8 Colorblindly is a free Chrome extension that applies color filters to any website to simulate different types of color blindness.

▶ **VIDEO 24.2**

Digging into the Accessibility Test in Chrome

The accessibility test built into Chrome is a fantastic starting point for checking your website. It provides a score and some helpful tips. Here's how it works.

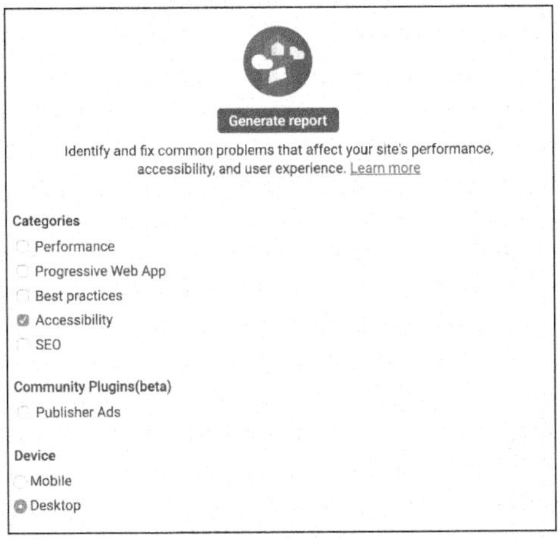

FIGURE 24.9 The report settings for the Audits tool in Chrome

To test accessibility with Google Chrome:

1. Visit your website in Chrome.
2. Open the DevTools by clicking the menu and choosing More Tools > Developer Tools.
3. Click the Audits tab.

   You may need to click the double arrow (») to reveal the Audits tab.
4. Deselect all categories except Accessibility (**FIGURE 24.9**).
5. Under Device, select Desktop.
6. Click the Generate Report button.

   The report gives you a score and a list of areas you can fix, as you saw in Figure 24.6.

To use WAVE for detailed testing:

1. Visit wave.webaim.org.

2. In the Web Page Address field at the top of the page, enter your website's URL.

   The test renders, and it gives you a detailed report of accessibility features, warnings, and errors (**FIGURE 24.10**).

   It also gives you a report on your color contrast (**FIGURE 24.11**).

This test is much more interactive and provides tons of detailed analysis to make sure your website is not only accessible but also web structured and free of markup errors.

VIDEO 24.3
Using WAVE

There are a lot of features in WAVE, so we walk through the interface to show you what the icons mean and how you can use the data provided by the test.

🏠	☰	ℹ️	⛓	○●
Summary	Details	Reference	Structure	Contrast

No contrast errors were detected in the page. Manual testing is necessary to test for other potential contrast issues.

Foreground Color
#0000FF

Background Color
#FFFFFF

Lightness

Lightness

Contrast Ratio: 8.59:1

Text Size:

Normal Text: Sample
AA: Pass
AAA: Pass

Large Text: Sample
AA: Pass
AAA: Pass

Desaturate page

Contrast is not tested when background gradients, transparency, etc. are present. A CSS background color that provides sufficient contrast must be defined when a background image is in place. This provides fall-back contrast in case images or CSS do not display.

FIGURE 24.10 The results of the WAVE test for Casabona.org

FIGURE 24.11 The contrast test results in WAVE

To test for color blindness with Colorblindly:

1. In Chrome, visit the Google Chrome Web Store (chrome.google.com/web-store) and search for *colorblindly*.

2. On the Colorblindly extension page, click the Add To Chrome button to install the extension. A new icon (👁) will appear in your browser bar.

3. Visit your website.

4. Click the Colorblindly icon.

5. Select the Green-Weak/Deuteranomaly option in the menu (**FIGURE 24.12**).

   This is the most common form of color blindness.

6. Review your website to make sure you can still read everything!

7. Repeat steps 5 and 6 for each form of color blindness.

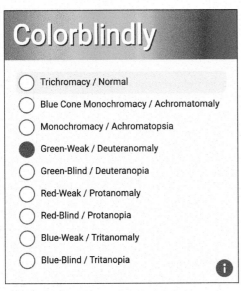

FIGURE 24.12 The forms of color blindness Colorblindly can simulate

Finding Your WCAG Rating

You may have noticed in all those tests that you weren't given a specific WCAG level rating. There's one more test you can conduct for that, using AChecker (**FIGURE 24.13**).

To check your site against WCAG level guidelines:

1. Visit achecker.ca/checker/.

2. Select the Web Page URL tab.

3. In the Address field, type your web-site's URL.

4. Click Options.

5. Under Guidelines To Check Against, make sure the most recent WCAG Level A option is selected.

   At the time of this writing, it's WCAG 2.0 (Level A).

   We're starting simple with WCAG Level A so that you can get the base-line issues fixed.

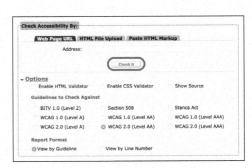

FIGURE 24.13 AChecker (achecker.ca/checker/) compares your website against the WCAG guidelines and shows you what you need to fix.

6. Under Report Format, select View By Line Number.

7. Click the Check It button.

On the Report page, you are given a list of issues you need to fix, broken down by line number, in order to become Level A compliant (**FIGURE 24.14**).

Wrapping Up

With that, you have enough tools to keep you busy! Over the last few chapters you've learned how to test your website, make it more performant, and make it more accessible. You're well on your way to becoming a fantastic web developer!

But in this chapter and throughout the book, you've seen references to another important aspect of web development: JavaScript. While that topic is too much to cover in this book, in Chapter 25 you will get a quick introduction to it as well as to some other technologies you might want to check out.

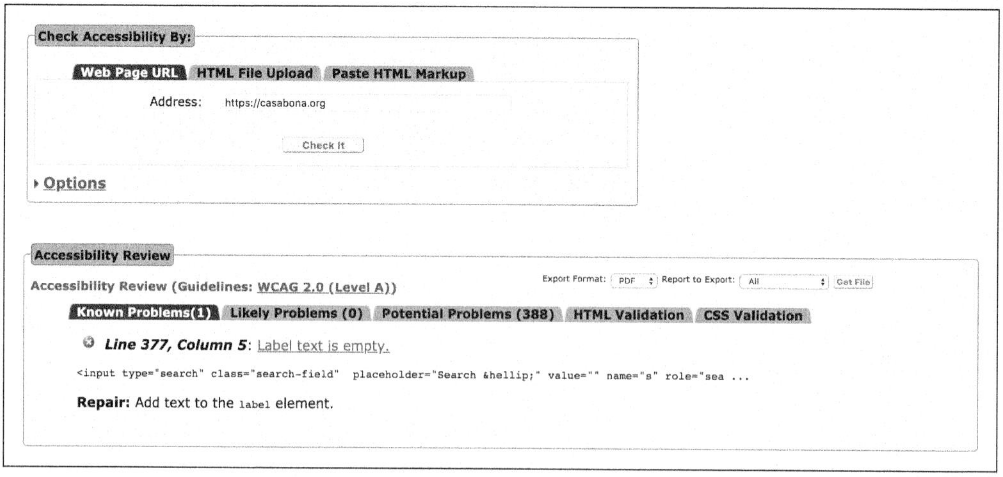

FIGURE 24.14 AChecker WCAG Level A results for Casabona.org

Going Beyond HTML & CSS

HTML and CSS form the bedrock of any website. And now you know how to structure and style webpages, as well as how to make them fast and accessible.

But they are only the beginning of your web development journey. Now that you know the foundation, it's time to show you a few tools worth looking at while you master HTML and CSS, starting with JavaScript.

JavaScript

You've seen the term *JavaScript* more than once in this book. You even got to write a tiny bit in Chapter 10 when you learned about local storage. But it hasn't yet been properly defined for you.

JavaScript is a programming language that is often used in web development. In the browser, it's a client-side language (like HTML and CSS). It usually adds dynamic features to a webpage in the form of manipulating elements, changing styles on the fly, advanced form validation, and more.

As you learn JavaScript, you'll want to strike a balance when using it. Loading too many different JavaScript files can make your page take longer to load. Using too much JavaScript can also affect your browser's performance, since it's executing code in real time.

If you've ever had a browser crash on you, there's a decent chance JavaScript was at least partially to blame.

The `<script>` tag

JavaScript is included on a webpage using the `<script>` tag, which you saw in Chapter 10. There are two ways to use the `<script>` tag:

- You can write the code inline—between the `<script>` and `</script>` tags—like you did with local storage.

- You can include the `src` attribute, like you did with the `picturefill.js` example: `<script src="picturefill.js"></script>`.

And as with the `<style>` tag, you can include the `<script>` tag anywhere within the `<head>` or `<body>` tags.

Although you won't learn how to write proper JavaScript here, you'll likely come across common JavaScript libraries (or applications) that you can use on your website without actually writing any (or writing very little) yourself.

Common JavaScript Libraries

There are tons of JavaScript libraries out there, and it seems new ones come out every week. You'll likely want to try your hand at a bunch once you get your legs under you, but I'd caution you to be judicious in what you decide to learn. In particular, when evaluating a library, make sure of the following:

- It has been around for at least one and a half to two years. That shows that the developers are invested in it.

- It is well supported by the developers and the users. More people using it means it's more likely to stick around.

- You actually need it! There's a Java-Script library for everything under the sun. But remember that the more resources you use, the heavier your page becomes. Only load the things you need to load.

Start with jQuery

jQuery (jquery.com) has been around for a very long time (especially in web years) (**FIGURE 25.1**). Even though its usage is on the decline, it's still a great way to dip your toe in the waters of JavaScript because it simplifies a lot of common actions without weighing down your site with excess code.

Here's how it works: you include jQuery on your webpage, and then you can use it instead of vanilla JavaScript (that is, regular JavaScript) to perform tasks like showing or hiding elements, fading elements in or out, and more.

TIP jQuery (and JavaScript in general) allows you to change areas of your website based on user interaction. Be mindful about using JavaScript when you should be using CSS.

FIGURE 25.1 The homepage for jQuery (jquery.com), a longstanding and popular JavaScript library

Other popular JavaScript technologies to consider

I recommend jQuery because its barrier to entry is a lot lower than that of other JavaScript libraries. But several have gained popularity and are worth considering because you'll likely see them come up a lot:

- React.js: Created by Facebook and made open source, React has found its way into lots of major projects, so this one is definitely worth looking into (**FIGURE 25.2**)

- Angular: This one was created by another heavy hitter, Google. It's been around a bit longer than React and is used to help with building single-page applications and websites (**FIGURE 25.3**)

FIGURE 25.2 React.js (reactjs.org/) is an open source library that has gained a lot of popularity in recent years.

FIGURE 25.3 Angular by Google (angular.io/) makes it particularly easy to create interactive experiences on both desktop and mobile.

Node.js® is a JavaScript runtime built on Chrome's V8 JavaScript engine.

Download for macOS (x64)

12.16.3 LTS
Recommended For Most Users

14.1.0 Current
Latest Features

Other Downloads | Changelog | API Docs   Other Downloads | Changelog | API Docs

Or have a look at the Long Term Support (LTS) schedule.

Sign up for Node.js Everywhere, the official Node.js Monthly Newsletter.

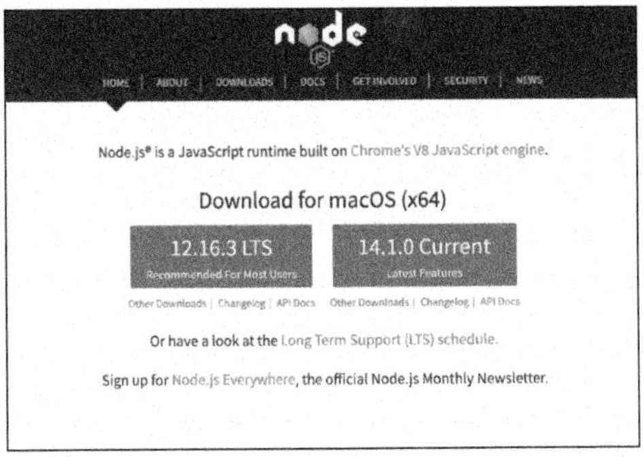

FIGURE 25.4 Node.js (nodejs.org/) is a bit different because it's not usually run in the browser.

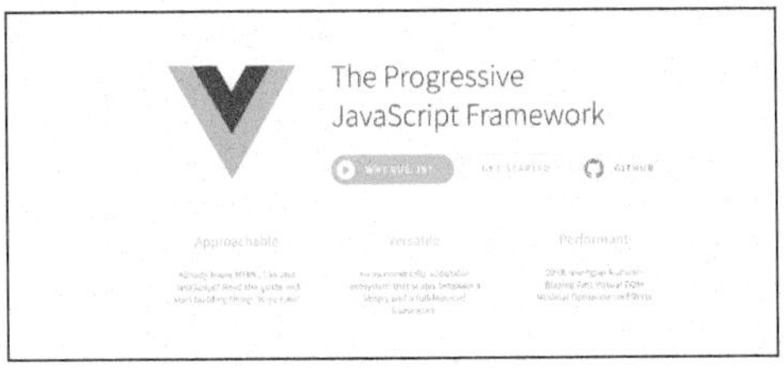

The Progressive
JavaScript Framework

FIGURE 25.5 Vue.js (vuejs.org/) is younger than the rest, but it's gained popularity because it has a low learning curve and is fast.

- Node.js: This is an open source library that's a little different from the others— it executes JavaScript *outside* your browser on a server, and is often used for tools that help you build websites rather than on the websites themselves. Node is very popular, so you'll definitely come across it (**FIGURE 25.4**).

- Vue.js: Finally, Vue is a relative newcomer in the space, but it has been adopted by many for its ease of use, especially when creating user interfaces (**FIGURE 25.5**).

Use JavaScript Only When You Need To

Once you learn JavaScript, you might be tempted to make changes to your CSS, or even to your content, using only JavaScript because it's easier. I strongly recommend you don't.

HTML, CSS, and JavaScript all have their place, and you shouldn't use JavaScript to change styles when CSS would be a better fit. Remember that adding JavaScript can impact performance in more ways than one.

As you evaluate whether or not to use JavaScript, ask yourself if it's something HTML or CSS can (and should) handle. If not, figure out how to add the script to your page while burdening it the least.

Version Control

Throughout this book, you've likely been making edits to your files, changing styles, adding and removing content, and then saving over the old changes.

While that's okay as you learn, in a more professional environment (especially working with teams), you'll want a way to be able to undo changes if you need to. That's where *version control* comes in.

Version control is the systematic management of changes to the pieces of a project. In the case of a website, you use version control to track and organize multiple copies of its files as they continue to be developed. You keep a single copy of your live site (called the *master*) and you create a development copy to work on (**FIGURE 25.6**). Each copy of the code is referred to as a *branch*.

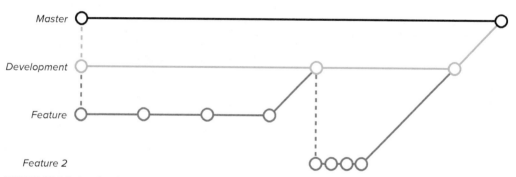

FIGURE 25.6 A visualization of master, development, and feature branches. Each circle represents a commit, and each dotted line is the creation of a branch. Each solid line is a merge.

Version Control Workflows

There are lots of opinions on what the proper version control *flow* should be. This book outlines the basic idea of version control, but individual teams implement their own processes.

In fact, the process outlined above is a popular one based on GitFlow (nvie.com/posts/a-successful-git-branching-model/). But there are many out there you can try based on project and team needs.

For smaller projects where it's just me, I've used a master/feature branch flow, where I create a branch for each feature, no matter how small, and then merge it back with the master when I'm done.

As you start to experiment with version control, the master/feature flow is a good way to familiarize yourself with the process.

How version control works:

- Your live site, the code that's currently uploaded to your server, is the master branch. This changes only when you're ready to launch a new version of your website.

- There is a second copy of the live site, often known as the development branch. This allows you to make changes to your website without irrevocably breaking your live site.

- Each new feature (design changes and new sections, images, or content) goes in its own *feature* branch. This lets you compartmentalize your changes, working on one at a time. Again, this makes it so you can work on one section of your website with the confidence that you won't break the entire site.

- Whenever you add a change and save it, it's called a *commit*.

- Once you're ready to add the new features to your website, you add them to the development branch. This process is known as *merging* and *pushing*. A merge takes your code and combines it with the development branch. A push sends your newly updated branch to the repository. The repository is where all the files and changes are tracked, and it can be a folder on your computer or it can be uploaded to a server that has Git enabled (more on Git in a moment).

  If you're working with other people, it ensures that you don't have any conflicts with another feature branch someone else is working on.

- Finally, once the development branch is in a state where you're ready to make the new site live, you merge the entire development branch into the master branch.

Use Git for version control

There are several version control tools out there (much like there are many JavaScript libraries), but *Git* is the clear winner (unlike with JavaScript technologies).

The great thing about Git is that it's free, and you can install it right on your computer—no additional tools needed.

However, the easiest way to get started is to sign up for a GitHub account (**FIGURE 25.7**). GitHub is a free tool that adds a nice interface and social interactions on top of Git.

You can then get the GitHub desktop client, which allows you to easily interact with GitHub. Create codebases (called *repositories,* or *repos*) and start playing around. You can even make copies of pre-existing codebases (like the one for this book). That process is called *forking*. Downloading the code that you want to make edits to is called *cloning*.

▶ **VIDEO 25.1**
Using GitHub

GitHub is a fantastic and free tool for use with Git. It's one of the easiest ways to get started with Git.

Here you'll learn how to interact with GitHub using the desktop app.

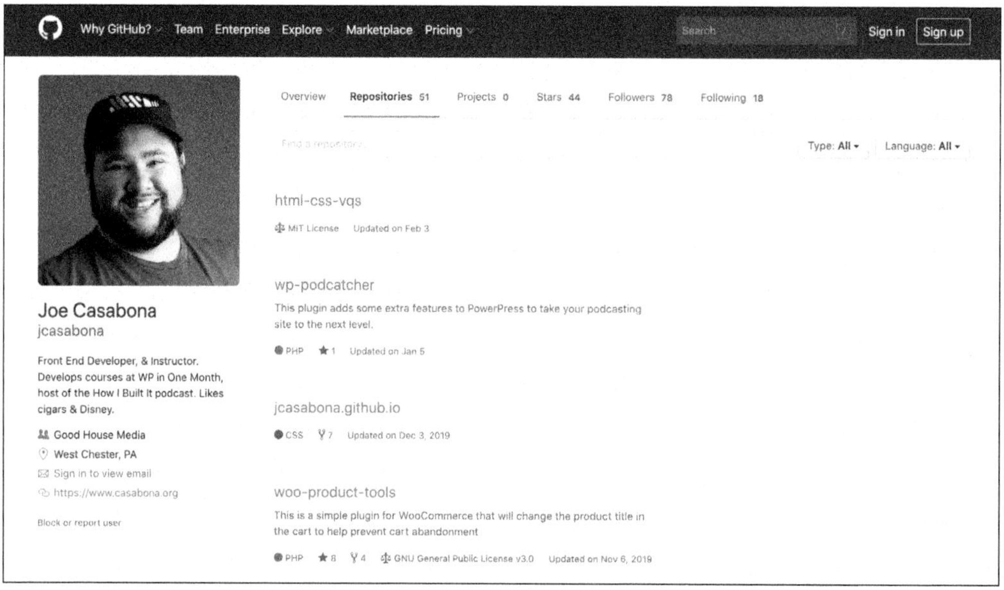

FIGURE 25.7
A typical GitHub profile. You can see information about the developer and the available repositories.

To create a GitHub account:

1. Visit github.com.

2. Fill out the signup form (**FIGURE 25.8**).

3. Verify that you're a human being.

4. Answer a few short questions about how you're going to use GitHub.

5. Verify your email address.

Now you're ready to start using GitHub!

To add a repository to your account:

1. Make sure you're logged in to your GitHub account.

2. Visit the GitHub repository you want to make a copy of. Try out github.com/jcasabona/html-css-vqs.

3. Click the Fork button on the top right of the page (**FIGURE 25.9**).

The repo is now part of your account! You can make changes to it without getting permission from the owner of the original codebase.

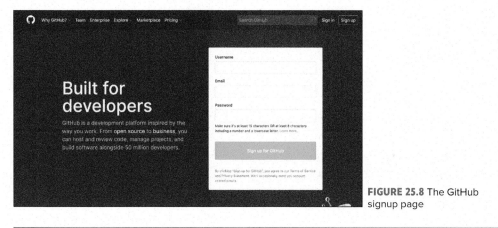

FIGURE 25.8 The GitHub signup page

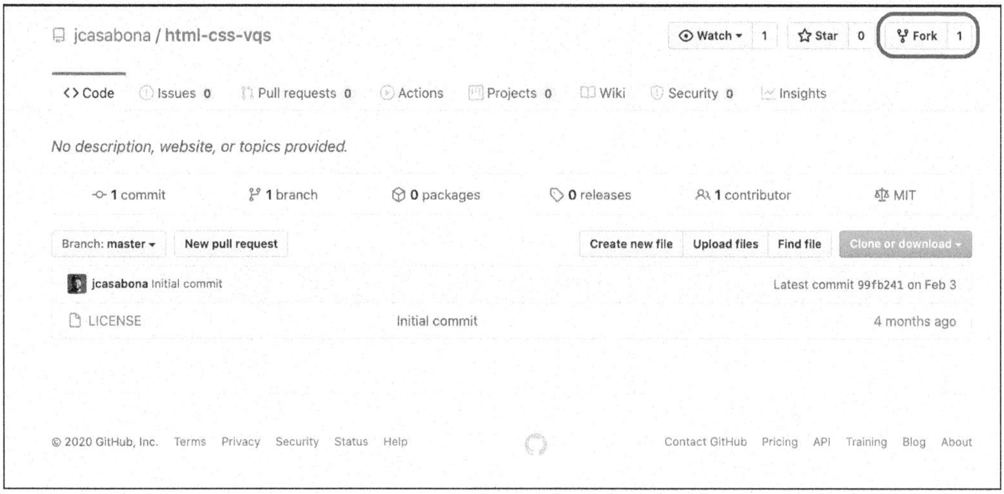

FIGURE 25.9 The Fork button lets you add a copy of the codebase to your account.

Build Tools

The final big concept in this chapter is *build tools*. We touched on this a little bit in Chapter 20 with CSS preprocessors, but there are a whole set of tools to help you build websites. They are called build tools, and they can do everything from setting up your folder structures and compiling Sass to checking your code for errors before you upload it to your server.

Developers like build tools because they automate a lot of complex processes for them, but they also complicate the overall web development process. Instead of opening up your text editor and writing HTML and CSS, you first need to learn to use the command line, install a set of tools, and configure everything properly. I personally try to avoid build tools unless I'm working on a big, complex project, or with a large team where consistency across work environments is important.

This is definitely the most complicated topic in this chapter, so we aren't going to dive deep into it, but I do want to share with you some popular build tools you might hear mentioned:

- Gulp and Grunt: I'm lumping these two together because they are so similar that distinguishing them on features won't yield much. Gulp (**FIGURE 25.10**) is a little newer and a little cleaner, which means it's a little more readable. Grunt (**FIGURE 25.11**) has been around a little longer and has more features and integrations.

FIGURE 25.10 Gulp (gulpjs.com) is a lightweight and popular build tool.

FIGURE 25.11 Grunt (gruntjs.com) is another widely popular, feature-packed build.

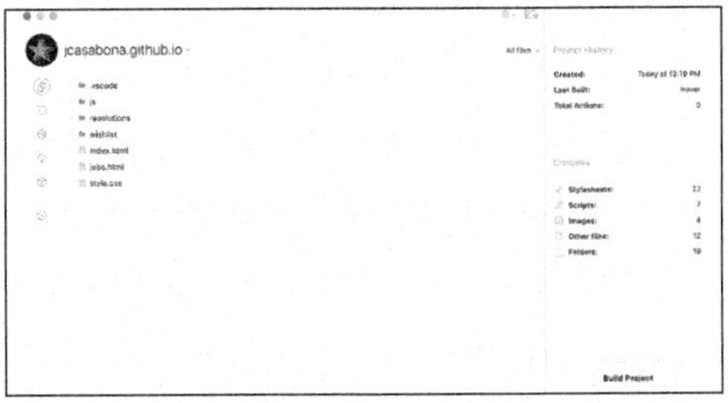

FIGURE 25.12 CodeKit (codekitapp.com) is a fantastic Mac app that puts a GUI on top of the command-line build tools. This is a great way get started with build tools.

- CodeKit: If you're a Mac user, CodeKit (**FIGURE 25.12**) is definitely the way to go when you're starting out. It has a GUI, which means you're not relying on the command line. It also means it's much easier for beginners to understand. That said, it might not (emphasis on might) be as flexible a tool as Grunt or Gulp, and its code may not be as portable as that produced by those tools.

CSS Frameworks

A *framework* is a codebase that you can tap into and use in your own projects. It will do a lot of the foundational work so you can focus on building new aspects of your website.

They work by providing you with a core set of CSS classes and base styles to give you a head start on your projects.

Another way to level up your skillset, especially with CSS, is to learn a popular CSS framework:

- Bootstrap: This super-popular CSS framework was started by Twitter and is used by thousands of web developers. It's great for making sure your CSS is rock solid and properly responsive. Get it at getbootstrap.com.

- Zurb Foundation: Foundation is a widely popular family of frameworks that provides not only CSS but also HTML and JavaScript. Developed by Zurb (get.foundation), it's fast and customizable, and it's used by brands like Mozilla, Disney, and Amazon.

- Tailwind CSS: Tailwind (tailwindcss.com) is a relative newcomer in the space. It touts itself as less "opinionated" than other frameworks because it provides you only the utilities you need without all the bloat of extra styles for things like buttons and cards.

Wrapping Up

As we conclude our journey together, I want to state that this chapter wasn't meant to overwhelm you. I wanted you to see what else is out there, and the likely candidates for what to learn next.

Learning a CSS framework can make you a better CSS developer. And JavaScript goes hand in hand with HTML and CSS. Checking out jQuery and familiarizing yourself with the complex world of web programming languages are good next steps, especially if you want to create websites professionally.

We're at the end of the book and what's next is a quick recap of what you learned, together with a few helpful resources.

Final Wrap-up

What's Next?

Congratulations! You've now completed *HTML and CSS: Visual QuickStart Guide*. We've covered a lot of ground, from basic HTML formatting and layouts to advanced techniques for styling text with CSS. We even took a look at important testing procedures, like those for rendering on mobile devices, performance, and accessibility. So what should your next steps be?

I recommend you continue honing your HTML and CSS skills. Here are a few useful resources:

- If you haven't checked out the videos that accompany this book, definitely do that!

- You can get exercises and common patterns for HTML and CSS at casabona.org/vqs/.

- CodePen has fantastic examples of clever HTML, CSS, and JavaScript at codepen.io.

- Try out the free tutorials at Codecademy: www.codecademy.com/learn/learn-html for HTML and www.codecademy.com/learn/learn-css for CSS.

In Chapter 25, I threw a lot of different tools at you. It can seem daunting. But the next language you should learn is JavaScript. As it turns out, Peachpit has a Visual QuickStart Guide for that too: www.peachpit.com/store/javascript-visual-quickstart-guide-9780133846089.

Finally, I want to hear from you! Let me know what you thought of the book and show me what you're working on. Find me on Twitter at @jcasabona.

Thanks for reading. I'm excited to see what you build!

Index

B

\<b\> tag, 30

background colors, 143, 167, 170, 217–219. *See also* colors

background images, 172. *See also* images

background transition, adding, 231–232

background-image property, 172

\<bdi\> and **\<bdo\>** elements, 33

blank value, target attribute, 43

block and inline elements, outlining, 49

\<blockquote\> element, 29

blog article layout, building, 54–56. *See also* **\<article\>** tag

\<body\> tags, 22, 147

boilerplate file, creating, 23. *See also* files

bold

  font-weight, 156

  text, 30

border attribute/property, 77, 172–173

box model, 46, 176–178

\<br\> tag, 31

browsers

  comparison, 8

  CSS (Cascading Style Sheets) support, 212–214

  Flexbox, 197

  Grid, 197

  support, 110

  testing, 276–277

  testing sites in, 272

  using, 13

build tools, 322–323

bulleted lists, 28

buttons, styling, 180

byline class, styling, 157–158

byte conversion chart, 291

C

caching files, 295

calculations with variables, 248–249

CanIUse.com, 111–112, 116, 212

Canva graphics, 68. *See also* graphics

\<canvas\> element, 113

capitalization of text, changing, 160

\<caption\> element, 76–77

cascade in CSS

  explained, 121

  and family relationships, 134

  specificity and precedence, 139–140

CDN (content delivery network), 295

centering elements, 183

checkboxes, creating, 94, 100

child

  family tree, 134

  indenting, 82

  relative link, 40

  selecting, 137

Chrome

  browser, 276, 304

  DevTools, 281–284, 290, 308–309

  extensions, 46–47

circle

  converting square to, 237

  element, 67

cite attribute, **\<blockquote\>** element, 29

classes. *See also* pseudo-selectors and -classes

  attribute, 53

  vs. IDs, 140

  naming, 133

  targeting elements by, 131–134

clear property, floats, 187

code

  indenting, 82

  marking up, 32

  tag, 32

codecs, 68–69

CodeKit build tool, 323

CodePen

  using with Sass, 253–255

  using for tests, 15

  using with tables, 78

color contrast, 166

color picker, Google Chrome, 103

color stops, 169

color wheel, 168

Colorblindly testing tool, 308, 311

colors. *See also* background colors

  in CSS, 164–168

  representing on computer monitors, 164

  RGB and RGBA, 167

  setting for styles, 165

color-scheme value, name attribute, 23

colspan attribute, 79–80

columns and rows

  extending, 79–80

  floats, 186

  Grid, 196–199

comma-separated list, 133

comments, adding, 20–21

compiling, 11

compressing images, 293–295

computer monitors, representing colors, 164

conic-gradient(), 169

content generators, 53

critical CSS, loading first, 296–300

CSS (Cascading Style Sheets). *See also* style sheets; styles

  animations, 236–239

  browser support, 212–214

links (*continued*)
    sections of pages, 41–42
    targets, 43–44
    URIs (Uniform Resource
        Identifiers), 43
lists, 28, 143
localStorage, 115

M

mailto: links, specifying, 43
main article section,
    creating, 54
Main page section, 50
MAMP (Mac, Apache, MySQL,
    PHP), setting up, 14
margins and padding, 179–183
marking up code, 31–32
markup, 2, 5, 274–276. *See
    also* semantic markup
matrix(), transform, 233
max attribute, forms, 102
max-width and max-height
    properties, 178
MB (megabyte), 291
media formats, 58–59, 68–69
media queries, 64, 196,
    216–217, 246–247
<meta> tag, 23
<meter> element, 105
method attribute, forms, 90
Microsoft Word document, 3
min attribute, forms, 102
minifying files, 291–293
min-width and min-height
    properties, 178
mobile vs. desktop layout, 222
monitors, representing
    colors, 164
monospace fonts, 146–147
month input type, 103
.MOV file extension, 68–69
-moz- browser prefix, 214
MP3 format, 71
.MP4 file extension, 68–69
-ms- browser prefix, 214

multimedia files, storing, 72–73
multiselect boxes, creating,
    98–99
MySQL web server, 14

N

name attribute, 23, 90, 92
name in URL, 37
naming
    classes, 133
    directories, 12
nav menu, making responsive,
    225
Nav page section, 50–52
nesting items, 121, 257–258
New York Times home page,
    46, 48, 176
Node.js library, 317

O

-o- browser prefix, 214
offline storage, 114–115
order-based selectors, 143
ordered lists, 28
outlining
    block and inline elements, 49
    elements with Wed
        Developer extension, 48
overflow property, 179
overflow-wrap property, 160
overlay, creating using z-index,
    192–193
overline, text-decoration, 156

P

<p> tag, 18
padding and margins, 179–183
page header, creating, 54
pages. *See* webpages
PageSpeed Insights, Google,
    288–289, 296
paragraph text, 18
paragraphs
    enlarging, 132
    and headings, 26–27

internal spacing, 160
    quoting with citations, 29
parameter value, adjusting, 104
parent, 40, 43, 82, 134
password field, aria-
    describedby attribute, 306
password format, forms, 94
paths, determining for files,
    13, 67
percentage (%), font-size,
    154, 177
performance, 286–290, 296
perspective(), transform, 233
PHP web server, 14
<picture> element, 64–65
p.intro class, 143
pixel density, 63
pixel vs. vector graphics, 59
pixels (px), font-size, 154
pixels, computer monitors, 164
placeholder attribute, forms, 93
plus sign (+), adjacent sibling
    element selector, 138
PNG (Portable Network
    Graphic) images, 59
polyfills and fallbacks, 111–112
polygon element, 67
polyline element, 67
position property, 187
POST value, forms, 90–91
<pre> tag, 32
prefixing tools, using, 213
preprocessors, CSS, 252–253
print style sheet, creating, 225
printer styles, adding to
    websites, 225–226
process.php file,
    downloading, 91
property, CSS, 122. *See also*
    shorthand properties
protocol in URL, 37
pseudo-selectors and -classes,
    141–142. *See also* classes;
    selectors
public_html folder, 14
px (pixels), font-size, 154, 177

tags (*continued*)
    `<aside>`, 52–53, 173
    `<b>`, 30
    `<blockquote>`, 29
    `<body>`, 22
    `<br>`, 31
    `<canvas>`, 113
    centering with margin:
        auto, 183
    changing, 19
    creating, 18
    `<code>`, 32
    `<dd>`, 81
    `<del>`, 31
    `<div>`, 53
    `<dl>`, 81
    `<dt>`, 81
    `<em>`, 30
    `<fieldset>`, 104
    `<figure>`, 62
    flow, 184–189
    `<footer>`, 56
    `<h1>`, 19
    `<head>`, 22
    `<header>`, 54
    `<html>` and `</html>`, 22
    `<i>`, 30
    `<img>`, 60–61, 63
    `<input>`, 90
    `<ins>`, 31
    `<legend>`, 104
    `<li>`, 28
    `<link>`, 127
    looking up, 111
    `<mark>`, 31
    `<meta>`, 23
    `<meter>`, 105
    overlapping, 190–191
    `<p>`, 18
    `<pre>`, 32
    vs. rulesets, 4
    `<s>`, 30
    `<script>` in JavaScript, 314
    `<section>`, 52

`<select>`, 96
selecting by relationships,
    136–138
and semantics, 2
setting styles, 131
`<small>`, 31
`<strike>`, 30
`<strong>`, 30
`<style>`, 124, 127
`<sub>`, 31
`<sup>`, 31
targeting, 122, 140–141
targeting by class, 131–134
targeting by tags, 130–131
`<time>`, 31
`<title>`, 22
`<u>`, 30
`<ul>`, 28
using, 18–19
viewing in browser, 19
Tallwind CS framework, 323
targeting
    elements, 122, 130–134,
        140–141
    media features, 227
targets, 43
`<tbody>` element, 76–77
`tel:` links, specifying, 43
templates, Grid, 210
testing
    accessibility, 307–311
    browsers, 276–277
    CodePen, 15
    critical CSS, 300
    devices, 276–280
    webpages, 107
    websites, 272, 274
text
    formatting, 156–158
    hiding, 160
    sizing, 154–155
    spacing, 159
    styles, 161
    transparency, 167

text editor, using, 10–11
text formatting
    forms, 94
    inline, 30–31
    overview, 26–27
`<textarea>` field, forms, 96
`text-decoration` property,
    156–157, 173
TextEdit, 10
`text-indent` property, 159–160
`text-shadow` property, 160
`text-transform` property, 160
`<tfoot>` element, 76–77
`<th>` element, 76–77
`<thead>` element, 76–78
tilde (~), general sibling
    selector, 138
`time` input type, 103
`<time>` tag, 31
`title` attribute, 61
`<title>` element, 22
TLD (top-level domain) in URL,
    37, 266
TLS (Transport Layer Security),
    266
`_top` link target, 43
`<tr>` element, 76–77
`transform` property,
    animations, 238
transformations, CSS
    (Cascading Style Sheets),
    233–235
transitions, CSS (Cascading
    Style Sheets), 230–232
`translate()`, transform,
    233, 238
TTF (True Type Font), 152
Twitter, offline storage, 115
two-column layout, at
    breakpoint, 223
`type` attribute, 92, 124
type selector, 130–131
typefaces. *See* fonts

videos (*continued*)

range input type, 104

registering domains, 267

relative links, 41

rental application, 102

resizing images, 63

responsive nav menu, 225

responsive three-column layout, 223

Sass CSS preprocessor, 257

schemas, 85

screen reader, 24

select and multiselect boxes, 98

setting styles on elements, 131

srcset attribute, 64

stacking order, 196

styles and markup, 5

styles and precedence, 139

styles vs. no styles, 5

SVG (Scalable Vector Graphic) images, 60, 67

tables, 78

tags, 19

targeting classes, 132

text transparency, 167

text-indent to hide text, 160

transformations, 233

transition functions, 230

two-column layout with floats, 186

typographic parameters, 161

unordered lists, 28

URLs (Uniform Resource Locators), 37

validating forms, 107

variables, 243, 245, 247

visual hierarchy, 4

W3C markup validator, 276

WAVE testing tool, 310

Web Developer extension, 48

Xcode Simulator, 280

viewport value, name attribute, 23

`:visited` state, 142

VS Code, 11

Vue.js technology, 317

W

W3C markup validator, 274–276

w3.org website, direction of text, 33

WAI-ARIA (Web Accessibility Initiative—Accessible Rich Internet Applications), 305–307

WAV format, 69, 71

WAVE testing tool, 308, 310

WCAG (Web Content Accessibility Guidelines), 307, 311–312

Web Developer extension, 46–48

web forms. *See* forms

Web Hosting for Students, 264–265

web server, mimicking, 14

`-webkit-` browser prefix, 214

WebM vs. Ogg, 69

WebP image format, 293

webpages

basic areas, 50

creating, 10

embedding content, 43

layout, 46–48

linking, 36, 41–42

outlining elements, 47–48

sections, 50–53

structuring, 22

testing, 107

URL (Uniform Resource Locator), 13

websites

making live, 269–271

pre-launch check, 268

reaching, 38

testing, 272, 274

week input type, 103

white-space property, 160

width property, 177–178

wildcard/universal selector (*), 144

wireframe, using, 50–53

Word document

converting to HTML, 31

example, 3

word-break property, 160

word-spacing property, 159

wrapper

class, 182, 188

converting to grid layout, 224

X

Xcode for macOS, iPhone emulation, 280

Y

Yoast SEO (search engine optimization), 84

yourbrowser.is tool, 279

YouTube.com, 73

YYYY-MM-DD type, forms, 102

Z

z-index, 191–192

Zurb Foundation framework, 193, 323